Times

For Li... and Law, Equal Rights and Industri...

NING, OCTOBER 1, 1910.

On All News Stands, Trains and Streets. 5 CENTS

# RECK THE
# ERIOUSLY INJURED

ver left eye;

Burned and cut

d back.

from window;

ed from second

left hand.

Jumped from

ned.

ver body and

ed and five chil-

ried.

e child.

three children.

one child.

one child.

and one child.

## CHIEF'S STATEMENT

CHIEF GALLOWAY, AT 3 O'CLOCK THIS MORNING, SAID:

"THAT THE BUILDING WAS WRECKED BY DYNAMITE SEEMS CERTAIN FROM ALL MY MEN CAN LEARN. THERE ARE ABOUT 100 PATROLMEN ON DUTY AT THE FIRE NOW, AND MOST OF THE DETECTIVES. WE HAVE FOUND SOME THINGS THAT SEEM TO US TO POINT TO THE AUTHORS OF THIS CALAMITY. WHETHER THEY WILL END IN ANY REAL RESULT IS IMPOSSIBLE TO TELL NOW, BUT I DO KNOW THAT WHETHER THEY DO OR NOT THE POLICE WILL KEEP AT IT WITHOUT REST UNTIL THIS WHOLE MATTER IS LAID BARE."

was a way out for brave men, and they took the desperate chance.

The explosion caught the working force unawares and many were buried in the ruins, while others jumped from windows, fell through the elevator chutes or climbed down fire escapes after receiving terrible injuries from flying timbers and debris.

A few in the building escaped uninjured.

Most of the injured were employed in the composing, stereotyping and press rooms, the greater number of those in the editorial rooms having finished their tasks and gone home.

The explosions were heard throughout the business district, and scores of persons going home in the 1 o'clock cars jumped out and joined the thousands of citizens who were pouring from downtown houses and hurrying to the fire.

Within five minutes the scene of the explosion presented a terrible spectacle, as the big building had burst immediately into flame and was doomed.

Great excitement seized the multitude and word quickly passed that scores of doomed persons were within the seething furnace. Desperate attempts were made by policemen, firemen and citizens to rescue those within, but the flames drove them back.

The terrible spectacle of persons attempting to escape from windows in the upper stories brought a cry of horror when they... to the ground. Or... framed in a window... up his hands and... the seething caldro... neath him.

Men poured from... broken limbs and... heads and bodies... forth were seized... borne to places of s...

Men begged to be... into the burning building, but officers with drawn revolvers and riot guns...

... borhood, but the cowards and murderers wer... gone.

Harry Chandler, assistant manager of the Times, had left the building a few minutes before the explosion. He rushed to rescue his imprisoned employes, but was driven back with the others, and with tears streaming down his face thanked God for those who were saved.

"The hounds!" he cried. "My poor men!" Then he hurried to the receiving hospital.

It may seem strange to say it that there was no panic; that no pandemonium broke out; that men fought and trampled one another to save their own lives.

No, these brave, the victims of the foulest plot of the foul union labor ruffians, shouted encouragement. Those temporarily overcome with the deadly smoke reached out a hand and helped their brothers. The women came first. There were shouts of "This way!"

Through the smoke, to the sound of the crackling flames, they plunged to the rear of the composing room.

### OUT OF THE JAWS OF DEATH

The escape from the city room and telegraph room on the third floor is little short of miraculous. In the former were Harvey Elder, assistant city editor; Mr. Lovelace, country editor; William E. Tribit, deskman. The reporters had all gone. Harry E. Andrews, managing editor, had left the city room a short half hour before the dynamiting.

In the telegraph room were H. D. Crane, assistant telegraph editor; R. L. Sawyer, chief telegraph operator, and Mr. McQuoddy, an operator. R. M. Whitney, telegraph editor, had left for home only a few minutes before.

When the explosion took place every man in both rooms sprang to his feet. One remarked sorrowfully. "That's the end." He felt the union laborites had done their worst. The men in the telegraph room ran into the city room, and the five stared blankly. Then came the glare of flames and the smoke. Immediately escape was cut off from the stairway leading to the pavement. Flames shooting him into the air cut off escape by the library... the job department. The...

... a fierce glare lighted up the room, walking in the center, searching a...

## N. Y. DEMOCRATS SELECT DIX FOR STANDARD BEARER

### State Chairman Finally Agrees to Run for Governor of the Empire State

### FULL TICKET IS NOMINATED

### When Independence League Is Mentioned It Is Greeted with a Storm of Hisses

ROCHESTER, N. Y., Oct. 1.—A state convention that will go into political history as one of the most remarkable in the history of the Democratic party closed this morning by nominating John A. Dix, chairman of the party's state committee and a wealthy Washington county business man to run on a progressive platform of the widest type.

Regarding the platform there was from the first little or no division of opinion.

But the candidate was not chosen until Charles F. Murphy, leader of Tammany hall, who by virtue of his 71 delegates was in a position to control the convention had canvassed the merits of no less than fourteen others.

"I said I would give them an up state candidate and I've done it," was Murphy's comment following the nomination.

[Associated Press]

ROCHESTER, N. Y., Sept. 30.—John A. Dix of Washington county was chosen candidate for governor by the Democratic convention tonight, while... delegates to the convention wait... hours in their seats for the formation or the slate.

The chief cause of delay was in... difficulty of filling second place...

# AMERICAN LIGHTNING

# AMERICAN LIGHTNING

TERROR, MYSTERY, MOVIE-MAKING,
AND THE CRIME OF THE CENTURY

## HOWARD BLUM

CROWN PUBLISHERS    NEW YORK

Published in the United States by Crown Publishers, an imprint of the Crown Publishing
Group, a division of Random House, Inc., New York.

www.crownpublishing.com

CROWN and the Crown colophon are registered trademarks of Random House, Inc.

Portions of this book appeared in slightly altered form in *Vanity Fair.*

Library of Congress Cataloging-in-Publication Data

Blum, Howard.

American lightning : terror, mystery, movie-making, and the crime of the century /
Howard Blum. —1st ed.

p. cm.

1. Bombings—California—Los Angeles—History—20th century.

2. Terrorism—California—Los Angeles—History—20th century.

3. Otis, Harrison Gray, 1837–1917.    I. Title.

HV6440.B58 2008

364.152'3097949409041—dc22         2008002974

ISBN 978-0-307-34694-0

Printed in the United States of America

DESIGN BY LEONARD W. HENDERSON

10 9 8 7 6 5 4 3 2 1

First Edition

*For Ivana,*
*with love.*

*And for*
*Sarah and Bill, Susan and David—*
*good friends.*

*"It's like writing history with lightning."*

—President Woodrow Wilson after viewing *The Birth of
a Nation*, the first movie ever shown in the White House


*"I know it's risky, but I still write history
out of my engagement with the present."*

—Richard Hofstadter

# CAST OF CHARACTERS

## Detectives

*Billy Burns:* The country's greatest detective, often called "the American Sherlock Holmes."

*Raymond Burns:* A son trying to win his father's love—and catch the bombers.

*Guy Biddinger:* Policeman, detective—and mole in the enemy's camp.

*Bert Franklin:* Former U.S. Marshal. His job for the defense: to ensure the jury votes for acquittal.

## Suspects

*J. W. McGraw:* A sawdust trail feeds speculation that he is the elusive Peoria, Illinois, bomb-maker.

*J. B. Bryce:* Purchaser of 80 percent dynamite from the Giant Powder company in San Francisco, explosives that are perhaps being used for more than "uprooting tree trunks."

*David Caplan (a.k.a. William Capp):* Anarchist with his own interest in purchasing dynamite.

*M. A. Schmidt:* Another anarchist, who pilots a boat at the center of the case.

*J.J. McNamara:* Engaging, handsome, lady's man, union official, and "a martyr to his cause."

*Jim McNamara:* Brother of J.J., on the run and potentially dangerous.

*Ortie McManigal:* Friend to the McNamaras. Out of work, yet not out of money.

*Harrison Gray Otis:* Cantankerous owner of the *Los Angeles Times* and a schemer determined to make a fortune.

## Lawyers

*Clarence Darrow:* Legendary defense attorney, drawn against his will into "the crime of the century"—only to be put on trial himself.

*Earl Rogers:* Defender of Darrow in the courtroom, and trader of punches with Billy Burns outside.

*Job Harriman:* Socialist candidate for mayor, Darrow's co-counsel, and, in time, Darrow's victim.

*John Fredericks:* A district attorney willing to make a deal—but only on his terms.

## Movie-Makers

*D.W. Griffith:* The most innovative filmmaker of his time, creatively energized by his unfolding connections with the trial's major players.

*Linda Arvidson:* D.W.'s actress wife, who is informed by her husband: "Don't think there is some other woman . . . It is not one, but many."

*Mary Pickford:* The first movie star and the focus of D.W.'s tormented thoughts.

*Sam Gompers:* Influential union leader, savvy to the connection between politics and theater, and authorizer of $2,577 to make "the greatest moving picture of the twentieth century."

## Journalists

*Mary Field:* Against Darrow's plea and despite his wife, she came to report on the trial—and share his life.

*Lincoln Steffens:* A muckraker intent on framing the trial in his terms: "justifiable dynamiting."

*E. W. Scripps:* Wealthy publisher and proponent of the view that the men killed "should be considered what they really were— soldiers enlisted under a capitalist employer."

PROLOGUE

# THREE LIVES

# PROLOGUE

---

As the detective made his way along a bustling Fourteenth Street in New York City on that late December day in 1910, he was confident that, after a frustrating month in Los Angeles, he was at least closing in on one murderer. "Every criminal leaves a track," Billy Burns was fond of telling his operatives, "that many times Providence interferes to uncover." Only in this grim case—the sordid murder of ten-year-old Marie Smith—an impatient Burns had decided he had no choice but to give Providence an inventive nudge. He walked toward his appointment at 11 East Fourteenth Street with great hopes for his plan.

The detective was also curious about the man he was going to meet. There had been a time, after all, when but for his father's misgivings, their lives might have followed similar paths. In high school in Columbus, Ohio, Billy Burns, the red-haired, freckle-faced immigrant Irish tailor's son, had performed in the Shakespeare Society's productions. He had won cheers and laughter—his first small thrill of celebrity—as a clog-dancing, thick-brogued Emerald Isle rascal in a comic routine he wrote for the school show. He had dreamed of a career on stage. But when his father insisted he get a job with a steady income, a government job, perhaps, Billy obeyed. He found work as an assistant operative in the United States Secret Service.

Tenacious, flamboyant, ingenious, and when the opportunity allowed, still theatrical, Billy Burns threw himself into each new puzzle. He rounded up the counterfeiters who had manufactured a hundred-dollar bill so nearly perfect it had fooled bank tellers throughout the country. He solved the mystery of how, despite a detachment of guards and meticulous security precautions, bags of Double Eagle twenty-dollar gold coins had been stolen from the San Francisco Mint. He foiled a plot to assassinate Julian, Lord Paunce-fote, the British ambassador to the United States. Posing as an insurance salesman, he spent months undercover in Indiana to identify and then track down the vigilantes who had broken into a small-town jail, abducted five gangsters, and left them hanging by their necks from the branches of an oak tree. On special assignment from President Theodore Roosevelt, Billy Burns had gone off to Oregon to build a case against a network of well-connected swindlers who were selling off large tracts of public land. And with the news of the Oregon indictments still echoing through the stunned corridors of power, the president sent his special operative off on another danger-ous mission: Billy Burns was to put an end to the cabal of mobsters and politicians who, backed up by bribes, beatings, arson, kidnap-ping, and murder, ran the city of San Francisco as their own fiefdom. It took several years, but once again, despite the risks, despite the ruthlessness and the institutionalized power of his opponents, Burns succeeded. Law and order were restored in San Francisco.

A twenty-two-year government career heralded in front-page stories had made Billy Burns famous. He was, the *New York Times* would soon declare, "the greatest detective certainly, and perhaps the only really great detective, the only detective of genius whom the country has produced." Comparable rivals, the London *Specta-tor* would concede, existed only in fiction: Burns was the "American Sherlock Holmes."

And now at forty-nine, Billy Burns was becoming rich. In September 1909 he had resigned from the Secret Service and joined longtime private detective William P. Sheridan in setting up the Burns & Sheridan Detective Agency based in Chicago. The agency, striving for both respectability and lucrative commissions, announced a policy of handling neither divorce nor strikebreaking cases. Still, jobs poured in; so many, that an overwhelmed Sheridan sold his interest, and on March 11, 1910, the firm became the William J. Burns National Detective Agency. Headquartered in New York, with regional offices throughout the country, the agency employed nearly twelve hundred operatives. Little more than two months ago, he and his firm had taken on the most monumental case of his career. "The crime of the century," the newspapers called it. But today he had returned to New York to help identify the murderer of a ten-year-old girl.

Short and rather stocky, a bit of a dandy with a fondness for three-piece suits and bowler hats, his hair and bristly mustache still crimson, a man with a banker's staid demeanor and a bartender's ready smile, at a glance an improbable detective, Billy headed up the wide stone steps of the Fourteenth Street brownstone that winter's day. He walked through the unlocked black entrance door and then crossed a narrow marble-floored vestibule to ring the buzzer affixed to the right of a pair of well-polished mahogany interior doors.

A door opened, and he was directed up a graceful, curving staircase to the top floor. He entered a large, open space illuminated by a harsh, white glow emanating from the banks of yard-long mercury vapor tubes suspended in orderly rows from the ceiling. Billy Burns walked across a ballroom that was now being used as the stage of the Biograph Film Studio and proceeded toward an oak roll-top desk in the corner. Near a small hill of rolled-up carpets and a pile of folded scenery was a tall, lithe man, dressed with meticulous care in a suit, tie, and, although indoors, a wide-brimmed hat. He held himself very erect, as if posing, his demeanor stern, somber, and imperial. His face was long and hollow-cheeked, and he had a tendency to stare; it was this habit, along with his prominent nose, that made him seem menacing, like a bird of prey. This was the man whose help the detective had come to ask—D. W. Griffith.

D.W., too, had once been a detective. Five years earlier on a stage in
San Francisco, David Wark Griffith had been Warburton, a cigar-
chomping private eye. And like his visitor, he had been relentless. To
get his man, he had donned a variety of farcical disguises—grizzly
bear, drunkard, even society dowager.

But D.W.'s days of playing detective, of scrambling for journey-
man roles in itinerant stock companies, of pursuing his more heartfelt ambition of writing stage plays, were now forever part of his
past. Growing up in rural Kentucky, he had had fantasies, he would
concede, "of fame and glory." By the time of his first meeting with
the celebrated detective, D.W. was on his way to achieving these
ambitions—and more. Still, the shape and circumstances of his sudden success had taken D.W. by surprise and no doubt would have
struck even Burns, with his greater capacity for skepticism, as nothing less than further proof of an "interfering Providence."

It had been only two years earlier that a thirty-three-year-old D.W.,
driven more by desperation than desire, had found his way into the
fledgling business of making movies. Full of high hopes, he had
come to New York with his new actress bride, Linda Arvidson, in
the summer to 1906 to be a playwright. But the farce he had written had run for just days in Washington and Baltimore. More
dispiriting, another recently completed play about the American
Revolution had failed to attract a producer. It would be months
before companies would be hiring actors for summer stock productions. And he was broke. He worried to a friend, "I'd lose standing
as an actor with theater people if they see me in a movie," but he
didn't know where else to turn. Resigned, he took the subway line
up to the Bronx to the Edison Studio.

His intention, however, was not to be cast in a film but rather to
sell a script. He had worked it all out: Since there was no on-screen

dialogue, he'd block out a scenario in hours; writers were never credited and therefore his playwright's reputation would not be tarnished; and the best incentive, a script could be sold for as much as thirty dollars. But no one at Edison was interested in his adaptation of *Tosca*.

Instead, he was offered a part. He was cast as the intrepid hero who climbs a formidable mountain to rescue a baby from the talons of an inert, and very obviously stuffed, eagle. He got an explanation about "foreground" and instructions to "keep in the lines" that marked the stage, and then without further preliminaries, the camera began shooting. After four days of shooting scenes both outdoors in New Jersey and in the Bronx studio, the one-reel film—905 feet—was completed. His week's pay was twenty dollars. "No one will ever see me," he rationalized to his wife Linda. In hopes of finding more easy paydays until the couple went off to summer stock, he joined the other actors who gathered at the nine A.M. casting calls at film studios around New York.

It was a good time to break into movies. The first large-screen movie theater had opened on Herald Square in New York City twelve years earlier. But much of the energy of the pioneers in the film business had been dissipated in bitter legal wrangling over patents on cameras and projectors. It was not until the end of 1908 that the major, feuding production companies had pragmatically banded together in the Motion Picture Patents Company. The MPPC members agreed that Thomas Edison—who had played only a small role in the actual inventions—would receive a royalty for his film equipment patents and that movies would be leased (not sold!) to exchanges that would distribute them to nickelodeons and the newer picture palaces. With that legal arrangement signed, the companies could now concentrate on making money and making movies.

And business boomed. For only a nickel, people discovered that they could buy nearly an hour of fun. They could watch three short reels of silent film and then sing along to the lyrics of a popular song that flashed onto the screen. By 1910 nearly 30 percent of the nation—an audience of 30 million people—went each week to one of the nearly nine thousand nickelodeons scattered around the country.

As people made this new form of entertainment part of their lives, entrepreneurs discovered that movies were a get-rich-quick scheme that really worked. For an investment of about two hundred dollars, and with little more effort than it took to hang a white sheet from the rafters, they could transform a storefront into a nickelodeon. Harry Warner was selling clothing in Pittsburgh near Davis's Nickelodeon when he presciently decided to change his line of work. "I looked across the street and saw the nickels rolling in," said the future movie studio mogul.

A constant problem, however, was the shortage of new films. The seven MPPC production companies were releasing between eighteen and twenty-one films each week, nearly two thousand a year. And audiences were still eager for more.

It was this small community of filmmakers, a fraternity of hustling businessmen and down-on-their-luck talent, an enterprise focused on churning out brief escapist bits of amusement, that D.W. reluctantly joined. He worked steadily during the spring of 1908 as an actor in Biograph productions and even succeeded in selling the company several scenarios. As he became part of the Biograph troupe, D.W., to his surprise, began to feel that there was something compelling, even intellectually exciting, about the world into which he had stumbled. "It's not so bad, you know," he told his wife, "five dollars for simply riding a horse in the wilds of Fort Lee [New Jersey] on a cool spring day." He suggested to Linda that she try to be cast in a film. But, he warned, "don't tell them you're my wife. I think it's better business not to."

When the time came to sign on for summer stock in Maine, D.W. was reluctant to go. "If this movie thing is going to amount to anything . . . we could afford to take chances," he reasoned to his wife. Linda agreed. "You don't know what's going to happen down at the Biograph . . . Let's stick the summer out."

So they stayed in the hot city, and events unfolded with all the rapid improbability and melodrama of a silent film plot line. "Old Man" McCutcheon, the director of the Biograph films, suddenly took ill; drink was the rumored cause. The company needed someone to take his place. In the early days of one-reel movies, a director's responsibilities were neither demanding nor creative. He'd choose the actors, make sure they stood within the marked lines on the set, and then step aside as the cameraman shot the film. Nevertheless, like a stage manager in the theater, a director's authority was necessary to move a production forward; and Biograph was contracted to release two new one-reelers each week. When none of the regular players wanted the job, it was suggested that D.W. seemed "to have a lot of sense and some good ideas."

After some hesitation, D.W. agreed to try to replace "the Old Man," but just temporarily. He was given a scenario about a child who was stolen by Gypsies, then rescued after tumbling over a falls in a barrel. *The Adventures of Dollie* was shot in four days, the whitewater exteriors in Hackensack in New Jersey, and Sound Beach in Connecticut. Piano wire steadied the floating barrel so the cameraman could get his shot. Linda played the distraught mother. The night the film was finished, D.W. would recall, his memory perhaps more accurate as metaphor than as fact, "I went up on the roof of my cheap hotel to watch Halley's comet flash through the sky. Down in the street Gypsy fortune-tellers were predicting a new era."

———

By the fall afternoon nearly two years later when D.W. met with Billy Burns, the "new era" had begun to take shape. With a storyteller's instinctive gift and an innovator's technical talent, D.W. had by that time directed nearly two hundred short films. Many of the works were remarkable: perfectly executed, affecting, and fully realized stories. He was starting out on a great and transforming cultural adventure, a man in the process of creating a new art form and a new industry. And now the country's most celebrated detective had come to D.W. to ask for his assistance.

It was Billy Burns who did most of the talking that afternoon. He made his proposal to D.W., and the director did not take long to consider it. Like the detective, he prided himself on being an intuitive psychologist; "I know how people think," he would say in an attempt to explain a bit of his talent. He believed film was "a universal language," that it had "a power" and could "strike hearts." Yes, he quickly decided, it was a plan that could work. D.W. told the detective that he would help him catch the murderer.

As they baited their trap, halfway across the country Clarence Darrow, the country's famous crusading attorney, the champion of populist (and often lost) causes, was trying to reinvent his life. Three years earlier he had charged into battle in defense of William "Big Bill" Haywood, a union official accused of murdering Frank Steunenberg, the fiercely antilabor former governor of Idaho. Full of Old Testament fervor, Darrow had raised his voice until it grew hoarse, pleading with the jury in the sweltering Boise courtroom, "Thousands of men, and of women and children—men who labor, men who suffer, women and children weary with care and toil—these men and these women and these children . . . are stretching out their helpless hands to this jury in a mute appeal for Bill Haywood's life." Haywood was acquitted. But Darrow nearly died.

Exhausted from the Haywood trial, Darrow had plunged into preparations to defend two of the union official's associates, when he took sick. At first he was diagnosed with the flu. Then he developed a violent pain in his left ear. "Excruciating," "unbearable," "a continuous orgy of pain" was how Darrow described his condition.

Doctors in Idaho, however, could not diagnose the cause. The only treatment was the codeine shots administered by his wife Ruby. The filing of the hypodermic needle points with emcry paper, the boiling of the needle, the measuring of the liquid—it started as a nighttime ritual. As the months passed, as the doctors remained puzzled, the doses of codeine and the frequency of the injections increased.

Unable to continue with the trial, Darrow decided to seek help from specialists. "Los Angeles," he decided, "looked beautiful from Boise . . . its sunshine and warmth, its flowers and palms . . . there I might recover." But he barely survived the sixty-hour train ride. And the physicians at California Hospital were baffled. They suggested it might be a case of badly overwrought nerves and the pain largely imaginary. In agony, Darrow was convinced he would die in Los Angeles.

The weeks passed, grim and hopeless, and Darrow decided that he might as well return to his home in Chicago to live out his last days. Resigned, he bought tickets for the train leaving at eleven that night. He returned from the ticket office when all at once he felt a new sensation in his ear. It was swelling. The next day the doctors operated. He had been suffering from a freak case of mastoiditis. If he had boarded the train, the cyst would have broken and he would have died on the way to Chicago.

But as he recovered, Darrow discovered more disconcerting news: He was broke. The stock market had plunged, and his wife, wary about exacerbating his illness, had not gotten him to sign the documents necessary for the sale of his investments. "Now I'll have to begin all over again," he moaned to Ruby.

And so at fifty-three, he started over. Once tall and hulking, his illness had left him weary and diminished. His face was etched with wrinkles, transfigured by his many battles. Yet like both Burns and Griffith, he believed in "the controlling power of fate in the affairs of life." As he saw it, instead of death, he had been granted "a continuance." Now he would change his life.

He would no longer champion causes. He would no longer cast himself as an avenging courtroom hero. He would make money handling corporate clients and grow old with Ruby. And he would never again return to Los Angeles. The city provoked too many memories of a time when he had settled into despair.

Yet before the next year was over, Darrow would return to Los Angeles. All his self-surrendering promises would be broken. All his reasonable plans would be demolished. And he would be brought lower than he had ever been brought before.

By then the detective and the director had moved on from their brief collaboration.

D.W., as requested, had provided Billy with a one-reel film about a kidnapped girl. The specific title has long been forgotten, but then there were many to choose from; villains terrorized helpless young women with a disturbing frequency in the director's work. With the can of film under his arm, Billy hurried down the block to the Fourteenth Street nickelodeon. He persuaded the owner to substitute the film for one of the reels in the scheduled program.

That evening Billy tailed the man he suspected of murdering Marie Smith. It was a night full of routine, a copy of the previous one. Dinner at Luchow's and then on to the nickelodeon. Only tonight the suspect didn't enjoy the show. The detective sat directly behind him, watching his target squirm in his seat. The suspect raised his head and stared at the ceiling, unable to watch the screen. And Billy knew he had his man. The movie had reached out to him, frayed his defenses, left him on edge. Within days Billy Burns would get the killer to confess.

But this case would be only a footnote to more momentous historic events when the lives and careers of William J. Burns, D.W. Griffith, and Clarence Darrow would intersect within months in Los Angeles. All three men would be caught up in "the crime of the century," the mystery, and the trial that followed. And in that swirl of events, three men, each deeply flawed, each goaded by a powerful ego, each in his way a practitioner of the actor's craft, each possessing a unique genius, would not only reshape their own lives and that of the times in which they lived, but they would help permanently transform the nature of American thought, politics, celebrity, and culture.

But first came the terrorist attack. The explosion. The twenty-one deaths. And the manhunt that would lead like a trail of bloody footprints back and forth across America.

PART I

---

# "DIRECT ACTION"

# ONE

---

I T WAS NEARLY midnight on September 4, 1910, in Peoria, Illinois, when the dark sky above the train yard opened and a pelting rain suddenly poured down. Surprised, the night watchman ran to a boxcar for shelter. That decision saved his life. He was safely inside when the bomb exploded. It was a clock bomb, rather crudely made but fueled by ten gallons of nitroglycerin. It had been placed under a nearby railway car transporting an eighty-ton girder.

The force of the blast knocked the watchman to the boxcar's wooden floor. Outside, the girder shot high into the sky. Shards of metal showered down, spears falling like iron lightning bolts amid the hard, hammering rain.

Within hours the president of the McClintic-Marshall Iron Works, the company that had fabricated the girder for a bridge being built across the Illinois River, hired the Burns Detective Agency to investigate the blast. A local Burns operative left his bed and hurried to the scene. Under a freight car carrying a second huge girder, he discovered a clock bomb that had failed to explode; the battery had lost its voltage. The clock had also been set for 11 hours and 59 minutes and 59 seconds. This would've allowed sufficient time for any escape. The culprits would be long gone, and, he anticipated, difficult to trace.

Outside the yard he found an empty nitroglycerin can and a small, neatly piled hill of sawdust. He brought the can and the unexploded bomb to the attention of the Peoria police captain at the scene. The captain glanced at the device, shook his head in a gesture of disgust at the criminals who had planted it, and then walked off to interview the night watchman.

Later, after the police had left, the Burns man retrieved the can and the bomb. He also gathered up the sawdust particles. He put all the evidence—the nitroglycerin can, the unexploded bomb, and the sawdust—into a large box and sent it to the agency's headquarters in Chicago.

For weeks the box sat on a shelf in the evidence room, ignored and unopened. It was only after the events in Los Angeles that Billy Burns began to suspect its significance.

# T W O

---

CALIFORNIA, HERE WE come! Over the hills and across the valleys of America, from the icy, windswept prairies and the snow-bound farmlands of the Midwest, people flocked to Los Angeles. As the twentieth century began, the city's chamber of commerce spread the word that sunshine would cure any illness, that ripe oranges hung from trees ready for the taking, and that fortunes could be made buying and selling parcels of land. The California Dream captured people's imagination, and day after day Southern Pacific and Santa Fe railroad cars filled with newcomers arrived at the Los Angeles station. In just a generation, this pueblo village dozing in the sunshine began to take shape as a city. By 1910 its population approached 900,000, and people were still pouring in. And as the city grew, as its inhabitants prospered, Los Angeles became a battleground.

It was a battle that was being fought all across America. In western mines, in New England mills, in New York sweatshops, in railroad cars traversing the nation, labor raged against capital. The nation was locked in a class struggle that threatened to erupt into the next civil war.

At one noncompromising extreme were unions such as the Industrial Workers of the World (IWW). They urged "direct action." Sabotage, violence—these were acceptable, even necessary, political weapons. The goal was to place "the working class in possession of the economic power, the means of life, in control of the machinery of production and distribution, without regard to capitalist masters."

For these radical unionists, "there can be no harmony between employer and employee."

In opposition, capitalists formed militant associations, organizations that were empowered by immense wealth, reinforced by private armies of goons, corrupt police, and hired detectives. They were led by men certain that material success was tangible proof of moral superiority. The associations held that profit must be maximized regardless of the human cost or suffering, and that no union man should be employed.

The nation was locked in an intense struggle over its future and over the quality of American life and justice. But nowhere in the country did the opposing armies of unions and employers collide with greater frequency than in Los Angeles. In the first decade of the twentieth century, the city had become "the bloodiest arena in the Western World for Capital and Labor."

This long-running confrontation was largely provoked by the sentiments, leadership, and intransigence of one belligerent and self-confident individual—Harrison Gray Otis.

Otis's was, in its meandering, unpredictable way, a typical California success story. He had come to California in 1880, at the age of forty-two, with no more specific ambition than to start over in the bright sunshine. He had been a hero in the Civil War, enlisting in his native Ohio as a Union private, and had risen, after fifteen battles and several wounds, to the rank of captain. But he had had no success in civilian life. His warrior's temperament had difficulty adjusting to the succession of menial jobs that came his way—clerk in the Ohio House of Representatives, and then a compositor, later a foreman, in the Government Printing Office. In desperation, he found a position as treasury agent of the Seal Islands in the Bering Sea. With only his wife Eliza for company, he endured a period of detachment and exile. A mountain of a man with a walrus mustache and a wild goatee, bristling with an instinctive aggressiveness, even his speaking voice a thunderous boom, Otis felt caged, his vitality drained, by his life in these bleak, barren islands. He served his three years and then headed to southern California, eager to pursue the vague yet restorative promise in endless blue skies and warm days.

At first Otis maneuvered to become collector of the Port of San Diego, but when this did not come to fruition, he tried something else. He raised Angora goats. A shepherd's life, however, did not suit the personality of a man who needed a more responsive audience. Once again he soon found himself grasping after something new. As a teenager he had worked in an Ohio printer's shop, and the experience was sufficient qualification to land him the editor's position at the *Santa Barbara Press*. Santa Barbara was a bucolic coastal village of two thousand, and the weekly published a folksy brand of neighborhood journalism. Otis enjoyed the work, but when Los Angeles's newest paper, the *Daily Times,* offered him a job writing editorials for a comparatively bountiful fifteen dollars a week, Otis, in his restless way, decided to accept.

He had not been at the *Times* very long before it became apparent that the paper was on the verge of bankruptcy. Unless investors could be found, it would cease publication. Otis was forty-four years old, and as he confided to his wife, he had come to the realization that he was running out of chances. Other considerations also had him thinking: His ego had taken to the power and posturing that comes with newspapering; and his instinct alerted him to a day when Los Angeles, although only a drab mud and adobe town of 11,000, would glisten with the shine of opportunity. Otis set out to raise the money needed to keep the *Times* going. When he succeeded, he was rewarded with a quarter interest in the struggling paper. Four years later, in 1886, he acquired total control. Otis was now sole owner, publisher, and editor in chief. He could run the *Times* as he saw fit, and unencumbered by

either doubts or hesitations, he did. As the city boomed, Otis transformed the *Times* not only into a commercial success but also into
a fiercely conservative, anti-union journal.

From the start, Otis came out fighting. The *Times,* like the city's
three other dailies, the *Herald,* the *Express,* and the *Tribune,* was a
union shop, and in the spring of 1890 he decided to do something
about that. Under Otis's leadership, the dailies banded together and
announced that they wanted the typographers to accept a 20 percent wage cut. The outraged typographers shot back with their own
ultimatum: The owners had twenty-four hours to sign an agreement
extending the existing pay scale for another year, or they would go
on strike.

The owners refused to accept the terms—at first. After only a
day, the *Tribune* signed. The *Express* held out for three days. The
*Herald* stood firm for three long and bitter months before it acquiesced. But Otis would not settle. The union men who had walked
away from their jobs, he announced, would never return. Their
positions would be taken by nonunion workers. Which, after all,
had been his objective from the start.

The *Times*'s pressroom became a combat zone. Union workers
fought with "scab" typographers brought in from Kansas City.
Otis, convinced of both the moral and the economic necessity of his
position, was relentless. News articles and vituperative editorials in
the *Times* kept up a continuous assault on the printers' union and
closed-shop unionism.

The dispute spilled out of the *Times* Building and spread across
the city. Pickets blocked the entrances of stores that advertised in the
*Times,* urging customers not to enter. Merchants who withdrew
their advertising were attacked by name in the paper as "cowards
and cravens." Unions throughout the country announced their support for the printers, and capitalist associations hailed Otis as a hero.

Within months a pressroom labor dispute had taken on a galvanizing momentum. The city was on edge, bristling with a combative politics. It was as if all of Los Angeles had chosen sides. When Eugene Debs, the Socialist Party leader, announced a national railroad strike, 100,000 Pullman workers around the country walked off their jobs. Los Angeles was immobilized. On June 27, 1894, cargo trains sat abandoned on the tracks. Nothing could come in or go out of the city on rail; and these new frustrations and deprivations ignited the already incendiary mood. Rioting broke out in the streets. The *Times* Building, a rallying symbol for both labor and capital, became the center of the conflict.

Blood spilled for an entire week. Union men and sympathizers attacked "scabs," ambushed paper carriers, and destroyed press runs before the issues could be distributed. Wielding ax handles, paid strikebreakers sought out union members and went after them with a professional, methodical violence. The fighting was hand to hand and unforgiving. Six armed U.S. infantry companies had to be deployed on the streets before the bloodshed could be stopped.

Otis was not deterred. The riots were, he firmly believed, only the opening salvo in a war that would not be over until the unions were driven out of Los Angeles. Compromise would be surrender. Rather than negotiate, he prepared for new battles. He now called himself "General." He christened his sprawling home "the Bivouac." He mounted a cannon on the hood of his limousine and made sure his chauffeur was prepared to repel, at his command, any enemy attacks. He modeled the paper's new printing plant on a fanciful vision of an impregnable fortress, complete with battlements, sentry boxes, and firing holes offering protected lines of fire at any mob that dared to storm his citadel. Impatient, full of a warrior's gusto, he waited for the conflict he was certain would come.

His greatest supporter was his son-in-law, Harry Chandler.

With unquestioning devotion, Chandler played the roles of ally, confidant, military aide-de-camp, and assistant publisher. He had quit Dartmouth at eighteen and headed west in the hope of curing himself of tuberculosis. Arriving in Los Angeles, he had found work in the *Times*'s circulation department. His rise was meteoric. As *Time* magazine glibly recounted it, "Young Chandler did his job so well that he attracted the General's eye, got a promotion, married the General's daughter." The two men were now a team, determined to bring Los Angeles into the new century as a bustling, nonunion metropolis.

Shrewdly, they recruited supporters. Otis gathered a well-heeled clique of bankers, merchants, and manufacturers into their own anti-union organization—the Merchants and Manufacturers Association or, as it became widely known, the M&M.

From its inception, the M&M was uncompromising. Either employers ran an open shop, or they would suffer consequences. Banks would summarily cut off the credit of offending businesses. Customers would be "persuaded" to go elsewhere. Organizers from the Citizens' Alliance, a national open-shop group, arrived to help the M&M attract members. Within weeks six thousand dues-paying, militant, anti-union employers joined up. The M&M became a powerhouse, and Otis, to his great satisfaction, was its guiding eminence.

The *San Francisco Bulletin* accurately captured the organization's spirit and tactics: "The Merchants and Manufacturers Association has one confession of faith, one creed: 'We will employ no union man.' The M&M also has one command: 'You shall employ no union man.' The penalty for disobedience to this command is financial coercion, boycott, and ruin." Otis did not disagree with this analysis. In fact, it filled him with pride.

Meanwhile the unions took anxious measure of the threat aimed at them, and they responded. In 1903 Samuel Gompers's American Federation of Labor (AFL) decided that an active and muscular central union organization was needed to confront the M&M. A Central Labor Council representing every labor group in Los Angeles was formed under the leadership of Patrick McCarthy, a San Francisco labor boss (and later mayor). McCarthy swore to re-create in Los Angeles what he had accomplished up north. San Francisco was a union town; its wages were on the average 30 percent higher than in Los Angeles. He vowed to go head to head against the M&M until workers' earnings in the two cities were equal.

Dozens of strikes broke out. There was a laundry strike, a brewers' strike, a bakers' strike, a butchers' strike. Each unfolded with its own bitter drama. Throughout the city buying a loaf of bread or a pint of beer became an earnest political decision. A customer's sympathies were revealed in nearly every purchase; he was showing either solidarity with labor or support for capital.

The *Times*'s editorials were shrill and unyielding, each one another hurled epithet. "Friends of industrial freedom," went one typically fervent manifesto, "must stand together and back the employers who are at present being assaulted by the henchmen of the corrupt San Francisco labor bosses. All decent people must rally around the flag of industrial liberty in this crisis when the welfare of the whole city is at stake. If the San Francisco gorillas succeed, then the brilliant future of Los Angeles will end, business will stagnate; Los Angeles will be another San Francisco—dead!"

The opposition shot back, aiming their most bombastic volleys at the target who, in their strident minds, personified all the unrestrained evils of capital—Otis. From the stage of the Simpson Auditorium in Los Angeles, Senator Hiram Johnson addressed a huge crowd:

"But we have nothing so vile, nothing so low, nothing so debased, nothing so infamous in San Francisco as Harrison Gray Otis. He sits there in senile dementia, with gangrened heart and rotting brain, grimacing at every reform, chattering impotently at all things that are decent; frothing, fuming, violently gibbering, going to his grave in snarling infamy. This man Otis is the one blot on the banner of southern California; he is the bar sinister upon your escutcheon; my friends, he is the one thing that all California looks at when in looking at southern California they see anything that is disgraceful, depraved, corrupt, crooked and putrescent—that is Harrison Gray Otis."

At the American Federation of Labor convention in Virginia in 1907, representatives from the typographers' union stood at the podium and declared that the many attempts to break the unions in Los Angeles had national significance. The M&M was the spearhead of an orchestrated campaign to destroy the entire American union movement. Otis, they alleged, had "unlimited financial backing" from capitalist organizations throughout the country. And his own personal wealth was considerable: He had earned a net profit of $463,000 in the past year from the paper. Otis had to be stopped—to protect unionism throughout the country. The typographers appealed for help.

The AFL passed a secret resolution: "A war fund for use in attacking the Los Angeles *Times*" was established.

## THREE

D. W. JOINED THE BATTLE. As opposing forces smashed into each other on the streets of Los Angeles, across the country on Fourteenth Street in New York City, D.W. offered up his own challenge. He, too, was concerned about the course of the nation's future.

*A Corner in Wheat* had only thirty-two frames, yet the argument made in the nearly 950 feet of film was more effective than any of Otis's dehumanizing editorials, more of a provocation than any picket line. D.W. Griffith had made an intellectual connection between the uproar in the world around him and the fanciful world that he was busily inventing in the former ballroom of a Fourteenth Street brownstone; and the result was a new, expansive way to communicate. With *A Corner in Wheat,* D.W. had created a succinct yet transfiguring masterpiece about the workingman's struggle to put a loaf of bread on his dinner table that struck deeply at the country's economic injustices. And he had marched the engaging and manipulative power of movies—a new cultural weapon—into the rough chaos of American politics.

"How can a movie be made without a chase? How can there be suspense? A movie without a chase is not a movie," people at the studio challenged when they heard D.W.'s plan.

D.W. heard them out. He was, by nature and southern breeding, a polite man. Besides, he didn't like to play the deep thinker. He wouldn't talk about art. "Art," he would say, making his point by joking about one of the leading men in his troupe, "in those days

merely meant Johnson's given name." But even as a fledgling director, he was determined to make movies his way.

When D.W. suggested consecutive scenes in *After Many Years*
showing the husband stranded on a deserted island, then a cut to
the dutiful wife waiting in their home for his return, the actors and
even Billy Bitzer, his cameraman, were incredulous.

"How can you tell a story jumping about like that? The people
won't know what it's about."

"Well," said D.W., "doesn't Dickens write that way?"

"Yes, but that's Dickens. That's novel writing. That's different."

"Oh, not so much," argued D.W. "These are picture stories.
Not so different."

D.W. would not be deterred. His vision was intuitive and visceral, and his confidence in his ability to tell a story was unshakable. Besides, Biograph was under contract to produce two films
each week. Every day was a race to a new deadline, and there was
little time for discussions. Moreover audiences liked what D.W. was
doing. People, as one early moviegoer observed, "sensed Biograph
pictures were 'different.' " D.W.'s name was not on the screen, but
on Mondays and Thursdays, the days when his films were released,
nickelodeons and theaters put up signs reminding the public that it
was "Biograph day." Nickels in hand, customers flocked to see the
new story the studio had filmed.

So D.W. was allowed, as his wife Linda put it, "to go his lonely
way . . . contrary to all the old established rules of the game." At
night in New York he would lie in bed in his tiny apartment in Mur-
ray Hill unable to sleep, excited by all the connections he was rapidly making, by all the possibilities he was envisioning. The studio
had told him to shoot pictures so that full-sized figures appeared on
the screen. This instruction troubled D.W. One afternoon he went
uptown to the Metropolitan Museum and studied how Rembrandt
and other great painters did it. "All painted pictures," he observed,

"show only the face." D.W. decided the day would come when he'd have close shots of the actors' faces in his films, too. He was like an explorer who had no map, only his instincts to lead him into this new territory. In two busy and fertile years, D.W. came to understand that film had a previously untapped power. A movie, he had begun to realize with his uncanny insight, could be more than just a well-told tale. "I believe," he said, "in the motion picture not only as a means of amusement, but as a moral and educational force."

At the tail end of 1909, the film he decided to make, *A Corner in Wheat,* was (like most of his early Biograph releases) a melodrama. But D.W. had deliberately shaped it with an distinctive ideological point of view. The country's many strikes, the muckraking journalists' attacks on greedy financial titans, William Jennings Bryan's passionate "Cross of Gold" speech at the 1896 Democratic Convention with its contrast between "the farmer who . . . toils all day" and "the man who goes upon the Board of Trade and bets upon the price of grain"—all the anger and rage of the era had seeped into D.W.'s nerves and now fed his imagination.

*A Corner in Wheat* was loosely based on a Frank Norris short story, although the author was never formally credited or, for that matter, paid. "We never bothered about 'rights,' " D.W.'s wife breezily conceded. "Authors and publishers were quite unaware of our existence." And Norris, in turn, had been inspired by the actual turn-of-the-century manipulations of Joe Leitner to control the Chicago Board of Trade wheat market.

The real-life scheme was cunningly complex, and Norris's fictive adaptation was part of a planned sprawling trilogy of novels. D.W.'s storyteller's gift compressed the sweeping scope of events into just three sparse and distinct strands. Each was controlled, unmannered, and very affecting. Audiences were introduced to farmers stoically working in a field; the Wheat King hatching his plot to control the market; and the city's downtrodden poor hoping to buy bread to feed their families.

During the course of the short film, no character from any of these settings journeyed outside his carefully delineated world. They did not speak to one another. They remained independent and self-contained. Yet D.W.'s deft parallel editing among the three strands was not just a technological innovation but an inspired act of story-telling. With subtlety and control, he succeeded in capturing the essence of the early-twentieth-century marketplace. His technique, his cutting between well-crafted and realistic scenes, created an uncanny feel both for the alienation in the American social experience and for the inescapable connections, the bread on the table, that bound the nation together.

D.W. did all this with poise and reserve, without histrionics. Still, the film brimmed with energy and a consistent point of view. The story built like a calm, well-reasoned argument, its discipline adding to the suspense, until at its end the audience was presented with three haunting images: The Wheat King, after receiving a telegram stating that he now controls the world's market in wheat, suddenly slips and falls into a grain elevator, the wheat enveloping him until only a single desperately grasping hand is visible, and then it too is engulfed and disappears; police, brandishing revolvers and clubs, charge at the enraged poor who, because the price of flour has doubled, can no longer afford to buy bread; and a solitary farmer, a pastiche of Millet's *The Sower*, working in a lonely field as night falls.

The unique and overflowing power in the film, its compassion and anger, did not go unnoticed. The reviewer in the *New York Dramatic Mirror* wrote: "This picture is not a picture drama, although it is presented with dramatic force. It is an argument, an editorial, an essay on a vital subject of deep interest to all . . . No orator, no editorial writer, no essayist could so strongly and effectively present the thoughts conveyed in this picture. It is another demonstration of the force and power of motion pictures as a means of conveying ideas. It is a daring step for the Biograph producers to take."

This "daring step" had one immediate consequence. D.W. had suggested to Henry Marvin, the president of the Biograph Company, that he be allowed to take the troupe to sunny California to shoot during the winter months. With the success of *A Corner in Wheat*, the front office agreed. Reservations were booked for the Alexandria Hotel in downtown Los Angeles.

# FOUR

---

As D.W. WAS shooting *A Corner in Wheat*, a new union offensive began in Los Angeles. The opening target was Hamburger's, the city's largest department store, with over thirty acres of floor space and two hundred employees. It was also the *Times*'s biggest advertiser.

The union tactics this time were mischievous, not violent. Telephone sales were shipped to homes whose residents insisted they had never placed the orders. Customers strolled through the store and made expensive selections, but after the goods were wrapped, they would inquire, "By the way, you don't advertise in the *Times*, do you?" When the salesperson answered yes, they would walk out in an indignant huff, without their packages and without paying.

Hamburger's response was inspired. The store announced a sale: "At Extremely Low Prices: A Large Supply of Strictly Non-Union-Made Clothing, Scab Overalls, and Women's Apparel." It was a huge success, and the store sent a list of all the names and addresses of the bargain-hunters to the *Times*. The paper gleefully reported that many of the customers were union men or their wives. A good deal, it observed with malicious relish, was apparently more important than supporting the cause.

The M&M countered the Hamburger's boycott with one of their own. Their target was the McCan Mechanical Works, one of the state's busiest foundries. David McCan, the independent-minded owner, had declared he would hire both union and nonunion men, asking "no questions other than whether the man is competent to do the work." The M&M decided that such a sentiment was reason enough to ruin him. And with a diligent campaign to persuade McCan's clients to take their business elsewhere, they came close to succeeding.

With grim inevitability, both sides within months escalated their activities. A new series of strikes rolled out. Carpenters, plumbers, plasterers, laundry workers, brewers—they all walked off. Life in Los Angeles was a nasty, politicized struggle. Then it got worse.

In the spring of 1910 a determined group of hard-edged San Francisco labor leaders—Olaf A. Tveitmoe, Anton Johannsen, Tom Mooney, and A. J. Gallagher—traveled south. They were the men who had transformed San Francisco into a city where the unions made their demands and employers had little choice but to accept or go out of business. Tveitmoe, called "the Viking," was as fierce and formidable as his nickname. He was six feet tall, weighed over three hundred pounds, and used a heavy cane to get about. He was also an intellectual, reading Greek, playing the violin, and translating plays from his native Norwegian into English. But above all else he was a dedicated union man, prepared to do whatever was required to help the cause. He arrived in Los Angeles with his associates, as Tveitmoe ominously promised, to give the Labor Council "some backbone." Their first strategic move was to bring the Structural Iron Workers into the conflict.

The ironworkers were tough men, familiar with danger. Their workday was spent on narrow girders hundreds of feet above the ground. They would not run or back down if attacked by scab armies. The council was certain it could count on them.

A letter, drafted by the council, was delivered to foundries throughout Los Angeles: On June 1, 1910, the ironworkers would walk off their jobs unless wages were increased. The *Times* gleefully reported the owners' response: They had thrown the letter into the trash. And so as promised, fifteen hundred ironworkers went out on strike.

A half-dozen other unions immediately left their jobs to show their support. Within hours, all over the city crowds of union pickets led by chanting ironworkers marched around factories.

Each protest was a taunting, menacing parade. The crowds dared the employers' goons to attack. It did not take long for the challenges to be accepted. Hired thugs and imported scabs charged at the workers. Stones were hurled, blackjacks swung, clubs slammed—each mean blow delivered with an ardent, powerful animosity. The city's streets were taken over by battling crusaders.

The Superior Court issued seven injunctions prohibiting the unions from demonstrating. The Los Angeles City Council passed a nonpicketing ordinance. The strikers ignored the injunctions and the ordinance, and charged the police who tried to disperse them. More than three hundred strikers were arrested, but the unions paid their fines, and they raced back to the streets. The violence grew more brutal; six deaths were reported. "Hate was in the air," observed a journalist covering the Los Angeles strikes for *Collier's*.

Then in the summer of 1910 the terror campaign began.

The first bomb was a fake. It was found at the Fourth Street construction site of the twelve-story annex to the Alexandria Hotel. Two developers, A. C. Bilicke and R. A. Rowen, had invested more than $3 million in this ornate five-hundred-room downtown showplace. Their investment was testimony to their faith in the city's future, to their belief that Los Angeles would continue to grow and that affluent visitors would come wanting a place to stay that rivaled the great hotels in New York, London, and Paris. Tapestries and rugs were shipped at outrageous expense from Europe to decorate the block-long lobby. A large glass chandelier that was rumored to have hung in a Bavarian palace now shimmered in the Alex's dining room. The hotel was an immediate success. It was *the* place to stay in Los Angeles. Its dining room was celebrated, liveried waiters pouring champagne into crystal glasses, presenting trays of briny oysters, and carving huge roasts from silver trolleys. And now Bilicke and Rowen had decided to add a new wing with rooms that would provide an uncommon luxury—private baths. But as the construction progressed, workers began to die.

A hoisting derrick suddenly toppled and came crashing to the ground. One worker was crushed to death; two were severely injured. The foremen could not understand how the accident had happened. Yet the next day the derrick fell again. Another worker was killed, and two more were injured. And now a possible explanation began to take shape: The dead workers were nonunion. "The scabs [were] killing each other through their own incompetency," insisted labor organizers.

As mournful workers carried the body of their dead friend, the second in as many days, out of the construction site, a fight broke out with the union pickets. The two sides traded punches, and the corpse fell to the ground. It was trampled. "CORPSE DEFACERS!" the *Times* screamed in ninety-six-point type on its front page the next day.

And now a bomb had been found at the Alex. When the police arrived to defuse it, they discovered after a cautious examination that the device was a hoax. A gas pipe had been filled with manure. A rusty dollar watch had been tied to it for effect.

The next bomb, however, was real. It had been placed at the block-long construction site for the city's new Hall of Records. Still, there was never any danger. The police were informed of its location hours before it had been set to explode. It was defused without incident.

The unions insisted that the bomb had been placed by minions of the M&M, a tactic to villainize labor. Capitalist organizations denied the accusation. An attack by "the labor-union wolves," the *Times* cheered, had been averted.

Yet throughout the city people trembled with a new fear. The possibility of a bomb exploding in Los Angeles had become very real.

# FIVE

---

THE INDIANAPOLIS ORPHEUM was that midwestern city's premier vaudeville house. It had been built at the turn of the century, a time when the discoveries of daring archaeologists in sandy deserts stirred the country's imagination. Life-size stone pharaohs wearing headdresses flanked the entrance. A gold-leaf frieze of invented symbols, a sort of hieroglyphics, ran across the top of the lobby walls. Throne chairs with carved serpent arms filled the reserved boxes. It was all meant to suggest that exotic adventures did not take place only in faraway lands. For the price of a ticket, customers could enter the Orpheum on Illinois Street in downtown Indianapolis and escape their dreary lives.

With the growing success of the nickelodeons, the Orpheum started "movie days." During the winter of 1910 *A Corner in Wheat* played at the Orpheum for several months. It was so popular that the film ran as a finale after the live vaudeville performances, too. Audiences came to be entertained, then found themselves sitting through an experience with an unexpected potency.

As it happened, one of the many customers to see the film at the Orpheum was John J. McNamara, secretary-treasurer of the Structural Iron Workers. The union's national office was on the fifth floor of the American Central Life Building in downtown Indianapolis, only a few blocks from the theater.

Still, J.J.'s taking time to go a movie was something extraordinary. His was a busy, accomplished life. He had quit school as a teenager and went looking for a job to support his widowed mother

and younger brother. Ignoring the danger, he signed on as an ironworker and spent a decade helping to erect scaffoldings for bridges
and skyscrapers. Popular and easygoing, a ready smile bursting
from his handsome boyish face, J.J. was elected as a delegate to the
national union convention and then at twenty-eight was appointed
to the full-time secretary-treasurer position. He went back to night
school, taking business courses, and then for two years he studied at
the Indiana School of Law. Now thirty-four, he juggled his union
job with other new ambitions—law, editing the union's *Bridge-
man's Magazine,* writing essays about economics and sociology, and
trying his hand at poetry. So perhaps it was J.J.'s expanding interest
in the arts that led him to the Orpheum. Or perhaps he was
attracted by what he had heard about the film's radical message.
But whatever the reason, that winter he saw Griffith's film. "A call
to arms" was how he described it.

A few months later a letter addressed to John J. McNamara arrived
at the union's downtown Indianapolis office. It had been sent from
Los Angeles, and the writer was Eugene Clancy, the head of the
Structural Iron Workers union in San Francisco.

"I have been here five days now," he wrote excitedly to J.J.,
"and they have started here the greatest strike any part of the
country has had in a long time . . . All the shop men of the Union
Iron Works and Bakers Iron Works and Llewellyn Iron Works are
quitting.

"Send Hockin at once," Clancy urged, requesting the presence
of veteran union organizer Herbert Hockin. "He will make his
salary—if not in money, in goodwill for the Iron Workers."

J.J., however, did not dispatch Hockin to Los Angeles. Instead,
he sent his younger brother Jim. His talents would be more appropriate. The letter, J.J. decided, was a call to arms, too.

Billy Burns had also been summoned to Los Angeles—his biggest client wanted him there. The Burns Detective Agency had been hired by the American Bankers Association, winning the contract away from the more established Pinkerton Agency. The association had 11,000 member banks, and now the Burns Agency was responsible for protecting all of them. It was a tremendous coup for Billy's new business, and he believed it would make him rich. The Pinkertons had accused Billy of underbidding, but he simply dismissed their complaints with a coy rejoinder: He promised to be too busy guarding banks to go after their racetrack business.

Billy booked his own train ticket. He needed to be in Los Angeles on Saturday afternoon, October 1, 1910, and he wanted to be certain there were no mistakes. He was to be the keynote speaker at the Bankers Association's annual convention luncheon.

Before leaving, he put his son Raymond in charge of the investigation of the explosion at the Peoria train yard. He was confident that a destroyed girder was not a major act of sabotage, certainly not the sort of case that needed his personal attention.

# SIX

CLARENCE DARROW DETESTED automobiles. He had returned to Chicago to begin what he hoped would be a new, lucrative phase in his legal career and was both surprised and annoyed by what he encountered. A parade of Model T's was motoring down Michigan Avenue. At the sight of all the noisy machines, all the backfiring traffic, the attorney's populist instincts failed him, and a curmudgeon's anger flared.

"No one can even guess at the cost of this new invention to the country or the change that it brings to life," he complained with the mixture of outrage and cynicism that was typical of how he increasingly looked at the world around him. "New roads have been built at great expense so men may ride quickly to some point so they can ride back more quickly if possible. Finance companies have helped the poor to get further into debt; an automobile complex demanding haste, change, and going and coming, has taken possession of mankind. With all the rest, it has furnished an extra harvest of unfortunates for our prisons."

But Darrow's was a singular crotchety voice. And as he conceded, it was too late to be a corrective. America's fascination with the automobile had taken firm hold. The Vanderbilt Cup auto race, in fact, had quickly become the country's largest spectator event.

Willie K. Vanderbilt, heir to his family's industrial fortune, had established the race in 1904 to encourage the country's emerging automobile industry. It was his hope that America would produce cars capable of competing with the sleek, fast European vehicles. In

1909 an American, Henry Grant, driving a big-wheeled Alco, won for the first time. The following year a half-million people would crowd the forty-eight-mile Long Island Motor Parkway to see if Grant would win the silver Tiffany trophy for a second time. Hoping to get a spot near the starting line, spectators on Saturday, October 1, 1910, began arriving in the chilly predawn mist, hours before the cars were in position.

The Edison Studios had filmed the 1908 Vanderbilt Cup race. Cameras had been set up along the route to maximize the opportunities for good shots, but the film was surprisingly dull. It did not capture the speed, the danger, or the excitement of the contest. It also didn't help that much of the footage was out of focus.

Willie Vanderbilt was very disappointed, but he still believed that a well-made film could help create even greater enthusiasm for his competition. He met with Henry Marvin, the former college teacher who was president of the Biograph Studio, and tried to persuade him to produce a movie about the 1910 race.

Marvin was intrigued with the idea, and he knew D.W. had a fondness for cars. The studio had bought a convertible for the director to drive to location shoots in upstate New York, and the filmmaker was so delighted that he had his initials painted in a discreet yet proprietary script on its door. Marvin did not wait long to tell D.W. about his conversation with the young heir.

D.W. mulled it over. A car race in a film was one thing. A film consisting of only a car race was decidedly another. D.W. wanted his movies to tell stories. The narrative could be suspenseful, heartwrenching, or politically instructive, but above all it must tell a story with a beginning, a middle, and an end. He would schematize these elements on paper for each scenario, and he would not begin shooting until the outline was clear in his mind. A self-contained narrative was the fulfillment of what D.W. believed movies should be all about.

D.W., of course, was shrewd enough to understand the journalistic potentials in the medium. He often talked about how the movie camera could be used to report on significant events. He anticipated the day when theaters would show newsreels. He simply didn't want to be part of it.

D.W. was adamant. He told Marvin he did not want to film the 1910 Vanderbilt Cup race. Anyway, he explained to his boss, there was no need for him to make a movie. The race will get plenty of play in all the newspapers.

D.W. was right. Six New York papers sent their reporters to Long Island to cover the race, and at least twice that number represented newspapers from around the country. The *Los Angeles Times* had even dispatched a reporter across the continent to witness the event.

At 12:30 A.M. on the morning of October 1, 1910, an anxious *Times* editor dictated a telegraph message to be sent to his race correspondent waiting in Mineola, Long Island. It was three hours later in the East, and the mechanics would already have begun fueling the cars.

"Send us a good account of the race," the editor instructed. "At the crack of the pistol, begin sending the actual scenes on the track."

Cy Sawyer was the night-shift telegraph operator, thirty-four years old, and fluent in Morse code. He quickly tapped the message in dots and dashes to New York.

At one A.M. Sawyer began sending a new message. On the opposite side of the continent, the New York operator started transcribing—when abruptly the line clicked, then fell silent. The connection between the country's two coasts had been broken.

TS, the New York operator, tapped anxiously, keying in the call letters for "Times Station," the code for the *Los Angeles Times*.

There was no response, and he continued to tap TS, TS. It was very frustrating. What if the line were still out at the start of the race?

At last the New York operator got a reply. It was from the chief of the Los Angeles Western Union office.

POOR OLD SAWYER WILL ANSWER NO MORE CALLS, it read. TS had been destroyed.

# SEVEN

THERE WERE A series of explosions, six in all, and they erupted in a rapid, booming, and terrifying succession. The first occurred at seven minutes after one A.M., and the noise was tremendous. A six-floor wing of the stone *Times* Building was thrown free of its foundation as if shoved by a malicious force. In the next horrifying moments, the building's south wall, the Broadway Street side, cracked. Deep fissures gouged the plaster, spread rapidly up the wall; and then all at once the entire south wall cascaded to the ground. Bricks and stone tumbled in a loud, crashing free fall. As the wall collapsed, five new explosions—sudden, deep, and intense—pounded through what remained of the two-winged structure. And fire raged.

The second-floor composing room burned like kindling. The wooden floor buckled, cracked, and then gave way. Huge linotype machines, heavy as railroad cars, rained down on the office floor below, smashed through the planks, and continued their descent until they landed with a tremendous thud on the basement gas mains. Rivers of gas gushed out, coursing in all directions, feeding flames and causing them to burn with a new intensity.

A firestorm shot up from the basement. Columns of intense red heat pierced floorboards, ignited ink barrels, and devoured huge rolls of newsprint paper. In less than four minutes the building had become a cauldron of smoke, heat, and flames.

At the time of the first blast, about one hundred people had been at work. On the upper floors, a thin late-night editorial and composing crew was hurrying to put the paper "to bed." Down below in the pressroom, the printers prepared the machinery; the first edition would have rolled off the presses at four A.M. Now they were all trapped. And escape would be a battle.

The first person to rush to the scene was a man wearing a woman's floral dress and a blond wig. Los Angeles police detective Eddie King had been working an undercover detail that night trying to catch the Boyle Heights rapist. Throughout the summer the rapist had been targeting women in the Boyle Heights neighborhood, and the police, with no clues and conflicting descriptions of the assailant, had decided to bait a trap with a decoy. But King, a hulking six-footer crammed into a tentlike dress and wearing a garish straw blond wig that barely covered his thick neck, had attracted only incredulous stares. Frustrated, his mood worked raw by the snide teasing that the backup officers had aimed at him throughout the night, King had been returning at one A.M. to the First Street police station. As he crossed Spring Street, the ground seemed to give way beneath his feet. He steadied himself, and all at once a catastrophic boom broke through the nighttime quiet. In the distance the sky lit up with a diffused glow. An earthquake, King decided. He ran full speed toward the eerie, unnatural light.

The *Times* Building was an inferno. King was overwhelmed. Instinctively he rushed toward the structure with the vague plan of saving someone. But the flames and the heat quickly stopped his advance; it was as if he were held back by an impenetrable wall. He had no choice but to remain on the street. He could stare at the galloping, uncontrolled fire, feel the scalding intensity of its heat, and listen to the miserable screams, the keening wails, of the people trapped inside. But there was nothing he could do. They were beyond his help.

Alerted by shouts, he looked upward. A crowd of confused, desperate faces appeared at the third-floor windows. The flames were moving toward them, getting closer. The heat was unbearable. So people started to jump.

It was a long way down. King watched men land on the hard concrete sidewalk. How must it feel, he thought, to have your entire existence come down to a single impossible choice: either you burn or you jump to your death. Tears in his eyes, he picked up one inert body after another and carried it across the street. He thought the corpses should be removed as far as possible from the fire's path. He didn't want them to be burned beyond recognition. He wanted relatives to be able to recognize their loved ones. He wanted families to be reunited one last time. He stacked the corpses in a pile like firewood. It was all he could do.

Inside, the exit doors had jammed. Perhaps the heat had melted the locks. Perhaps the doors had not functioned for years. Whatever the cause, there seemed to be no way out. Still, a group of engravers on the sixth floor refused to give up. There was nowhere else to go, so they headed for the roof. It was rough going, a journey through smoke and flames, but they kept at it and in time succeeded in reaching the rooftop. Only now they were trapped.

Opposite the roof, across an alley, was a rooming house. They could see the adjacent building's roof, but it was too far to jump. The engravers yelled for help. They hoped someone would hear them and rescue them before the fire climbed higher.

They yelled, their voices shrill pleas above the noise and tumult and confusion of the blaze. And finally they were heard. Residents at the rooming house hurried to the roof. But they didn't know what to do. They stared across at the men trapped on the other side. They could feel the heat of the fire, and their eyes burned from the smoke. They saw what it was like to be in the *Times* Building. But they had no way of helping the engravers. All they could do was look at the trapped men across the alleyway.

At last, a ladder was found. It was carried to the rooming-house roof. Only it was too short. It almost reached across the alleyway but not quite. So one man lay down on the rooming-house roof and leaned over the edge, his arms dangling in the air as he grasped the ladder. Behind him several men held his legs in place. The ladder now stretched across the alleyway. The man holding the ladder had powerful forearms, but it still required all his will, all his concentration, to keep the ladder steady. It seemed impossible that he would be able to hold the ladder in place for long. But there was no alternative. It was the only way.

One by one the engravers crawled on their hands and knees across the ladder. They tried not to rush. They tried not to panic as the smoke intensified. When the ladder started to shake, they kept going. They knew they could not stop. There was no other escape. All six men made it across the alleyway to the rooming house.

Harry Chandler was also fortunate. The assistant publisher had left the building only moments before the first explosion. His father-in-law, Harrison Gray Otis, had not been in the building either. He was in Mexico, sent by President William Howard Taft to represent the United States at the Centennial of American Independence.

Churchill Harvey-Elder was the last man to jump from the building. Recently promoted to assistant night editor, he had earlier returned from dinner at Tony's Spanish Kitchen on North Broadway to find his mother in the newsroom. Proud of her son, she wanted to see him working at his new, important job. She watched him with a beaming pride for a while, and then he walked her to the door.

Nearly two hours later he was in the city room when the explosion occurred. He tried to escape down a flight of stairs, but the flames pushed him back. In just an instant the flesh was seared from his arms and chest. He retreated, moving back from the fire until he was up against the windows on the First Street side of the building. There nowhere else to go, so he crawled out onto the ledge. It was hot to his touch. He was three stories above the ground. The fire was moving toward him. Smoke attacked him. His burns were incredibly painful. He did not know what to do. He had run out of options.

Then he heard shouts coming from the street. He looked down and saw two fireman and a policeman holding a net. From this height, the net looked very small. But they were yelling at him, pleading with him, to jump. Harvey-Elder realized it was his only chance. He jumped.

He missed the net. He landed on the concrete. But he was still alive when they carried his body to the ambulance. He hung on to life at Clara Barton Hospital for a few more hours, and then at seven-thirty that morning he died. Harvey-Elder's was the final death.

In all, twenty-one people died. They were editors, linotype operators, printers, pressmen, compositors, telegraph operators, and Harry Chandler's secretary, who had decided to linger in the office for a few minutes after his boss had left. Sixteen of the dead men left behind widows and children. Seventeen people were injured. The building was a ruin.

But there still was a paper to get out. Eyes brimming with tears, Harry Chandler addressed the survivors. He assembled them on a street within view of the smoldering building. The air was heavy with a noxious, charred smell. The ambulances, bells clanging, continued to take away the dead, their colleagues.

The publisher, Chandler explained, had been fearful that the paper would be attacked. As a contingency, he had months earlier set up an auxiliary newsroom and composition plant. It was just a few blocks away on College Street. The owners of the *Los Angeles*

*Herald* had agreed that the plates could be run off their presses. They had two hours to get the first edition out.

As Harvey-Elder lay dying at Clara Barton Hospital, a one-page special edition of the *Los Angeles Times* ran off the borrowed presses. An eight-column streamer stretched across the entire page: UNIONIST BOMBS WRECK THE TIMES.

The front page also carried "A Plain Statement" signed by Harry E. Andrews, the paper's managing editor. It read:

> The *Times* building was destroyed this morning by the enemies of industrial freedom by dynamite bombs and fire.
>
> Numerous threats to this dastardly deed had been received.
>
> The *Times* itself cannot be destroyed. It will be issued every day and will fight its battles to the end.
>
> The elements that conspired to perpetrate this horror must not be permitted to pursue their awful campaign of intimidation and terror. Never will the *Times* cease its warfare against them . . .
>
> They can kill our men and can wreck our buildings, but by the God above they cannot kill the *Times*.

Even on that first day, as the story was told in headlines across a shocked nation, not everyone was as certain as the *Times* editors about what had caused the explosion. Many people had the suspicion—and some had the firm belief—that the obvious cause was too obvious.

# EIGHT

---

$I$N BILLY BURNS'S orderly world, tardiness was an unforgivable sin. He would not tolerate it when his agents were late, and his usually genial mood would quickly turn sour and often abusive. He lived his own life, too, by a precisely calibrated timetable; punctuality, he lectured his four sons, was the necessary foundation for a logical mind. So on Saturday morning, October 1, 1910, Billy's anxieties lifted when his train pulled into Los Angeles station at eight. He was right on schedule. He'd have sufficient time to go to his hotel, freshen up from the journey, get his suit pressed, review his speech one last time, and then head to the American Bankers Association luncheon.

His satisfied mood was reinforced when he looked out the train window and saw Eddie Mills, from his Los Angeles office, waiting on the platform—just as scheduled. Mills would help with the bags and then drive him to the Alexandria Hotel. Perhaps there would even be time for the two of them to catch up over breakfast. Billy loved a good breakfast. "A good day needs a good start" went another of the precepts he repeatedly shared with his sons.

He hurried to the platform to meet his agent. Only then, as he looked into Mills's somber face, did Billy realize something was not right. Mills handed him the morning papers, and he read the shocking headlines: twenty-one dead, the *Times* Building destroyed.

On the ride to the Alex, Billy could see a column of gray smoke rising high in the downtown sky. The smell of fire, of seared wood and stone, remained strong in the air. Within moments Billy felt as if the awful smell of disaster had become trapped in his lungs. It

coursed through him like a plague. He was visiting a ruined city.
They drove as close as they were allowed to the scene, and Billy saw
people crowding the police lines. He imagined that many were the
wives and children of the dead waiting for the bodies to be pulled
from the ruins. It was heartbreaking. And futile. His mind raced.
Billy thought about Otis. He detested the man. A price had been put
on Billy's head, and Otis and the *Times* had supported—even
encouraged—the men who had wanted him murdered.

It was only five years ago when, on secret orders from President Teddy Roosevelt himself, Billy Burns had gone off to San
Francisco to make a case against a well-connected group of, as
the detective called them, "rich crooks." He succeeded in getting
Abraham Rueff, the city's political boss, to confess to taking a
fortune in bribes. Rueff then testified against Mayor Eugene
Schmitz, and he, too, was convicted. But after the indictment for
bribery of Patrick Calhoun, the president of the United Railroad, a man whose patrician pedigree and polished demeanor
symbolized, in Billy's prickly immigrant mind, elitism and ruling
class arrogance, the campaign against corruption in San Francisco turned dangerous.

The home of the chief witness Billy had recruited was blown up.
A prosecutor, Francis Heney, was shot, the bullet slamming through
his jaw. The editor of the *San Francisco Bulletin*, Fremont Older,
was kidnapped at gunpoint. An assassin was hired to shoot Billy,
but the detective learned of the plot and arrested the man.

Calhoun, however, did not in the end need to have anyone
killed. He escaped conviction thanks to the indispensable help of
Earl Rogers, a bombastic yet clever criminal lawyer. Rogers came
up with a malicious strategy: Calhoun would, with his intransigent
demands, force the unions to declare a strike against his railroad;
then, he'd rush to the paralyzed city's rescue by breaking the strike.

Carrying out the plan required twelve hundred strikebreakers, but in the end Calhoun defeated the union.

Harrison Gray Otis had made sure Calhoun became a hero. The San Francisco papers were pro-union, so Otis had special editions of the *Times* shipped north daily and distributed on the San Francisco streets. Each edition lauded the brave Calhoun and attacked the vindictive strikers. Thanks to Otis's flattering editorials and disingenuous reporting, Calhoun's accomplishments grew into legend. And the jury would not convict the man who had seemingly saved the city; the incriminating facts of the bribery case were simply a tedious irrelevancy.

Billy, although personally sympathetic to the workingman, could also understand in principle Otis's commitment to the anti-union cause. However, the detective was too strong a moralist to believe that Otis's unscrupulous actions had any justification. The publisher had championed a guilty man, a man who had conspired to have the detective killed. Otis's actions, Billy was convinced, were driven by a diabolical ethic: He would do whatever was necessary to achieve his ends.

But this morning Billy could not help but be affected. The mood of the frightened, damaged city reached out to him. *Another earthquake,* he decided, *would not have created such fear.* He understood too well the sort of man capable of such destruction. *A cunning, heartless ruthless enemy of society. A homicidal manic.*

Billy hoped the man responsible would be caught soon, before he could strike again. But it was, he also knew, not his personal concern. Or his case. He had come to Los Angeles at the request of his biggest client to deliver a speech.

Billy enjoyed speaking to audiences. Always the actor, he knew how to reach out to a crowd. He'd offer up accounts of his famous cases, playing up the suspense and the danger as he built to an inevitable conclusion—the great detective getting his man. And he loved the applause.

He was in his hotel room, reviewing a draft of his speech to the bankers one final time, waiting impatiently for his breakfast to be delivered, when the house phone rang. The caller was George Alexander, the mayor of Los Angeles. He was in the lobby and wanted to come up.

Billy told the mayor his room number and waited. He had no doubt as to why the mayor wanted to speak with him. But his mind was set. He would not take the case. He had a new company to build. He did not want, or need, to be involved in another time-consuming and politicized investigation, another San Francisco. He had already confronted too many powerful adversaries in his lifetime. Besides, he was scheduled to give a speech in less than three hours.

"This certainly is a stroke of luck," Mayor Alexander said as he pumped Billy's hand. "You being right in the city at a time like this." He was an older man, in his seventies, and with his long white goatee and a bit of the brogue from his native Scotland in his voice, he struck Burns as a comical figure, the sort of engaging character you'd see on stage in a vaudeville farce. But this morning Alexander was dour and mournful. Los Angeles had been attacked, and its mayor was frantic with concern. How many more bombs would explode? How many more people would be killed? The mayor needed the famous detective's help.

"I wired all over the country in an effort to find you," Alexander went on with genuine amazement, "only to learn that you were due here in Los Angeles this morning. It seems like fate." He appealed to Burns to take the case. The detective must apprehend the men responsible for the twenty-one deaths, "no matter what the cost and no matter who they are."

Billy considered. He was flattered by the mayor's personal appeal. He knew the entire nation would focus on this case. A success would add another dimension to his celebrity. A triumph would bring new clients to the Burns Detective Agency. He even already had a theory about who might be involved. But still he hesitated.

His graft investigation in San Francisco had created too much ill-will. Too many well-connected people in California had wanted him to fail, and Billy was certain they would eagerly work against him again if they had the chance. He feared that Otis would actively obstruct his investigation. Los Angeles was the publisher's home territory, a city where his influence was immense. Billy doubted he had the resources, the insider's knowledge, to challenge Otis in his own town—and prevail.

"Mayor Alexander," he said at last, "I have certain very influential enemies here in Los Angeles owing to some investigations I have made in the past. They will try to thwart me at every turn."

But Billy also knew it would be the biggest case of his, of any detective's, career. He wanted the job—if he could get it on his terms.

"I accept the responsibility of this investigation on the condition that I will be obliged to report to no one—not even you—until the job has been brought to a successful conclusion."

He needed his independence; he was convinced it was the only way his investigation could succeed. Billy, adamant, went on: "My connection with the investigation should be kept an absolute secret."

Mayor Alexander agreed without hesitation. He had done his job—he had hired the country's greatest detective.

Billy Burns was pleased, too, energized by the mystery he'd be delving into. Without feeling any guilt, he quickly canceled the day's

previous commitment. Priorities, he decided with a bit of philosophy, had rearranged his orderly world. As soon as the mayor left, he
called his Los Angeles office and told Malcolm MacLaren, its manager, to inform the bankers that they'd need to find someone else to
talk at their lunch. He regretted this last-minute cancellation, but he
hoped they'd understand. William J. Burns would be occupied solving the crime of the century.

# NINE

---

An hour later, as Billy at last was eating his breakfast, an agitated Mayor Alexander returned to the detective's hotel room. He brought news, and all of it was bad.

Two more bombs had been found. Police Detective Tom Rico had been part of a group of officers searching the Bivouac, Otis's mansion fortress on Wilshire Boulevard, when he noticed a suitcase wedged into the hedges. Assisted by other officers, Rico carefully removed the suitcase and carried it to a far corner of the vast green lawn. He was slitting it open when he heard a whirring sound. "Run!" he yelled. The officers had dived into a drainage ditch when the bomb exploded. The blast dug a crater out of the lawn, but no one was hurt.

The second bomb was discovered at the home of Felix Zeehandelaar, the secretary of the Merchants and Manufacturers Association. For years he had been the object of union barbs; "Zeehande*liar,*" strikers had taunted. Now he had become a target.

Once again it was Detective Rico who had noticed a suspicious suitcase. But this time the bomb didn't go off. The police had succeeded in cutting the wires. The device was intact.

"I'll want to see it," Billy told the mayor. He kept, however, another thought to himself. It was quite a coincidence that Rico had found both bombs. Perhaps it was even something more than a coincidence.

"Agreed," said the mayor. The defused bomb had been taken to police headquarters on Second Street; the detective could examine it at his convenience. But, the mayor continued, his voice suddenly faltering, there was another problem.

Billy did not speak. He had seen too many men make agreements, give their word, and then walk away from their promises. He knew what was coming, and he prepared himself. He wanted to react with calm dignity, not with anger. His temper was famous, and he had grown old enough to be embarrassed by it.

The mayor's words came out slowly, forming uneasy sentences. It was the manner of a man who was unpersuaded by his own logic or reasons. There were "political realities" in Los Angeles, he explained. At their last meeting perhaps he should have disclosed the situation to the detective with more clarity. He had needed, of course, to inform General Otis and the Merchants and Manufacturers Association, as well as the Citizens' Committee, of Burns's appointment to head the investigation.

So much for the mayor's promise, so much for secrecy, Billy thought. But now that the damage had been done, temper would accomplish nothing. Resigned, he let the mayor go on.

These groups, the mayor said, wanted their own representative to work with Burns. They felt they needed someone who would report to them on the course of the investigation. Bombs had been planted at *their* homes. For their own safety they insisted on knowing what progress, if any, was being made.

"They've picked a man, Mr. Burns."

"Who?" Billy asked.

"Earl Rogers."

Billy felt as if another bomb had just exploded. This was the man who had represented Patrick Calhoun. The man who had been on the side of all that was corrupt in San Francisco. It would have been difficult to suggest a more inappropriate individual. Still, Billy measured his words:

"He's a lawyer, not a detective, and what you need at this time is the service of the latter. Besides, I cannot cooperate with Rogers."

Mayor Alexander tried to persuade Billy, but the detective cut him off.

"Turn the entire matter over to the M&M and the Citizens' Committee. I quit."

Billy remained in his hotel room, brooding. He told himself he had done the right thing. He had had no choice: He could not work with Rogers.

But at the same time he also realized that if he was truly resigned to leaving the investigation and to relinquishing the opportunity to solve the crime of the century, at this moment he'd be on his way to the Bankers Association to give his speech.

He waited.

Billy was relieved when the house phone finally rang. Mayor Alexander was on his way up.

Alexander did not argue or try to reason with the detective. With a politician's well-practiced canniness, he offered up a very personal plea.

"If you refuse to consent to act with Rogers, I will always be blamed if we fail to apprehend the men responsible," the mayor said. "My administration would be discredited . . . I need your help, Mr. Burns." His voice quivered as he spoke, and Billy felt the emotions were genuine.

Billy understood that this was his last chance. The mayor could not be expected to beg him again. "A great detective requires great cases"—that was another of his precepts. Billy believed in his talents, but his vanity demanded that others acknowledge his skills, too. The apprehension of the men responsible for the destruction of the *Times* Building, for twenty-one deaths, would bring him national acclaim. He had grown used to the power and thrill of celebrity. A case of this magnitude would ensure his fame. He weighed all that was to be gained, and he made his decision: He would have to tolerate the presence of Earl Rogers. He'd simply have to find a way to prevent the attorney from meddling.

Billy, however, did not rush to share his change of heart. With a natural showman's timing, he let a few reflective moments tick away. Then: "I think I can bury the hatchet with Mr. Rogers," the detective announced.

"Wonderful, wonderful," the mayor rejoiced.

The two men soon left the Alexandria Hotel. They were going to police headquarters. The detective would be briefed by Chief of Police Galloway. The mayor had also arranged for Rogers to meet them in the chief's office. But Billy had his own agenda. At headquarters he'd get a close look at the suitcase bomb recovered from the Zeehandelaar residence.

# TEN

---

I N  N E W  Y O R K  the news of the disaster in Los Angeles continued to fill the front pages. Five days later the *New York Times* reported that bodies were still being removed from the charred rubble. The National Association of Manufacturers met that first week of October in Manhattan and sent Otis a telegram urging him to continue to battle "for industrial freedom." At a large, boisterous rally on Union Square speakers speculated that the explosion might have been an accident, "caused by gas, which several in the building smelled during the evening." While on nearby Fourteenth Street, D.W. already had Los Angeles on his troubled mind.

His troupe would be leaving for California in six weeks. Only now they would be forced to make the trip without the director's favorite leading lady. The "Biograph Girl," as audiences had taken to calling her, the country's first genuine movie star, had abruptly left the company. Mary Pickford had sailed to Cuba with her new husband to shoot movies for Carl Laemmle's Independent Motion Picture company.

D.W. felt not just disappointed but betrayed. Mary—born Gladys Smith—had walked into the Biograph studio as an accomplished teenage stage actress, but D.W. always believed he had discovered her. In his director's mind, she was his creation. He had been the first to understand the engaging power that Mary's tender, wonderfully expressive face would have on the big screen.

It had been a warm May morning in 1909 when sixteen-year-old Mary, as she would remember it, "belligerently . . . marched up the steps of Biograph" for the first time. With the family short of funds, and no new play on Mary's schedule, her mother had insisted that she audition for a role in the movies. Reluctantly Mary obeyed. "I was disappointed in Mother: permitting a Belasco actress, and her own daughter at that, to go into one of those despised, cheap, loathsome motion-picture studios."

Mary took a seat in a corner near the door, deliberately tucking herself away as if trying to hide. She was wearing a blue-and-white-striped dress and a rolled-brim straw sailor hat with a dark blue ribbon. Short golden curls bobbed around a fresh, angelic face. Her large hazel eyes shined magically. She looked not more than fourteen, but there was a maturity and confidence in her controlled demeanor. Despite her efforts to remain aloof, it did not take her long to get noticed. In the dressing room, the actors who had been playing craps starting talking.

"There's a cute kid outside. Have you seen her?"

"No. Where is she?"

"She's been sitting out there in a corner by herself."

Bobby Harron, the prop boy, told D.W. about the "good looker" who had the actors buzzing. Curious, the director went downstairs to see.

D.W. looked at her appraisingly. It was, Mary felt, "a manner that was too jaunty and familiar." But the director was intrigued. "She was small—cute figure—much golden curls—creamy complexion—sparkling Irish eyes, but eyes that also had languorous capabilities."

He decided to give her a screen test. In the basement dressing room, Mary was handed a costume. D.W. thought the young girl might be right for Pippa in *Pippa Passes,* the Browning poem he was hoping to shoot later that summer. He applied the makeup himself, asking about her theatrical experience as he worked. His manner was professional, yet Mary could not help feeling there was something intimate and presumptuous in his touch. He was "a pompous and insufferable creature" and she "wanted more than ever to escape."

But Mary was led to the top-floor ballroom studio, presented with a guitar, and D.W. instructed her to pretend to play it. Without further preliminaries, the camera started rolling. Owen Moore, the troupe's rakish leading man, walked onto the set. He took one long look at Mary and in his lilting, musical voice wondered, "Who's the dame?"

Mary was shocked. She was not accustomed to being referred to in such a vulgar manner, and she began to admonish Moore.

D.W. cut her off. "Never, do you hear, never stop in the middle of a scene. Do you know how much film costs per foot? You ruined it! Start from the beginning!"

Mary bristled at the reprimand, but she began again from the top. When she finished, she was convinced she had brought nothing to the scene. She returned to the basement dressing room and changed into her blue and white dress, certain she would never again enter the Biograph Studio. But D.W. was waiting for her.

"Will you dine with me?" the director asked.

He was old enough to be her father! Besides, Mary had never been out on a date. She curtly refused.

D.W. was not put off. He told her to come back tomorrow, and he offered the studio's standard fee, five dollars a day.

"I'm a Belasco actress, Mr. Griffith, and I must have ten."

D.W. laughed. "Agreed! Five dollars for today and ten for tomorrow. But keep it to yourself. No one is paid that much, and there will be a riot if it leaks out." And he insisted on walking her to the subway, doing his best to hold his umbrella over her golden curls as a late-afternoon spring rainstorm pelted New York.

From their first encounter, D.W., in his direct, instinctive way, had been attracted to Mary as a woman, and as a screen actress.

And Mary, shrewd and pragmatic, had been willing to learn from
D.W., and manipulate him.

The next day Mary began her film career, playing the pretty daughter in *The Violin Maker of Cremona*. It screened later that week in
the brownstone's second-floor bedroom, which had been converted
into a projection room. The reaction, according to D.W.'s wife, was
unanimous: "The studio bunch was all agog over the picture and
the new girl."

Mary quickly became D.W.'s favorite, and he used her often.
The camera would focus on Mary, and her desires, instincts,
impulses, and thoughts seemed bared on the screen for the audience
to see. Her versatility was also unique. She could be cast in roles
beyond her years, in comedies or melodramas, as a scrubwoman or
a society woman, an Indian squaw or a choir girl.

Movies were new to Mary, but they were also new to D.W.
With discipline, spontaneity, and a good deal of squabbling, they
worked together to expand the medium's artistic possibilities. They
were pioneers, and they fed off each other's instincts and experi-
mentations.

Mary, for example, thought the elaborate screen gestures used
by the other actors were too exaggerated, more like pantomimes.
She conducted herself on screen with a stage actress's subtlety and
control. At first D.W. threatened to fire her unless she gave more
histrionic performances. But after he watched her on the screen, he
came around to embracing her realistic acting style. It was, he realized, more suitable for the stories he wanted to tell. It made them
more believable.

Yet D.W., too, had his own expectations for a performance.
While filming the climax of *To Save Her Soul*, when the villain
waves a revolver at Mary, D.W. became annoyed. Mary was not
showing sufficient fear.

He rushed onto the set, grabbed Mary by the shoulders, and shook her violently. "I'll show you how to do this thing!" he shouted. "Get some feeling into you, damn it! You're like a piece of wood."

Without thinking, Mary bit him on the hand. "What gave you the right to lay your hands on me?" she shouted. Then she stormed from the set.

Shaking, raging, Mary was walking down East Fourteenth Street when D.W. caught up with her.

"I'm sorry," he said. "You must forgive me. I know you can do that scene. Let's try once more."

D.W. led her back to the studio. He didn't bother with a rehearsal.

"Come on, now," the director instructed. "Let me see the real Pickford! I know you can do it!"

The experience, the fight with D.W., had left Mary seething with emotion. Now she trembled at the sight of the gun and tears rushed down her face. Her fear was palpable. The scene played out perfectly. And D.W. had learned an important lesson about the efficacy of a director's belligerent authority.

Mary's magnificent face, and the many animated masks she could put on at will, encouraged D.W. to try new things. "Come on, Billy," the director ordered his cameraman late in the afternoon while they were shooting *Friends,* "let's have some fun. Move the camera up, and let's get closer to Mary."

It was a startling suggestion. But Billy Blizter carried the unwieldy one-hundred-pound camera forward and took the shot.

It was the first close-up in the history of pictures. They viewed it that evening in the Biograph projection room.

"Pickford, what do you think?" asked D.W.

At first Mary had been disconcerted by the sight of her own face magnified on the screen. But she quickly grasped that such shots could be effectively used to communicate emotions. "I think you'll do more of that, Mr. Griffith. Maybe even closer."

"You're right, but something's wrong with the makeup. Can you tell me?"

"I think there's too much eyebrow pencil and shadowing around my eyes."

"You're right, Pickford."

In such a collaborative fashion, they made movies and invented an art.

Working with D.W., Mary became the first movie star. The films gave no screen credits, and none of the players' names were ever mentioned in advertisements, but that did not matter. Audiences recognized her face. They called her "Goldilocks" or "The Girl With the Curls." Mostly, though, she was known as "The Biograph Girl."

Fan letters arrived at the Fourteenth Street brownstone. "You know," a surprised yet impressed D.W. told his wife, "we are getting as many as twenty-five letters a day about Mary Pickford."

"Why, what do you mean, letters about her?"

"Every picture she plays in brings a bunch of mail asking her name and other things about her."

"You're not kidding?"

"Of course not."

"Did you tell her?"

"No. I don't want her asking for a raise in salary."

But D.W. did not need to tell Mary. She would walk down Fourteenth Street or ride on the subway to her home in Brooklyn, and people would recognize her. It was not just gratifying; it was exciting. Mary, shrewdly, began to realize that her growing celebrity brought with it a commercial power. Audiences were going to theaters and nickelodeons to see her. She deserved a larger share of the money that was pouring in.

She was already imagining a more glorious future. "Someday I am going to be a great actress and have my name in electric lights over a theater," she said with complete assurance to a group of Biograph actors over dinner at Cavanagh's on East 23rd Street. She had a vision of the movie star, the American idol, she would become. But Mary also understood that to achieve such transforming fame, she would need to burst out of D.W.'s controlling, and often patronizing, grasp.

They argued, ostensibly about money. Mary was earning $100 a week in the fall of 1910 when Carl Laemmle's Independent Motion Picture company (IMP) offered her $175. D.W. refused to budge. And IMP also promised to display her name in theaters. D.W.'s own name was not credited; he would not allow one of his players to gain recognition that was denied to him.

But the roots of the breakup ran deeper. Mary felt her talents and her celebrity were constrained by D.W. At Biograph, he was the star. Now she could become one.

After Mary left, D.W. went around the studio like a man in mourning. He would need to find another ingenue to replace her for the trip to Los Angeles. In the meantime, he would focus on scenarios that featured older, more mature women. But with Mary's absence, he began to examine the nature of the attentions he had rained on her. His thoughts remained unarticulated, yet they were a torment. They pounded through his consciousness with the force of a compulsion. Mary, the teenager who looked young enough to be his virginal daughter, was the embodiment of deeper desires. D.W. was drawn to attractive young girls. He needed them in his films, and in his life. The prospect of being in California without Mary left him deadened. His only comfort was the hope that someday she would return to his troupe, and to him.

# ELEVEN

---

**T**HAT FALL DARROW'S life, too, had its secrets. Of course, a woman was involved. He had returned to Chicago with a practical vision of his future and quickly set to work. He ignored the many calls that arrived from all over the country begging him to rush to the defense of one after another victimized populist hero. Instead, he stayed close to home, lending his name to a few local causes but devoting most of his time and practice to well-paid tasks for the Chicago Title and Trust Company. At nights, rather than the swirl of earnest political meetings that had been so much a part of his previous life, he returned home to his wife Ruby. He tried to find comfort in her companionship, familiarity, and stability. In Los Angeles Darrow had come close enough to death to resign himself to its ineluctable pull. When to his great astonishment he was granted a reprieve, he vowed to take advantage of this second chance. He would live a more reasonable and settled existence. Only this too, he came to discover, was a sort of death. He realized this when he fell in love.

Mary Field was a woman of immense vitality and she channeled her intensity and passion into the great causes of her times. She had come to Chicago from her native Detroit because she wanted to help integrate the flood of recently arrived immigrants into the American Experience. She found work and a home at the Maxwell Street Settlement and was drawn into the impoverished lives and socialist politics of the city's Russian-Jewish immigrants. Their oppression, first by the czars and then by the Chicago police, became hers; and as she absorbed their experiences, she was further radicalized.

She met Darrow in the spring of 1909 at a rally to protest the extradition to Russia of Christian Rudowitz, a czarist dissident. The crowd was large and dangerous; Rudowitz's deportation, they knew, would ensure his death. When Darrow spoke, his words offered hope and the possibility of a legal solution. The crowd at once grew silent and attentive. Field, too, was swept up in Darrow's oration. She was certain of the deep well of his commitment. He was the sort of man it would be an honor to love. Emboldened, she introduced herself to the famous attorney after the rally.

Darrow shook hands with a short, tiny actually, dark-brown-haired thirty-year-old woman. She had a firm handshake and a steady smile. It was a candid greeting, and Darrow understood its implicit invitation. Did he try to resist? Perhaps. But his life had grown tedious. He suffered from a malaise more painful than the sickness that had previously brought him to despair: death without dying. In time, inevitably, Mary became his lover.

He called her Molly, and she called him Darrow. He was more than twenty years her senior, celebrated and accomplished, but it was Molly who controlled the relationship. Her ideals, her expectations, prodded Darrow. To her, he was unique, one of those rare individuals "who have loved and served their fellow men with sincerity of heart." Darrow, weary after fighting for so many causes, tried to find the energy and the clarity of purpose to be the man she saw in him. Her faith aroused him. They talked about Tolstoy, read poetry aloud. At night she would unpin her long, dark hair, and her heavy tresses would cascade down the pillow and fall around the two of them, hiding the couple away in a secret world.

But guilt ate at Darrow. He was betraying Ruby, and, he came around to conceding to himself, he was also betraying Mary. He could not leave Ruby; she was the anchor that weighed him down, yet at the same time she kept him moored. And if he wasn't going to marry his Molly, what would become of her? She was young, and she needed to make her own life unencumbered by a middle-aged married man.

Their parting was a sadness. It would not do for her to remain in Chicago; proximity would bring memories and new temptations. Darrow gave her some money and wrote a letter of introduction to his friend Theodore Dreiser. The author, after the negligible sales of his first book, *Sister Carrie,* was now editing a women's magazine, *The Delineator.* Molly went off to New York with the hope of becoming a writer.

The week of the explosion in Los Angeles, Mary's first article appeared in *The Delineator.* Dreiser was enthusiastic, and other editors noticed the piece, too. John Phillips, at *America Magazine,* wrote her: "That piece of yours in the *The Delineator* was a beautiful thing . . . and I may tell you that it is only now and then that I feel envious of what I see in other magazines." Her pieces started appearing in *America,* too.

Darrow was impressed and a little surprised. "You have gone so far I can't see you anymore," he wrote her. And he missed his Molly. "No one else," Darrow told her in another of his ardent letters, "is so bright and clear and sympathetic to say nothing of sweet and dear." "Am tired and hungry and wish you were here to eat and drink with me and talk to me with your low, sweet, kind, sympathetic voice."

He told her that he would come to New York to see her. He planned to move there so that they could be together.

But even as Darrow wrote those words, he was not convinced. He could not leave Ruby, and the prospect of his being with Molly again was, he knew, simply an old man's wishful thinking. His life would have to go on without any feelings of love.

As Darrow resigned himself to the vast unhappiness of his stolid life in the Midwest, a life without Molly, as D.W. traveled to Los Angeles wrestling with his own ambitions and demons, a telegram arrived at the Burns Detective Agency in Chicago.

In Los Angeles, Billy Burns had examined the suitcase bomb that had been found in the shrubbery outside Felix Zeehandelaar's house. A New Haven Clock Company alarm clock and a No. 5 Columbia dry battery were fastened by a copper wire to a small board. One piece of brass had been soldered to the alarm key on the clock, and another was fastened by a screw and a bolt to the board. These were the two contact points. When the alarm rang, the current would shoot from the clock to the battery and ignite the dynamite. It was a simple but lethal device. The explosion would have been devastating.

As powerful, the detective realized with a sudden intuition, as the blast that had rocked the Peoria train yard earlier last month.

The next day Billy sent a telegram to his son Raymond in the agency's Chicago office. He wanted the operatives who had worked on the Peoria investigation to come immediately to Los Angeles. They were to bring with them the package containing the evidence gathered at the train yard.

He waited impatiently for Raymond's response. When no telegram arrived, Billy assumed that the operatives were on their way; they had left Chicago in too much of a rush to pause to send a telegram. But on the third day a telegram arrived at the Alexandria Hotel. Its message was terse and utterly demoralizing: The Peoria evidence was missing.

# PART II

---

# MANHUNT

# TWELVE

---

**B**ILLY BURNS LIFTED his water glass high into the air as if to make a toast. But rather than offering up a conventional salute, he leaned across the dining table at the Alexandria Hotel, fixed his district manager with a steady, thoughtful stare, and shared another of his often-recited maxims. "Find the motive," he lectured Malcolm MacLaren, "and in due course the criminal will be revealed."

It was January 1911, just three months after the destruction of the *Times* Building. The detective, after a quick business trip to New York to work on a murder case and then home to Chicago for the Christmas holidays, had been back in Los Angeles for little over a week. While he was away, there had been another bombing in the city. Early on Christmas morning a series of explosions had rocked the Llewellyn Iron Works. A night watchman had been injured, and the plant had been severely damaged. His men had searched the ruined building but had not been able to find the remnants of a bomb. He did not know if this latest blast was tied to the *Times* explosion. Perhaps it was the work of someone inspired by that disaster, acting for unknown and very personal reasons. These questions reinforced Billy's growing sense of urgency. He feared there would be more explosions, more deaths. But he had no answers. All he could do was to sift through a thicket of possible clues and intriguing rumors, trying, as he put it, "to unravel the mystery."

It was a frustrating time. Throughout the nation prominent figures were voicing many deeply believed—as well as many self-serving and politically inspired—theories about who was to blame

for the blast. But there was little hard evidence. Billy had suspected
the Peoria bomb might reveal a promising lead, but until it could be
found—and he still had hopes it would be located—he had no
choice but to pursue other inquiries.

For weeks he had been stymied, but now at last he felt that one
investigative avenue loomed with a measure of promise. "A possibility," he said with a careful guardedness. Still, he felt confident
enough to try it out on MacLaren; after all, Mac was the L.A. native
and would have a first-hand appreciation of the stakes—and
whether they could lead a man to commit murder. Or more accurately, the detective realized, twenty-one murders.

So he had summoned his district manager to dinner in the Alex's
grand dining room. Not even waiting for the meal to begin, Billy
rushed into his presentation. He kept his glass high and, always full
of theater, let the glow of the dining room's crystal chandelier reflect
on it as though it were a spotlight. "The motive," he then suggested
to MacLaren, "might very well be in this glass—water!"

In arid southern California, water was the elixir of fortunes, Billy
began, as if at last delivering his lecture to the bankers. It was a
commodity as rare and as precious as gold. And the future—as well
as a robber baron's treasure—belonged to those visionaries who
could manipulate Nature and bring the revitalizing flow of water to
the vast hot, sandy California wastelands.

Harrison Gray Otis was driven by such ambitions, the detective
told Mac as he settled into his story. And Otis's and his partners'
attention was focused on a sun-baked strip of land 250 miles north-
east of Los Angeles, close to the Nevada line—Owens Valley.

Nearly ten miles wide and one hundred miles long, the valley
would have been simply another scorched stretch of desert if
not, Billy explained, for one redeeming and fateful bit of geology.

Running through its center was the Owens River, an icy, permanent stream of clear mountain-fed water. Over the generations, a series of prosperous towns had popped up on both banks of the river, and the valley bloomed.

In the early 1900s the good life in the valley promised soon to get even better. The U.S. government had come to help. J. B. Lippincott, the smooth-talking chief engineer of the U.S. Reclamation Service, arrived and went from ranch to ranch explaining that the government was determined to bring water to over 200,000 acres of adjacent desert land. This land would be irrigated at government expense by government engineers. It would be, he conceded, a complex undertaking involving an intricate network of canals and sluices. But in time this tract of desert would bloom, too. And best of all, Lippincott told the ranchers, when the construction was finished, they would be able to buy back the irrigated land from the U.S. government at the bargain price of $23 an acre. There was one small catch: To avoid delays, Lippincott urged the valley residents and their municipal water companies to turn over their rights and claims to the undeveloped desert land and to the Owens River water. The government, he promised, would protect their interests. The transfer of ownership was merely a legal technicality. The land and the water rights would be returned to the original owners once the project was completed.

What a deal! the ranchers thought. They would sign over worthless desert land, and then after it was improved at the government's expense, they would buy it back for a song. With no investment of their own, a valueless asset would be transformed into something substantial. The trusting ranchers eagerly complied, and the government survey of the valley began. The fieldwork dragged on for several years, producing a flurry of maps and charts and stream measurements.

Unknown to them, a bemused Billy went on, the real hub of
activity was down in Los Angeles—in the offices of a cabal of politicians and businessmen. And a deal too good to be true would prove
to be just that.

Lippincott was a fraud. He did work for the federal government, but he was also receiving a salary from the city of Los Angeles. And he had known that the Owens Valley reclamation project
would never happen because all along another, grander plan was
covertly taking shape.

The well-coordinated plot proceeded on several fronts simulta-
neously, said Billy. In Owens Valley, as the government engineers
scurried about, two men appeared. The one who did all the hail-
fellow talking was Fred Eaton, a former mayor of Los Angeles. The
other, scholarly and taciturn, was William Mulholland, chief of the
Los Angeles Water Department. Eaton introduced himself as Lippincott's agent, and using the government-funded surveys of the
valley as his guide, he began buying additional land.

But Eaton wasn't purchasing land for the government. He was
the front man for a group of Los Angeles businessmen—Otis
prominent among them—who had other plans for the Owens River.
They wanted to bring its water to Los Angeles.

Their intention was to construct an aqueduct into the river and
then divert this stream of water to the city 250 miles away. It would
be a complex engineering feat and a costly one. Under Mullhol-
land's supervision, however, the plan for the world's longest aqueduct was secretly formulated.

Once Eaton had acquired all the necessary land, the government
officially announced that it was no longer interested in developing
Owens Valley. On cue, with the front page of the *Los Angeles Times*
leading the way, the plan for the aqueduct was revealed in 1906 to
the city's citizens. And with this front-page story, a public relations
campaign began.

The *Times* hammered away, relentless in its doomsday fervor. Without the aqueduct, the city's future would be dire. A single drought would ruin Los Angeles. Expansion, prosperity—all would be impossible. The bustling metropolis would revert to the parched desert town it had once been. The city had only one hope: The voters would have to approve $22.5 million in bonds to build an aqueduct from the Owens River to Los Angeles.

Concerned, even frightened, the voters dutifully fell into line, Billy explained. The sale of the bonds was approved. And the release of the bond money allowed the first part of the scheme to be realized. Eaton and his clique of money men—including the publisher of the *Times*—resold, at an enormous profit, the land they had acquired along the Owens River to the city of Los Angeles. They made a fortune. But only a small fortune. The truly big money, Billy noted with genuine awe, would be earned once the aqueduct was completed, and the rest of their insiders' plot could come to fruition.

Suddenly Billy's narrative came to a halt. One moment he had been going on in his intense, rapid-fire way, poised to reveal to MacLaren the final, audacious component of Otis's scheme. Then, abruptly, he was distracted. The dining room, he realized, had turned quiet, an unnatural hush descending like an enveloping veil. Curious, he looked up and saw that people had stopped eating and talking. Everyone appeared to be following the progress across the room of a retinue of women. They were young, giggly, a bit flamboyant, and very glamorous. They moved with a confidence, a recognition, that all eyes were on them.

Leading the pack, striding very purposefully as though oblivious to the commotion their presence was causing, was a familiar face. On the other side of the vast room, D.W. Griffith stopped at a table covered with a starched white cloth and set with heavy silver.

The director stood very erect, waiting until the ladies were seated. He remained in this position for several moments, motionless and quiet, like a conductor preparing to lead his orchestra into the opening notes. At last, full of ceremony, D.W. took his seat. As if on command, the women at the table immediately turned their attention toward him.

# THIRTEEN

---

THE TROUPE HAD made their way across the country to Los Angeles in style. They had traveled in reserved coaches with red leather seats on trains renamed in their honor the *Biograph Special*. Conductors eagerly saw to their needs. Stewards hovered attentively in the dining car, and they had a generous three-dollar allowance to spend each day on food. In San Bernardino all the ladies were presented with bouquets of sweet-smelling carnations. When they arrived in Los Angeles the principal players were, to their surprise and delight, booked into the Alexandria, the city's finest hotel.

Gone were the days of traveling with theatrical stock companies from small town to small town. No more paying with their own money for railroad sleepers and greasy meals. No more finding themselves dropped at the train station at dawn and every hotel in town fully booked. They had been lifted out of the scramble of their previous lives. The movie business was booming, and they were part of it.

That night, sitting in the hotel's splendid dining room, full of a sense of the glittering enterprise that was their new calling, they listened as D.W., as usual, took center stage. He grew voluble when he had had a few glasses of wine, and it was his practice to use these communal meals to share a bit of what he had in store for the troupe. He was always open to their ideas, as long as he had the final say.

He had plans, he revealed, for "something *grand*." He wanted them to take a second try at a story he had filmed before, Tennyson's tale of an ocean voyage and doomed love, *Enoch Arden*. But this time it wouldn't be shot in a Fourteenth Street ballroom in front of painted studio sets. He'd do it "right," outdoors, by the sea. And if it took more than one thousand feet of film to tell the story, well, he'd figure out a way to get the exhibitors to accept such an unprecedented length. First thing, though, he needed costumes. There was nothing of any use in Los Angeles, so he announced that he was sending one of the actors in the company, George Nichols, up to San Francisco to check out what was available at Goldstein & Company, the theatrical costume shop.

D.W. had a few less ambitious scenarios in the works for this western trip as well. One of them had been taking shape in his mind for a while, but it might just as well have been inspired by the conversation that was going on across the dining room. Its plot, too, involved the scarcity of southern California's most precious commodity. He called it *The Last Drop of Water*. D.W. wanted to shoot the film in the desert not far from the city, in a place called the San Fernando Valley.

Billy, meanwhile, had resumed his conversation with MacLaren. When he had first spotted D.W., he had considered walking across the room to tell the director how the murder case on which they had collaborated had unfolded. But then he decided not to disturb Griffith during his meal. He'd corner him later, perhaps in the hotel lobby, where the gentlemen gathered after dinner to smoke their cigars. Besides, he was eager to get on with his story. He wanted Mac to appreciate the brilliance of Otis's scheme, and the windfalls it promised. And he wanted to know whether Mac believed such a treasure was motive enough for a man to conspire to blow up his own building and kill twenty-one people in the process. Billy quickly picked up his narrative where he had left off—in the heat and dust of the San Fernando Valley.

The San Fernando Valley seemed as unlikely a place for a real estate investment as it was to shoot a movie. Its 150,000 acres, more or less, of sun-bleached, bone-dry desert land were hospitable only to horned toads, rattlers, and tarantulas. Still, it had one potential virtue—it was a mere twenty miles from Los Angeles. As the city grew, far-seeing speculators realized that this forsaken valley would acquire a new significance. Perhaps someday it could even become a suburb dotted with picket-fenced homes for people who worked in downtown Los Angeles. But this sort of nearly magical transformation, subdividing a wasteland into tree-shaded plots of green lawns and bright flowerbeds, would require—water.

And so from the start, as the machinations covertly unfolded to bring the Owens River water to Los Angeles, the plotters, Billy explained, had another equally furtive agenda. Otis and his son-in-law Harry Chandler, along with a group of their friends, had been buying up the San Fernando Valley. The land went for a song; the gloating sellers were only too eager to take the fools' pennies.

Otis and his fellow investors, however, knew they would have the last laugh. They mortgaged a large chunk of their personal fortunes, confident that their stakes would in time be multiplied many times over. Developing the land would cost them millions, but after the houses were built, the roads were paved, and the schools were erected, they would own a city-size southern California suburb.

In the fall of 1910, after years of steady acquisition, the Los Angeles Suburban Home Company—the conspirators' front organization—was ready to begin the first phase of development. The company hoped to turn 47,500 acres of desert into a sprawling subdivision of comfortable single-family homes. Homes whose faucets and garden hoses flowed generously with water siphoned off from an aqueduct ostensibly constructed to serve Los Angeles. Water brought to the valley by city taxpayers' millions.

Only now, Billy pointed out, there were uncertainties. The aqueduct was still not completed. In next year's municipal election, the voters would be asked to approve another round of expensive bonds to fund the project. This time the public might not be so easily persuaded. The city's growing Socialist Party was grumbling that "handing the aqueduct water over to the land barons" for their own private use in the San Fernando Valley was a scandalous theft of a public resource. It was a pretty persuasive argument; the voters might very well listen. If the Socialists won the 1911 mayoral election and pushed George Alexander out of city hall, then the San Fernando Valley would never get a drop of city water. And Otis, Chandler, and their partners would have lost millions.

MacLaren listened with mounting interest, but he was puzzled. He did not understand how the city's possible abandonment of the aqueduct project and the potential collapse of the San Fernando Valley development could be tied into the bombing of the *Times* Building. His boss had promised to provide a motive, but if one was there, he still didn't see it.

Billy, however, would not be rushed. His mind enjoyed a good puzzle; and perhaps even more, he wanted Mac to appreciate the deductive brilliance of his solution. Ever the performer, he continued to tease.

What have we established over the last three months? Billy asked. Then without even pretending to wait for a response, he answered his own question. Nothing, he said. Only accusations, theories.

Bodies were still being dug out of the rubble, but Otis and the M&M were certain they knew who was to blame. Immediately they had pointed their fingers at labor. Called it a terrorist attack, a dynamite plot to intimidate the capitalists.

Others had said a gas leak had caused the explosion. MacLaren nodded in agreement. The *Examiner,* he knew, had reported that people had been smelling gas in the building all evening. The paper quoted a boy from the pressroom: "The gas has been terrible all night. Everybody noticed it." According to this theory, the leaking combustible gas accidentally ignited the highly inflammable stock of printing materials stored in Ink Alley, a corridor outside the *Times* Building.

Eugene Debs, the railroad union leader and Socialist Party presidential candidate, Billy went on, had another theory. Just a week after the explosion, Debs had written an article in *Appeal to Reason* stating that "the *Times* and its crowd of union-haters are the instigators." In subsequent issues he had posed incriminating questions: "Wasn't it strange that all the big officials and chief editors were out of the building when the explosion occurred?" "Why was Otis out of town at this time?" "How did Harry Chandler just happen to be on the street?" And when a gloating Debs uncovered that Otis had recently taken out a $100,000 insurance policy on the *Times* Building, even the paper had to respond. An indignant *Times* editorial struggled to dismiss the implications as preposterous: "Some of the more hardy of the *Times'* enemies industriously spread the report that the *Times* had blown up its own building and killed its own men for the dual purpose of getting the insurance and fastening the crime on organized labor."

Lots of finger-pointing, Billy went on, but the crucial questions had not been answered: Why did Otis need the insurance money? Why did the building reek of gas? Why would Otis have been so determined to brand organized labor as bomb-makers and murderers? Why would he have blown up his own building?

That was where, Billy suggested, Otis's scheme to bring water to the San Fernando Valley fit in. It provided a motive. And once this missing piece was in place, logical answers fell into place, too. Look at it this way, the detective suggested.

Otis needed the insurance money because the valley development had dragged on and expensively on. It had drained him. The $100,000 would help handle his cash-flow problem for the short term, especially if he put off rebuilding the offices that had been blown up. Or maybe he'd never replace the building. The paper, after all, had not missed a day's circulation, despite the destruction of its presses and offices.

But what if the houses in the San Fernando Valley were never built? What if a new Socialist mayor and city council put an end to his scheme? What if a new administration prohibited water's being drained off from the city's aqueduct to irrigate the valley? Well, Otis and Chandler would stand to lose a fortune. Maybe they'd be wiped out, ruined. One hundred grand of insurance money would sure come in handy. It was a fortune—enough to keep the *Times* going for a year or two.

But, Billy raced on, as if following a well-marked trail, what if there was a way of pocketing $100,000 and at the same time ensuring that the project would go forward? Would Chandler and Otis be interested? Well, if people believed that labor was capable of planting dynamite and killing innocent people, it sure would make a lot of people angry. Who'd vote for the Socialists, a party aligned with murderers? If Alexander and his cronies were reelected, then the aqueduct would be built, the San Fernando Valley would get all the water it needed—and Otis would reap his millions.

"That motive enough for you?" asked Billy, full of triumph.

MacLaren started to respond. But before he got very far, Billy was interrupted by a tap on his back. The detective turned to see Harold Greaves of his Chicago office standing behind him.

Greaves held a long box under his arm.

# FOURTEEN

————————

**T**HREE DAYS LATER George Nichols took the train to San Francisco to rent costumes for D.W. As it happened, Billy was also on his way to San Francisco. But the detective did not take a direct train. He didn't dare. First he needed to lose the man who was following him.

Billy had noticed the tail the morning after his dinner with Mac. He had been leaving the hotel, on his way to police headquarters, when he suspected he was being watched. From the corner of his eye, he glimpsed a man in a brown suit and a brimmed hat. Quickly he improvised a plan. Looking back into the lobby, he recognized one of the ladies who had been seated at Griffith's table. Abruptly he turned and went to speak with her. The talk was all contrivance, Billy introducing himself and asking that his greetings be conveyed to Mr. Griffith. Still, Billy did his best to let it go on a few awkward moments longer than necessary. When Billy finally exited the hotel, he saw that the man in the brown suit was still there. Now the detective had no doubts: He was being watched. He only wondered for whom the man was working. Otis? Labor? Billy instinctively clutched the package his agent had delivered more tightly under his arm and continued on his way. The detective hoped what was inside would help him discover who was so very interested in the progress of his investigation.

At headquarters Greaves, his Chicago operative, joined him, and together they met with Police Chief Galloway. Greaves was a tall, hulking presence, by nature terse and blunt, and he had no trouble intimidating witnesses. He towered over Billy, but his manner around his boss was always deferential and often obsequious. From Billy's perspective, Greaves was a conscientious agent, particularly valuable when a hardcase needed to be persuaded, but despite his talents Billy found it a struggle to be in the man's presence. That morning Billy focused his attention entirely on the police chief.

With great ceremony, Billy opened the carton he had been carrying. Inside was the unexploded bomb that had been recovered in September from the Peoria train yard. The chief looked and didn't understand; for an uneasy moment he thought another bomb had been found in his city. Billy calmed his fears but offered no further explanation. Instead, no doubt enjoying the mystery he was creating, he asked the puzzled chief to please produce the device that had been recovered from the home of the M&M secretary. The chief immediately dispatched an aide.

Billy waited with a building sense of anticipation. The course of his investigation was, he felt, about to be determined. As he had worked it out in his mind, there were only two possibilities. If the bombs were similar, then the culprits were part of a larger, nationwide terrorist conspiracy: labor versus capital. If not, then all his suspicions about Otis would have to be explored. Either way, the case was about to take a dramatic turn.

As soon as the device was delivered to the room, Billy began his inspection. There was an alarm clock manufactured by the New Haven Clock Company and a No. 5 Columbia dry battery. He picked up the clock and held it close to his eyes. Soldered to the alarm key was a tiny piece of grooved brass. Wires ran from this piece of brass to another brass plate fastened to the battery board by a simple screw and nut. When the current ran between these two contact points, the dynamite would explode.

He then turned to the Peoria device. He looked at the clock and the battery. With great care he examined the brass plate grooved to fit the winding key, the soldering technique, and the screw fastened to the battery board. When he was finished, he paused, more for effect than to work things out.

There is one essential difference in the two devices, he explained at last. Nitroglycerin was the explosive component in the first bomb. The Los Angeles bombs were primed to ignite dynamite—a powerful and rarely fabricated 80 percent charge. Other than that—

"Identical," he announced triumphantly. The two bombs, he said, were made by the same person. It wasn't simply that the alarm clocks and batteries were manufactured by the same companies. The wiring, the soldering, the brass plates—it was as if the bomb-maker had left his signature, Billy told the chief.

The chief was impressed. But at the same time he realized they were no closer to identifying the person who had made the two bombs. And without this vital information, they could not discover who had planted them, and why.

I really don't see, Mr. Burns, how we're farther along in this investigation than before, the chief demurred. He was clearly grow-ing impatient; so much for the great detective.

Billy listened without interrupting. He seemed to be enjoying the moment. Then he spoke. "Let me inform you of something we have been fortunate to keep secret. A little pinch of sawdust taken as a sample in the railyards in Peoria came in very handy," he revealed.

It was Harold Greaves who had originally followed the sawdust trail, but it was Billy who told the story. Along with the unexploded bomb, an empty nitroglycerin can had been found last September near the train yard. "Knowing that nitroglycerin could not be trans-ported on railroad trains," he began (according to an account he wrote years later), "we felt that it must have been manufactured within easy reach of where the explosion took place." Days after the explosion, teams of Burns's operatives fanned out around Peoria.

They found one distributor, then another, and another. It didn't take them very long to discover that the nitroglycerin could have been bought from any of more than a dozen sources. How would Burns's men determine where the bomb-maker had made his purchase?

"One of the essential features which go to make up the efficient detective," Billy often lectured, "is the vigilance over small details." At the train yard, such vigilance, he explained, had resulted in the discovery of another clue. A pile of sawdust lay near the abandoned can. Dutifully, it had been gathered up and sent on to the agency office in Chicago. It was this mound of sawdust, Billy told Chief Galloway, that had provided the first big break in the Peoria bombing. He was now confident it would also help him find the man who had blown up the *Times* Building.

Harold Greaves had been ready to give up. For weeks, Billy told the chief, his operative had been traveling in an expanding circle around Peoria and had little to show for his efforts. It wasn't that his investigation had produced no results. Rather, his search had been too successful. He already had a long list of names of men who had purchased nitro. But he had no definitive way of knowing which of them, if any, had used the explosive to build a bomb. It would take months, years perhaps, to investigate all the suspects. And it was just as likely they all were innocent.

Frustrated and exhausted, weighed down by the growing enormity of the challenge, Greaves went off to interview still another nitro distributor, this one in Portland, Indiana. Fred Morehart was a garrulous man and glad to have company, even if it was the laconic Greaves. Without much prodding, Morehart confirmed that he had sold several crates of nitro to a stranger a month or so before the Peoria bombing.

The buyer had introduced himself as J. W. McGraw. Said he

worked for G.W. Clark & Co. in Peoria, and they had some hard rock that they wanted to blast. Nitro, McGraw explained, would do the trick better than dynamite. Morehart was reluctant to sell explosives to a man he didn't know, but McGraw pointed to the ring on Morehart's finger. I'm a Knight of Pythias, too, he announced. That assuaged some of Morehart's suspicions; members, after all, joined the fraternal order to work for universal peace. Then moving quickly to seal the deal, McGraw took a thick roll of bills out of his pocket and peeled off three twenties as a down payment. The final payment would be made, McGraw promised, when the crates of explosives were delivered.

The delivery arrangements struck Morehart as odd, but he went along with them. According to McGraw's instructions, Morehart was to load his wagon with the explosives and drive to a road intersection two hundred miles away. McGraw would be waiting there with his own wagon.

A few days later Morehart met him at the designated junction. McGraw, Morehart explained, seemed familiar with the proper method for handling the explosive and with the laws concerning its transport. That helped to assuage Morehart's doubts, and he carried the nitro out of his transport crates and loaded them into the other wagon. "I got my money, and that was that," he told Greaves. "Never saw McGraw again."

But Greaves was curious. The delivery arrangement was not only irregular but, to the detective's mind, furtive. He asked Morehart for directions to the intersection where the nitro had been transferred from one wagon to the other.

Two days later Greaves was standing at the spot. He didn't know what he was looking for, but he began walking around, eyes to the ground. Lying amid the tall grass by the side of the road he saw something. Scattered like rubbish were the papers that Morehart had used to wrap his cans of nitro. When the cans were put in McGraw's wagon, the papers apparently had been discarded. Greaves knelt down to get a closer look at one of the wrapping papers and saw that the remnants of a coarse sawdust still remained in the folds. Greaves collected the sawdust, filling two glass vials he carried with him; a detective, he had been tutored, must always be prepared to preserve evidence.

In Chicago, the sawdust from the Peoria bomb and the sawdust gathered from the roadside were placed under a microscope. They were identical. Greaves had identified the bomb-maker—J. W. McGraw.

As he concluded his story for the chief of police, Billy began talking much too quickly. That was his habit; when the thrill of a new chase loomed, words would gallop from him. His men, Billy went on rapidly, had immediately checked out the company McGraw had claimed to work for in Peoria, only to find that it didn't exist. But Morehart, he said, had provided "a good description of McGraw": mid-thirties, chubby, medium height, bushy mustache, dark eyes. "Next was to get his signature. Greaves hunted through the various hotels in the town around Portland and finally came to a register in Muncie, Indiana, with the name J. W. McGraw upon it. Greaves made a tracing of this signature."

I'm certain, Billy continued, that the bombings in Peoria and Los Angeles involved the same man. We found where he bought the nitro. And now we are going to find where he bought the dynamite.

"Then," Billy announced with confidence, "I will be one step closer to finding the elusive J. W. McGraw."

Just as D.W. learned that San Francisco was the place to rent costumes, Billy quickly discovered that the unique 80 percent dynamite used in the Los Angeles bombs would also likely have been purchased up north. The Bay Area was dotted with companies that manufactured the explosives needed for construction work. San Francisco, he decided, would be his destination, too.

Accompanied by Greaves, suitcase in hand, he took a taxi from the Alex to the train station. He bought two tickets to San Diego. Both men boarded the express, traveling south down the California coast, and entered a first-class compartment. Greaves hoisted his boss's suitcase into the baggage rack above Billy's seat, and the two men settled in. But as the train was about to depart, Billy stood and announced that he was going to the lavatory.

Billy walked into the facilities and then immediately walked out. He kept on walking, leaving the train and heading into the crowded terminal. As the train pulled away, he was already in a cab, driving downtown. It was the start of a long, circuitous trip to San Francisco, but Billy was confident he had lost the man in the brown suit. And that he was on his way to find J. W. McGraw.

# FIFTEEN

A S BILLY BEGAN his manhunt up north and D.W. motored to Santa Monica to scout oceanfront locations for *Enoch Arden*, Darrow settled in. To his great satisfaction, the lawyer had recently signed a long-term lease on the apartment he had previously been renting month to month. When the nearly penniless Darrow had returned to Chicago resigned "to begin all over, be a slave to that irksome law work," he had moved into an inexpensive apartment in an unfashionable neighborhood near the University of Chicago.

His seventy-five dollars a month got him nine rooms and views from the large bow windows looking straight out toward Lake Michigan and the trees of Jackson Park. He had the walls connecting a string of boxy rooms demolished, creating a grand sunlit space that he lined with shelves to hold his book collection. This imposing room served not only as his library but also as a place for entertaining. Sitting in his favorite wicker rocker adjacent to the fireplace, a glass of dry Italian wine in his hand, Darrow was a convivial and eclectic host. He enjoyed the challenge of vigorous ideas, and he deliberately pushed conversations until they became, to his amusement, heated debates.

One evening each week the Evolution Club would convene in his apartment. Other nights groups of instructors and professors from the university assembled in his book-lined sanctuary and discussed great issues. The victimization of the working man. The rapacity of capital. The existence of God. Often renowned thinkers, activists, politicians, and journalists appeared and took part in the give-and-take. Jane Addams, Harold Ickes, William Jennings Bryan,

Joseph Medill Patterson—all were guests. Yet Darrow, cantankerous and often mischievous, always remained the focus of attention. Robert Hutchins, the scholarly, liberal-thinking president of the University of Chicago, remembered, "When I think of Clarence Darrow, I see a tall, majestic man debating with our faculty members, opposing their views, defending their rights, holding long, quizzical, deliberate conversations with them in the dark red library of his apartment on East Sixtieth Street, plumbing and challenging them, taking their measure." These evenings in his apartment brought Darrow great pleasure.

His days, however, were less satisfactory. As a partner in Darrow, Masters and Wilson, he handled a diverse caseload—tax problems for International Harvester, corporate reorganizations for William Randolph Hearst and his newspapers, and for the city of Chicago, zoning matters. He avoided great causes and instead focused on using his lawyer's license and his celebrity to make money. The routine was numbing, but Darrow persevered. After two years he had paid off nearly $15,000 of his debts. And he finally felt confident enough in his financial future to sign a long-term lease on the apartment he had grown to love—his sanctuary, his stage.

Life, a weary and resigned Darrow tried to persuade himself, could be measured out in small pleasures, not great passions. And he tried not to think of Mary Field or wonder about her days and nights in New York.

# SIXTEEN

---

THE GIANT POWDER WORKS was housed in a red-brick warehouse just a short walk from Fisherman's Wharf in San Francisco. The busy, well-established concern specialized in fabricating powerful explosives for the building trades. When Billy walked through the company's front door, he had already been in the city for a day, working his methodical way down a list of firms that sold sticks of 80 percent dynamite. So far he had nothing to show for his effort. He had found no records of sales to a J. W. McGraw. Nor had he found any suspicious purchases in the weeks before the L.A. bombing.

But he wasn't discouraged. He had spent most of his adult life knocking on doors and asking questions. He still enjoyed the hunt. He always "played the game hard," he told his operatives. In this case, however, the stakes had increased in importance. He felt as if the entire country were watching, waiting for him to solve the mystery. He was determined to get his man. And if the L.A. bombing was in fact tied to the one in Peoria, he was on the trail of a much larger, possibly nationwide conspiracy. He could not even begin to guess at how many people might be involved.

Giant Powder that afternoon churned with activity. People had lined up to make purchases, and an annoyed Billy had to wait before he got someone's attention. When he was finally able to speak to a salesman and identify himself, the man was impressed and became quite excited. Billy's reputation was well known in this city; there was even a squat, derby-wearing red-haired detective in the *San Francisco Examiner* funny pages named "Hot Tabasco

Burns." The manager was summoned, and then he was joined by the secretary of the company. They were all eager to help, to cooperate with the famous detective. The order books were sent for and swiftly reviewed.

And there it was. On September 16 a large order had been placed for 80 percent dynamite. Bruce McCall, the clerk who had made the sale, was summoned. He remembered the circumstances quite clearly.

The day before the sale, McCall began, he had received a phone call from a man representing the Bryson Construction Company of Sacramento. He needed the 80 percent explosive. Could Giant handle the order? McCall told the men to come by, and it all would be arranged.

When the customer appeared the next day, McCall immediately grew suspicious. The buyer introduced himself as Bryce. I thought you said on the telephone the name was Bryson? challenged the salesman. No, the customer insisted, you must have misheard me.

Bryce went on to explain that his company had been trying to uproot some stubborn tree stumps on a job in Auburn, California. After a couple of stump-pulling machines had been broken in the process, it was decided that blasting would be the only way to get the job done.

The salesman cut him off. Eighty percent is way too powerful. It's used for demolishing rock formations. You can buy something cheaper and still get your job done.

Bryce, though, was insistent. He had a contract with a man named Clarke, and the contract specified 80 percent gelatin. Either you sell me what I want, he announced indignantly, or I'll take my business elsewhere.

Fine, McCall thought. Customer wants to spend more money than he has to, well, that's not my problem. He told Bryce, We don't have 80 percent in stock, but give me a day and we can make some up. The price was $82.10. Pay now and you can pick up the dynamite at the company's factory on the other side of the bay. You got a boat? the salesman asked.

We'll take care of it, Bryce assured him, and asked for directions. Bryce took a flat package from the inside pocket of his coat pocket and removed four twenty-dollar bills. That caught the salesman's eye.

"You don't see paper gold certificates too often here in San Francisco," McCall told Burns. "I figure Bryce has to be from out of town, maybe back east. Right?" he asked.

People were always doing that to Billy, trying to show him that they could play the master sleuth, too. Sometimes he'd throw out a bit of praise and pretend he hadn't thought of that, exuding, "You know, that's good, damn good bit of detecting." This afternoon Billy was in no mood to play games. The case was too important. He simply kept a guarded, noncommittal silence.

After a moment, the salesman picked up his story. The rest of the money was paid in silver. But, he concluded, there was something "wrong" about the entire transaction. "I didn't like the look in his eye," he said.

Billy had let the salesman tell his story without interruption. When a witness was eager to cooperate, when his memory was sharp, the rule was, you sat back and listened. But now that McCall's account was finished, Billy posed the one question he had been waiting to ask. Any chance you can recall, he wondered with a casualness that was all disguise, what this Bryce looked like?

Once again the salesman was a perfect witness. Bryce was thirty-two or thereabouts, five foot ten perhaps, maybe 190. Lots of wavy, sandy hair, blue eyes, or sort of grayish. And dressed like a gentleman, in a sack coat, with a four-in-hand tie.

It wasn't McGraw, Billy realized at once.

And if he wasn't McGraw, who was he?

And where was McGraw?

The puzzle grew even more complicated when Billy went to the Giant manufacturing plant. The big box of a building fronted the bay near Oakland. Bryce, he learned, had not come to pick up the order. Two other men had arrived with a letter signed by Bryce authorizing them to accept the delivery. One of the men did most of the talking. His name, Billy learned, was Leonard: dark hair, even darker eyes, about five foot ten and thin, perhaps 160, and wearing a derby hat. The way he talked, his entire manner, suggested he was educated, possibly a college man. Said he had killed a lot of jackrabbits while blowing stumps with dynamite; he seemed to know how to handle explosives. The other man was short and swarthy, with jet-black hair parted in the middle and sharp, distinctive cheekbones. He didn't talk much, but when he did, he had an accent. Asked where he was from, he said he was Spanish. His name was Morris, only he pronounced it Mor-*rice,* with the accent on the last syllable.

Neither of them, a frustrated Billy realized, could have been J. W. McGraw. The descriptions were too far off. So who were they? The bomb in Peoria and the bomb recovered in Los Angeles were identical. The planting of two identical devices within about a month was not a coincidence. How many people were involved in this? First McGraw. Then Bryce—or was it Bryson? Then Leonard. And Morris. What had he stumbled into? How large was this conspiracy? Who was behind it, paying the bills, choosing the targets?

Billy found the stock clerk who had helped Leonard and Morris carry the crates of nitro down the dock. He had also helped the two men load their boat. In answer to Billy's question, the clerk said

sure, he remembered the boat. Just the kind he'd want to own someday. At least a twenty-six-footer, he said, with a twelve-horsepower
engine. A beauty.

The name? Billy, full of patience, wondered. Think you can
remember?

The clerk thought for a moment.

"The *Pastime*," he said finally. "Yes, the *Pastime*. That was it."

# SEVENTEEN

---

$A$s BILLY BEGAN searching the docks around San Francisco Bay for the *Pastime*, D.W. was also looking for a boat. In his director's eye, the opening frame of *Enoch Arden* had taken shape: sailors boarding a tall-masted sailing ship as they prepare to set out for a long voyage, the vast gray sea stretching into the distance in the background. Finding the proper ship would be as difficult—and as crucial—as casting the actor to play Enoch. That first shot had to convey grace, majesty, vulnerability, and a bit of the magic of a bygone era. Movies, D.W. understood, were a series of pictures, and like a painter he was fastidious about the details. He hunted up and down the southern California coast for his perfect ship.

On these excursions he was often eager for company, and he looked to the Biograph actresses to join him. D.W. did not, however, extend invitations as much as he made demands. He felt it was his director's right, and he began to exercise it with a promiscuous authority.

His wife Linda was a member of the company, and they shared a suite at the Alex, but nevertheless in California many women caught the director's eye. A building tension was unavoidable. "There was hell to pay," his cameraman, Billy Bitzer, observed. But D.W. was undeterred. Success, D.W. had discovered, was liberating. It provided him with a justifying logic that the once-struggling actor could never have understood. The scouting trips for the sailing boat grew more and more frequent, and he found many willing and convivial companions.

———

After Mary Pickford abruptly left the Biograph studio, D.W. had sent a telegram to Blanche Sweet offering her forty dollars a week to join the troupe for the California trip. She had acted in movies when she was younger, but she had missed the thrill of a live audience and soon returned to the theater. D.W. remembered her as a slim, girlish actress, her talents modest, but he hoped she could replace Mary as his screen ingenue—and that her dewy adolescent beauty could assuage the intense loss he felt by Mary's sudden departure. But the actress who arrived in California was not the girl he had once directed. Blanche at once realized his disappointment. She also understood its cause. She had become more womanly, "grown in all directions," she frankly conceded. D.W., she had perceptively intuited, preferred his leading ladies to project a child's innocence and vulnerability. The director wanted victims, not heroines. From the day Blanche appeared at the Alex, they clashed. "I was always a rather independent child," she said without apology. "I was rebellious. I wanted to do what I wanted to do and he was a very dominating man." D.W. soon went looking for companionship elsewhere.

Dorothy West was more to his liking. In close-ups, her face did not have the riveting attraction and energy of Mary's or even Blanche's. Her actress's power was also more ordinary. When Dorothy joined the troupe two years earlier, she had been cast in supporting roles—a ghetto child, a frail Italian peasant maid. But in time D.W. saw something in "little Dorothy," as the players took to calling her, that affected him. In *The Golden Supper* he cast her as the beautiful princess.

"Aren't you taking a chance?" he was asked. "I can make them all beautiful," D.W. answered, full of a self-satisfied confidence. Dorothy realized his transforming power, too, and was deeply grateful. The director had given her the most wonderful of gifts. He had made her a star, and she reciprocated with her love.

D.W.'s relationship with Harriet Quimby was more complicated. It was respectful, full of passionate admiration. She was a
journalist, had published theater criticism, and had flown a plane
across the English Channel. In 1911 alone she wrote four screen-
plays that D.W. went on to direct. The director was less imperious,
less domineering in her presence. When she gave him a ring that
winter in California, D.W. wore it proudly.

In San Pedro, D.W. finally found the old, tall-masted ship he had
envisioned. He had the antique towed up the coast to Santa Monica. By the time it arrived, Linda had made a discovery, too. She had
stumbled on a love letter that her husband had received.

The writer of the letter has long been forgotten. And in truth,
her identity was unimportant even at the time. It could have been
composed by any of D.W.'s many companions, or perhaps it was
dashed off by an aspiring actress whom he had briefly met while
casting a film. But the letter was tangible, heartbreaking evidence.
Linda could no longer delude herself. Her humiliation was complete. A rageful anger coursed through her. She confronted her
husband.

But D.W. refused to apologize or even yield. He was defiant,
not contrite. Linda did not want to leave him, to walk away from
their exciting life, but his imperiousness left her no choice. With
regret, Linda announced the marriage was over. She wanted a legal
separation.

D.W. showed no sympathy. Unrepentant, and fearful that Linda
might have a change of heart, he attacked. He wrote her a letter that
he said was "the solemn truth." But it was truth dipped in acid.
"Turn your face to your own future," he advised. "After your discovery of that letter written by a certain other woman I have not
been able to see how we could possibly live together any longer."
Relentlessly, vindictively, he kept twisting a razor-sharp knife:

"There were others before her, and there are sure to be others just as objectionable in every way after her . . . I am better off morally, and all ways, outside of marriage and so will you be . . . Don't think there is some other woman in this case. It is not one, but many."

And so D.W. moved out of their suite in the Alex. But not out of the hotel. He simply found another room, on another floor.

Like his life, his work continued with little apparent disruption. The costumes had arrived from San Francisco, and the sailing ship was in place, so D.W. moved forward with *Enoch Arden*. For a week the company shot exteriors on the beach in Santa Monica. They arrived at dawn and rented a shack from a Norwegian fisherman to use as a dressing room. The days were long, but D.W. did not seem to notice. He was consumed by the movie he was making.

D.W.'s vision was disciplined and uncompromising. Each of the many characters was introduced with a close-up. Every frame was meticulously arranged. The lighting was executed with great precision. The opening backlit shot of Enoch and the rest of the crew going off to sea on their doomed voyage had a solemn beauty. With this film D.W. was intent on proving that he was an artist, and that a film could be a work of art. He had begun to understand his talent, and now he wanted audiences to appreciate it, too.

He shot the film in two reels, an unprecedented indulgence. But if he were to tell the important, complex, and affecting stories that were taking shape in his mind, films would need to be longer. The exhibitors complained, but since it was D.W. they reluctantly agreed to show one reel on Monday, the second on Thursday. The demand to see the entire film was so great, however, that theaters soon began screening both reels on the same program. D.W.'s vision had triumphed.

Linda's performance in *Enoch Arden* was masterful. With an actress's long-practiced discipline, she found a level of professional detachment and played one of her final roles for her husband. She was cast as Enoch's long-suffering wife, Annie Lee, and received praise for her "sea eyes." She had no trouble evoking the melancholy of a woman left behind.

Like D.W., Darrow was growing restless. His settled, undemanding life was squeezing all the energy out of him. He felt separated from any feeling of love, for Ruby, for his work. His will was deadened.

He missed his Mary.

Guilty yet desperate, he took a train to New York. Mary was sharing an apartment with Ida Rauch, the actress who had founded the Provincetown Players. The two women had become part of a lively intellectual circle. Their friends were artists and activists caught up in trying to shape the new century: Theodore Dreiser, the novelist and journalist; Max Eastman, the editor of *The Masses;* the reformer Frederick Howe; the sculptor Jo Davidson. In their presence, with his Mary, Darrow's spirits lifted.

But in time he returned home. He was too old to start a new life. He would live with the compromises he had made. "I miss you all the time," he wrote to Mary. But he stayed with Ruby in Chicago, certain that this time he would not leave, or see Mary again.

# EIGHTEEN

---

WHERE WAS THE *Pastime?*

Billy had been searching the bay docks for the motor launch but without success. He had reviewed the city licenses, only to find no registration record for a boat with that name. He had hoped the *Pastime* would be the clue that would lead him to the three mystery men who had purchased the dynamite. He had left Los Angeles convinced he "was getting nearer to the heels of the men." But now he was stymied.

Where had he gone wrong? He forced himself to review all he had learned since arriving in San Francisco. Perhaps there was a clue, a hint, he had missed. Methodically, he ran the interview at the Giant Powder Works through his mind—until something the salesman said took on a new significance. *You don't see paper gold certificates too often here in San Francisco. I figure Bryce has to be from out of town.*

Bryce, Billy suddenly realized, wouldn't own a boat. He didn't live in San Francisco. He'd have rented one.

Billy immediately concentrated his investigation on boat rental agencies. But this, too, seemed to be a dead end. He found no record of a rental launch called the *Pastime*. Yet Billy was tenacious; he felt he was on the right path. His busy days in San Francisco had left him charged. He never considered abandoning the chase. And finally at a rental dock in Oakland, the detective found the boat he was looking for.

Only it wasn't the *Pastime*. This boat was called the *Peerless*.

Yes, Billy learned from the dock manager, three fellows had

come by to rent a boat near the end of September. They put down a deposit of five hundred dollars cash—imagine people willing to hand over that kind of money, he gushed, still impressed. The next day they had returned the boat. He could give only a vague description of the trio, but there was nothing in it, Billy noted, that would rule out their being Bryce, Leonard, and Morris. But what really interested Billy was what the manager had discovered after the launch had been returned. The bow and stern had been freshly painted. Even the name had been redone. Why on earth would someone do that? the manager wondered.

Maybe we can find out, Billy suggested. If he could scrape away some of the new paint, he'd pay for the boat's being painted once again.

The manager was bewildered but intrigued. He agreed, and very carefully Billy began to remove the new letters. Slowly, a letter at a time, a faint palimpsest was revealed. It was a single word: *Pastime*.

When the men signed the rental contract, Billy asked, did they include an address?

Let me check, the manager agreed. Then he walked down the dock to his office.

Billy waited impatiently by the boat. A cold wintry breeze was coming off the bay. Yet he hardly noticed. He was consumed by his hope that at last the case would finally be moving forward.

You're in luck, the manager announced when he returned. He had the contract in his hand, and he offered it to the detective. Directly below the renter's name was an address in San Francisco.

The address was a vacant lot. It took all of Billy's discipline to control his disappointment. The bay wind continued to blow, and a stiff chill ran through him. But Billy stood on the sidewalk staring out at the empty space for quite a while. He remained as motionless as a statue, and all the time his mind whirled with activity.

Frustrated, he tried to put the pieces of the puzzle into place. The men were from out of town, yet they were familiar enough with the city to know the precise address of a vacant lot. That meant they knew this area. Why? Perhaps, he speculated, they had holed up in a nearby rooming house. Yes, that would make sense, Billy told himself. The neighborhood was near the docks, near where they'd have unloaded the launch. It'd been too risky to travel across San Francisco carrying cases of dynamite. They'd have stayed close. The more he thought it through, the more he grew convinced. Yes, Billy decided, the trio would have gone to ground somewhere not far from where he was standing.

Billy went block by block, from house to house. He could not find anyone who had rented a room to any of the three men. Where did I go wrong? he asked himself. What did I miss? He had a strong intuitive conviction that he was on their trail, following their foot-steps, but somehow they had managed to elude him. All he could do, he wearily resolved, was retrace his steps.

Billy returned to the vacant lot and for the second time that day set out to inspect the surrounding streets. He turned a corner, and this time he focused on something he had previously ignored. It was a deserted house. Peeling paint, shutters hanging at angles, windows punched out. He might as well see what was inside.

The front door opened with a push. The floorboards creaked with each step he took. Under the stairwell, he found a door that led to the cellar. It was a cave of shadows. A strong smell of mildew rose up in his nose. He kicked at piles of dirt and rubble but found nothing.

He headed back up the stairs and made a room-by-room inspection of the first floor. He entered each room slowly, not knowing what to expect. Every new step was a decision. It was easy to imagine that someone—or no less likely, three men—were hiding, waiting to jump him. But there was no one. The rooms held only the dust and dirt of abandonment.

Billy went on to the second floor, still cautious, still attentive to every stray sound. He entered one room. Empty. Then another. Empty. But as he stepped into a back room, he saw something: a canvas tarpaulin covering a pyramid of wooden boxes.

With that discovery, he abandoned any pretense of stealth. He rushed ahead and pulled off the tarpaulin. He counted ten boxes. Each one displayed the name of the Giant Powder Works and was stamped DANGER! EXPLOSIVES.

With great caution, he opened each box. Eight of them held sticks of 80 percent dynamite. The remaining two were empty. Based on the contents of the other boxes, Billy calculated that forty-eight sticks were gone. That was enough to make three bombs. One for the *Times* Building. Another for Otis's house. And a third for the M&M secretary. He had found the bomb factory.

But where were the bombers? There was not a trace of them anywhere in the house. It was as if they had vanished. Nothing had been left behind.

But then, Billy realized he was mistaken. They *had* left two clues. There was the dynamite—only he had already exhausted that lead. And there was the canvas tarpaulin. What could a piece of canvas tell him? he wondered.

Billy held the tarpaulin in his hand, absently running his fingers over the fabric. He was concentrating, not knowing precisely what he was attempting to discover. And then he understood. The canvas was stiff to his touch. Stiff as new. It had just been purchased. He needed to locate the store where it had been sold. Perhaps he'd learn something that would put him back on the trio's trail.

Assisted by a task force of San Francisco police, the next day Billy made inquiries at stores throughout the city. The police had the descriptions of the three men and asked the store owners if they could recall selling a tarpaulin to someone who bore a physical resemblance to any of the trio.

In a hardware store off the Embarcadero, the owner remembered selling canvas to a man who fit the swarthy Morris's description. Only he had called himself William Capp. And Capp had had the canvas delivered. The address was 1565 Grove Street.

Billy hurried to the address. It was a rooming house. Billy found Mrs. Lena Ingersoll, the landlady, and introduced himself. She had never met a celebrity before and became very enthusiastic. She was eager to help. She wanted to be part of something larger and more significant than her daily routine.

Only she insisted no William Capp had ever lived in her house.

But the canvas was delivered here. We were given the address, Billy challenged. He tried not to sound desperate.

Don't know about any canvas, the lady said.

There was an odd coyness in her voice. And now Billy understood. She was taunting him, another civilian trying to demonstrate that she, too, could play detective. He let her go on.

'Course, she said, there was a David Caplan who had roomed here. She had been sure he was up to no good. That's why, the landlady explained, she'd kept a real good watch on him and his friends.

You should be the detective, not me, Billy congratulated her. If she wanted praise, he'd give it. He needed to learn what she knew.

It took some time, but she shared everything. Two friends were always visiting this Caplan. There was a ruddy-faced man who Billy was certain was Leonard. And a taller man who resembled Bryce. She even knew the rooming house down the street where Bryce had rented an apartment.

Maybe you want to hire me? she asked Billy as he was getting ready to leave.

Let me think about that, he said politely. And with a tip of his derby hat, he hurried off.

It was the San Francisco police who gave Billy the rest of the information he needed. They had a file on David Caplan. He was a well-known anarchist; and further cause for law enforcement's concern, his wife was a relative of the country's most famous trouble-making anarchist, Emma Goldman. Once Caplan was identified, Leonard's real name was revealed, too. He was Caplan's friend, another anarchist, by the name of M. A. Schmidt. Everyone called him Schmitty. Bryce—or Bryson?—however, was more of a mystery. He had left the rooming house about the time of the bombing in Los Angeles without leaving a forwarding address. All Billy could discover was that he had bought a train ticket to Chicago.

The case was suddenly moving forward, but Billy felt no sense of triumph. The truth was, he was more perplexed than when he had arrived in San Francisco. This was not what he had expected.

There was nothing to connect Otis to the bomb-makers.

Organized labor also seemed not to be involved.

But why would anarchists want to bomb a train yard in Indiana and a newspaper office in Los Angeles? The bombs were too similar to be a coincidence. And where would anarchists get the funds to finance such a widespread terror campaign? And what about McGraw, the mystery man who had bought the dynamite in Indiana? Where did he fit in? Was he the mastermind?

Adding to his concern and bewilderment, another bombing occurred. This one was in Milwaukee. A coal storage facility had been blown up. Billy sent his men to investigate, but for now he could only wonder if it was also the work of anarchists. If in fact it was anarchists he was really chasing.

Billy did not have the answers to any of his questions, but he was determined to find them. He told his son Raymond to try to pick up Bryce's trail in Chicago. He would go after the two anarchists, Caplan and Schmitty. If he found them, perhaps they would lead him to the person in charge.

The next evening Billy slipped out of the city. He made sure no one was following him, and then he boarded a train to Tacoma, Washington.

# NINETEEN

---

**B**ILLY'S DESTINATION WAS a hardscrabble settlement of cabins scattered about the woods circling the icy blue waters of Carr Inlet, just off Puget Sound. This was the Home Colony. In 1898 the Mutual Home Association had bought up 217 acres of rural land in the Pacific Northwest "to assist its members in obtaining and building homes for themselves and to aid in establishing better social and moral conditions."

For Home's twelve hundred inhabitants, "better social and moral conditions" meant a free-spirited, utopian anarchism. It was a communitarian philosophy that opposed private ownership. Instead, property should be collectivized, shared by all members of the community, and distributed freely and equitably. Government, the residents of Home believed, was evil, a force that restricted freedom and self-interest. Their universal credo: The state should be overthrown.

Caplan's wife lived in the settlement. Schmitty, according to police reports, had often been observed there, too. The two men would feel safe, even protected, among their fellow anarchists, the detective predicted. Until Billy Burns surprised them.

Billy despised anarchists. In his long career he had arrested murderers, thieves, swindlers, and crooked politicians, but he had a singularly deep, visceral hatred for anarchists. He thought they "lived without any regard for a single decent thing in life." "They exist in a state of free love, are notoriously unfaithful to their mates thus chosen, and are so crooked that even in this class of rogues there

does not seem to be any hint of honor." That is, their way of looking at the world directly challenged his orderly, patriotic, churchgo-
ing, monogamous, achieving middle-class life. And that, he knew
with unshakable certainty, was an unforgivable crime.

Not that Billy had ever conversed in any meaningful way with
an anarchist or, for that matter, read any of the movement's contentious pamphlets or wishful treatises, all widely distributed at the
turn of the century. His knowledge came from less authoritative
sources. After the Haymarket Riot in 1886 and the assassination of
President McKinley in 1901, the vilification of anarchists as bombthrowers and assassins, as unscrupulous foreign agents preparing to
engage in any manner of violence to destroy the social order, was
standard shrill fare in the popular press. The more unspeakable the
crime, the greater the certainty with which newspapers would point
at "the red nihilists" as the chief suspects.

Anarchists were stock villains in the movies, too. In *The Voice
of the Violin* D.W. had cast a clique of bulging-eyed, wild-haired,
foreign-looking political schemers to play the bad guys. Yet the plot
of this 1909 one-reeler was grounded in melodrama, not radicalism:
A hapless violin teacher is recruited into a bomb conspiracy—only
to learn to his horror that the target is the father of the student with
whom he has fallen in love. To save the girl, he must risk his own
life by betraying a cell of dangerous and vindictive anarchists. In the
end, love prevails. This was the film's only message. Politics was an
irrelevancy. Anarchists, in the director's calculations, were simply
an easy plot device. They were seedy stock characters that audiences
would rise up and root against as soon as they appeared on the
screen. They were perfect foils for his heroes.

Darrow, as in most things, had a more nuanced outlook. He
thought that anarchists were perceptive when they argued that
government was evil because it reined in individual liberties. And
he agreed that wealthy special interests—railroads, capitalist

organizations like the Merchants and Manufacturers Association—had unjust powers that allowed them to manipulate workers' lives at will. But his hard-fought life in the courtroom had made him too much of a pragmatist ever to become a true believer. "I think you folks are right—but not altogether right," he had chided in his mocking way at an anarchist rally in Chicago. "Your idea of free associations would have worked in a handicraft stage of society like we had in Kinsman [Ohio] when I was a boy, but you fail to take into account the growing machine age."

But not even the anarchists in the Home Colony were of one mind on all issues. By the winter of 1911, when Billy headed north to hunt for Caplan and Schmitty, the inhabitants had dissolved into two feuding factions: the "nudes" and the "prudes." At issue, the focus of much earnest debate, were such lofty philosophical concepts as "individual freedom" and "group responsibility." The galvanizing incident, however, was more mundane. The nudes had gone swimming in the inlet without their bathing costumes. This libertine excess so outraged the prudes that they reported the nudists to the county authorities. Squads of wide-eyed police descended on the colony, and the offenders were arrested and summarily jailed. When Jay Fox, the editor of *The Agitator,* the colony's paper, wrote an editorial defending a person's right to swim in the nude, he was charged with encouraging "disrespect for the law." He spent two months in jail. Billy thought the sentence was too lenient.

The detective entered the colony disguised as a hunter. Instead of his customary derby, he wore a peaked hat with flaps that covered his ears. His Chesterfield topcoat was replaced by a hip-length red and black plaid jacket. According to the cover story he had quickly invented, he was hoping to bag some venison for his family's table.

He hadn't come alone. The colony was as big as some cities, and the woods offered plenty of places for a resourceful man to hide.

From the first day, he had deployed a team of his veteran operatives as backup. They went around with maps and surveying equipment; if anyone asked, the vague explanation was that they were working on a county engineering project.

Billy's plan was simple. First he'd locate Caplan and Schmitty. He'd spot them in the colony; or he'd bribe a greedy anarchist to give them up; or paying no mind to federal laws about the privacy of the U.S. mail, he'd intercept a letter sent to Caplan's wife, or to his good friend Jay Fox, the radical newspaper editor, that would disclose where the men had gone to ground. Then Billy would "rope" them.

"To rope a man is to gain his full confidence," Billy would explain. "And that is even better than an arrest." If he could rope Caplan and Schmitty, get them scared enough to cooperate with him, then they'd lead him to the man in charge. For Billy had become convinced: "The dynamite outrages all over the country were directed from some headquarters and by some master mind." But from where? And why? Who was behind this terrorist scheme? He hoped to find a piece of information in the colony that would send him farther along on the trail.

But the detective soon realized that his plan was in danger, and that he was the problem. After only a few days traipsing around the woods and making small talk at the general store, Billy appreciated that his hunter's disguise was unconvincing. He was uncomfortable playing the role of a pudgy, middle-aged woodsman. And he looked ridiculous, like a plaid tea cozy, he conceded. The chances of his cover being blown, of someone's staring too long at his absurd getup and finally recognizing the well-known detective, were too great. He decided to withdraw to a warm hotel room twenty miles away in Tacoma and let his operatives continue the investigation in the colony. He insisted, however, that they report to him daily in writing.

Assistant Manager C.J.S. reported:

Today at 7:30 A.M., in company with Investigator H.J.L., we proceeded to acquaint ourselves with conditions surrounding Home Colony and its residents.

Our pretext as surveyors permitted us to move around without attracting attention. We found that a number of the community occupy residences in places isolated in the timber and not easy of access. We located the residence of Jay Fox, who is supposed to be connecting with Caplan . . . we found numerous places where Caplan could remain in safe hiding.

Assistant Manager C.J.S. reported:

Today at 7:30 A.M., in company with Investigator H.J.L., I took up a surveillance on the residence of Jay Fox . . .

Assistant Manager C.J.S. reported:

Today at 7:00 A.M., having learned that the Anarchists were to hold a meeting in Tacoma to commemorate the Haymarket Riot in Chicago . . . I watched the departure of the Home Colony contingent on the 8:00 A.M. boat . . . It was decided that I proceed by launch . . . I then proceeded to where the Anarchists' meeting was being held . . . I did not see Fox. Neither did I see anyone answering the description of Caplan depart from the hall. At 11:45 P.M. I discontinued.

H.J.L. reported:

I resumed investigation here today at 7:00 A.M. covering the outgoing boat to Tacoma to ascertain whether Fox sent out any mail . . .

The lady who handled the letters for Fox on the steamer Monday was Mrs. B, an English woman, who lives on a remittance and also writes for the magazines. She has a husband here. They are divorced. She rents a house here, and stays two or three days out of the week here, and while here, she and others of the "free love" faith hold a drunken carnival.

The Jewish tailor, F., is pretty sore at the Fox family and might have some information.

Investigator H.J.L. reported:

We are getting acquainted very nicely, going along very slowly and feeling our way and the cover is first class. We have created no suspicion . . . I have become acquainted with the three store keepers, all friendly and will talk.

For weeks the undercover investigation dragged on. And each day, or so it seemed to a restless Billy, he received another telegram from the Chicago office reporting a new bombing. There had been explosions in Springfield, Illinois; French Lick, Indiana; Omaha, Nebraska; and Columbus, Indiana. Billy wanted to believe he was on the trail of the masterminds and that his men in the colony would at any moment inform him of the arrests of the two anarchists. But the string of new bombings frayed his confidence. He grew impatient. And scared. What have I missed? he asked himself. Is this a fruitless diversion, or am I still on the right trail? There were nights when he could not sleep. If new explosions caused more deaths, he knew, they would be his responsibility, the results of his mistakes. And the nation would curse his name.

# TWENTY

I N TACOMA, BILLY was growing tired of waiting in his hotel room. He needed to keep busy. When the local police chief told him there had been labor troubles up in Seattle the previous summer and that a building had been blown up in August, Billy decided to investigate. He had no reason to believe the Seattle explosion was tied in any way to the ones in Los Angeles and Peoria. "Not even a hunch," he would later admit. It was just that his men were in the Home Colony while he sat indolently in his room reading their reports. This inactivity gnawed at his sense of his own importance. This was the greatest case of his career, a mystery the entire nation was waiting for him to solve. He wanted to be the detective who uncovered the telltale clue and broke the case. He had to play an active role.

He arrived in Seattle without a predetermined course of action, but one quickly developed. His first stop was at police headquarters, and of course, the chief was only to happy to meet with William J. Burns. Without delay, Billy was escorted to the chief's office.

We don't have a lead on the bombing, the chief told him as the two men shared a drink. And, truth is, Mr. Burns, I doubt we'll ever solve this case.

Did you try finding the source of the dynamite? Billy suggested casually. He did not want to seem as if he were telling the Seattle authorities how to manage their investigation. He simply explained that approach had moved the Los Angeles case forward.

That's the problem, the chief complained. It's as easy to buy dynamite in this city as it is to buy a beer. Seattle, he explained, was the West Coast teaching center for the construction trade. We got maybe a dozen trade schools that'll sell you dynamite and then show you how to use it. Whoever planted the bomb could've been enrolled in any of them. But there's no way of knowing. It's not that we have a name, someone to look for, the chief complained to his famous visitor.

But Billy had a name. In fact, he had three—Bryce, Leonard, and Morris. And he had their descriptions, too.

He went from school to school. Then he discovered that "J. B. Bryce" had been enrolled last summer in the Seattle Trade School for a week-long blasting course. The teacher, J. D. Waggoner, gave Billy a description of his pupil that left no doubt: He was the same Bryce who had purchased the 80 percent dynamite from the Giant Powder company. The dynamite used in Los Angeles.

Bryce? Sure, I remember him well, the teacher told Billy.

Now why is that? You must have dozens of students going through here each week, the detective challenged. Instinct made him wary. The worst kind of witness was not the man who couldn't remember, but the one who invented memories.

Waggoner wasn't put off by the rebuke in Billy's tone. Patiently he explained that in addition to teaching demolition, he also owned a shop that sold explosives to the construction trade. Bryce had come to him to buy a length of coil. He planned to blow some big rocks and needed the coil to set off a spark that would ignite the dynamite.

What's so unusual about that? Billy wondered.

Nothing, Waggoner agreed. It was just that Bryce had shown him a small can containing two sticks of dynamite. The can was marked "Portland." Now that surprised me, Waggoner said. I didn't know they made dynamite down in Portland, and I told Bryce that.

Not Portland, Oregon, Bryce had corrected. Portland, *Indiana*.

An instant connection was made in Billy's mind. Bryce had purchased dynamite from the very place where J. W. McGraw had bought the explosives for the Peoria attack. Bryce and McGraw had to be two different men—their descriptions did not match at all. But somehow, Billy knew, they were connected. To the Peoria bombing. To Los Angeles. And now to Seattle. What was he up against? he wondered. What sort of conspiracy was this? What was the connection?

The mystery kept growing, expanding, but Billy felt he was making progress. It wasn't clear to him yet, but he was confident he was getting closer. He just needed to understand how all the disparate elements fit together.

Anything else this Bryce happen to mention? Billy tried.

Well, Waggoner went on, I had asked him what was he doing in Portland, Indiana, buying dynamite. Long way from Seattle, you know. So he told me it was near where he was working at the time. In Indianapolis.

That night an excited Billy sent a telegram to his son Raymond in Chicago. He sent the message in the work code that he and his son had devised long ago. Caution was necessary; a detective could never tell who'd be intercepting his messages.

The telegram was delivered to the Chicago office the next day. Raymond made quick work of breaking it down. Its message: LIKELY BRYCE IN INDIANAPOLIS.

An exhilarated Billy returned to Tacoma. But his buoyant mood was short-lived. Bad news was waiting for him. The source was not the Home Colony but Los Angeles. His enemies were on the attack.

Leading the charge was Earl Rogers, the attorney whom he had first battled during the political corruption trials years earlier in San Francisco. Rogers now worked for Otis and the M&M, and he was

making headlines accusing Burns of swindling the city of Los Angeles. Months had passed, Rogers told reporters, but what had the
great detective to show for all the money he had been paid? There
was no evidence, no leads. Burns had no idea who had blown up the
*Times* Building. And no less infuriating, Burns wasn't sharing what,
if anything, he had so far uncovered. How do we know, an indignant Rogers ranted, that Burns has done anything? For all the citizens of this great city know, Burns has simply pocketed the
taxpayers' dollars.

Otis, too, was upset. He didn't trust Burns, and the fact that the
detective was working in secret only increased his suspicions. What
was Burns up to? he fumed. Was the detective building a case
against labor or against him? Anything was possible, Otis feared.
On Otis's instructions, Rogers urged that a grand jury be convened
to investigate. The district attorney was too cowed to disagree.

Mayor Alexander was subpoenaed and told to produce Billy's
investigative reports. But he had none. Billy had sent him nothing.

Then Malcolm MacLaren, the manager of Los Angeles office of
the Burns Detective Agency, was called to the stand. The district
attorney again demanded that Billy's reports be handed over. Mac
truthfully testified that he had never received a single one.

That night the L.A. office of the Burns Agency was broken into.
Desks were rifled. The contents of filing cabinets were strewn about
the floor. But if the thieves were looking for the reports detailing
Billy's search for the men responsible for the bombing of the *Los
Angeles Times,* they did not find any. Anticipating trouble, Billy had
sent all his files to Chicago. They were locked in a safe deposit box
deep in the vault of the First National Bank.

Neither the grand jury nor Otis and the men in the M&M were
able to learn anything about the progress of the investigation. But
that did not prevent the city from taking action. Mayor Alexander
needed Otis's support in the upcoming election, and he caved to the

publisher's will. He announced that he would immediately stop all further payments to the Burns Agency. Burns would not get another penny from the city until he produced results.

Billy was devastated. How was he going to pay the dozen or so men he had working on the case? Over $100,000 was pledged in rewards for the apprehension of the person or persons responsible for the twenty-one murders, but before Billy could receive any reward money, he'd have to solve the case. After months spent following an inconclusive trail, Billy knew that wouldn't be easy. He needed the monthly retainer from Los Angeles to finance what he suspected would be a long and expensive investigation. He had collected lots of leads, but he still was not sure where they were pointing. There was a likelihood, a strong one, that he might never catch the men responsible. If he borrowed the money to keep the investigation going and failed to solve the crime, he'd never be able to repay his creditors. He'd be bankrupt, penniless and ruined after a lifetime's work. All because of his vanity. His refusal to concede that Billy Burns couldn't solve every mystery. What about his responsibilities to his wife Annie? His four children?

But in the end Billy decided it was a gamble he had to take. "As long as there was a chance to get Caplan or break out a trail to him," he said, "I was going to stick." He couldn't imagine failing. He was the greatest detective the world had ever known. He would get his man. It was humiliating. It made him anxious. But he borrowed $14,000 and stayed on the case.

Then all at once his faith seemed justified. He got his big break. His men in the colony sent an urgent report. Fox had a visitor. "He was a peddler of notions, women's goods, etc. He was a loud-mouthed Jew and a strong Anarchist . . . he answers the description of Caplan, as to height, color, and age."

Billy rushed to the colony. He did not even bother with his

hunter's disguise. He didn't care if he was recognized. He was going to get Caplan, and no one was going to stop him. But when he cornered the man and started to question him, he realized "he was not the man I wanted." The peddler was not Caplan.

On the ferry trip back to Tacoma, Billy was as low as he had ever been. Maybe he should give up. He'd have to learn to live with his failure, his embarrassment, but it would be better than dragging his family into bankruptcy. Every detective, he tried persuading himself, encounters a case he cannot solve. Perhaps this was his.

He entered the hotel and was heading sullenly to his room when the manager approached. Telegram, Mr. Burns, he announced as he handed Billy the yellow envelope.

What now? Billy wondered. More bad news?

He waited until he was in his room to open it. It was from his son Raymond, sent from Indianapolis, and it was in code. He began to decipher it, slowly at first and then with increasing excitement. Raymond had spotted someone in Indianapolis. Only it wasn't Bryce. It was J. W. McGraw.

## TWENTY-ONE

BOVE ALL ELSE, twenty-five-year-old Raymond Burns
wanted to please his father. Raymond knew he was a disappointment to the detective, but he felt it was not all his fault. True, Raymond deserved some blame. There was no doubt he had made a
mistake three years ago in San Francisco. He had been given a great
responsibility—a great opportunity—and had let his father down.

That unlucky Friday the thirteenth, in November 1908, had
begun, Raymond recalled with remorse, with such promise. At
breakfast his father had informed Sherman, Raymond's younger
brother, that he wouldn't be able to attend his football game at
Lowell High School as he had promised. Threats had been made
against Frank Heney, the prosecutor who was trying the case
against Abraham Rueff, the city's former mayor and a leader of the
corruption ring. Billy needed to be in the courtroom at Heney's side.

What about George? Sherman had asked. The oldest brother,
his father explained, had left town yesterday for Reno. He was pursuing Peter Claudiannes, a suspect in the attempted murder of a witness in the trial. That was when Raymond spoke up. Go watch
Sherman play, Dad, he urged. He'd take the detective's place in
court. He'd protect Heney. He was twenty-two; he wasn't a kid.
Billy mulled in silence for a moment. C'mon, Dad, Raymond
repeated. At last Billy acquiesced. Be on guard at all times, he told
Raymond. The chances of anything happening are slim, nevertheless be on guard.

As a trial recess ended, as people filed back in, as Raymond
bent over the courtroom stove giving the fire a stir, a man in a black

overcoat moved toward the prosecutor. He pulled a revolver from his coat pocket and fired. The sound boomed through the confined space, and Raymond turned at once. He leaped at the shooter, knocking the pistol out of his extended hand before another round could be fired. But it was too late. Heney had collapsed facedown on the prosecution table, blood was forming a deep red puddle beneath his head. The bullet had sliced through his jaw and gone on to lodge in his neck. Heney was still breathing when he was rushed to the hospital, but death seemed imminent.

The next morning Billy Burns emerged from the hospital to address the crowd of reporters; they had been waiting all night for some news. "Frank is going to make it," he announced. "You folks know," he added with a relieved laugh, "how hard a lawyer's jaw muscles are."

But Billy had no jokes for Raymond. He could not forgive the boy's failure.

Three years later Raymond could understand both his culpability and his father's continued anger. But he also believed this was only a partial explanation for the relentlessness in his father's attitude. The larger, unarticulated reason was not his fault.

Raymond could not help it that he was not George. George was his father's favorite son. George, the tall, thin handsome one, who had followed his father into the Secret Service; the charmer who dated showgirls and palled around with George M. Cohan. But now George Burns, the designated heir to the nationwide Burns Detective Agency, was gone. In May 1909 George, not yet thirty, had contracted tuberculosis. He died in a hospital in Monrovia.

Billy was bereft. His pain was such that he was unable to express his sorrow; it was beyond words. Raymond suffered through the detective's silent bitterness and felt his cold, sorrowful glare. In time, Raymond understood that words were unnecessary.

He knew what his father was thinking: The wrong son had been taken from him.

And so when Raymond had received the telegram from his father announcing that Bryce was in Indianapolis, he was determined to track him down. He wanted to prove to Billy that he could get the job done. He wanted to demonstrate that although he could not replace George, he, too, was his father's son.

He left Chicago promptly, and on the train to Indianapolis he worked out a plan of action. First, he would check the phone books to see if a J. B. Bryce or Bryson was listed. If that failed, he would try to find where Bryce worked. Since Bryce was familiar with dynamite, Raymond reasoned that he would most likely be employed in the construction business.

The Structural Iron Workers headquarters was in downtown Indianapolis. Raymond assumed that an unemployed worker returning after some time on the coast would stop by the union offices to see if any job sites were hiring. Raymond understood, of course, that the union would not cooperate with him or anyone connected with the Burns Agency; organized labor had made it clear that they believed that they were being set up to take the fall in the Los Angeles bombing. But Raymond had a description of Bryce. The union offices were on the fifth floor of the American Central Life Building on First Street. He'd hang around the lobby and wait till he spotted Bryce. It wasn't much of a plan, but all he could do was hope that it would work.

It didn't. When he arrived in Indianapolis, Raymond discovered that no Bryce or Bryson was listed in the phone book. And after three days of wandering through the lobby of the American Central Life Building and loitering on nearby street corners, he was beginning to attract attention. Soon either he would be arrested, or a couple of burly union members would drag him off to show him what they thought of spying private investigators.

On the fourth day, Raymond found an office in a nearby building that gave him an unobstructed view straight into the lobby of the American Central Life Building. It cost him a few dollars, but no one minded if he sat for hours and stared across the street.

Another day passed. Then someone making his way toward the elevators caught his eye. It wasn't Bryce, but something about the man seemed familiar. Raymond couldn't quite place what had gotten his attention. Perhaps he knew the man from some other case? Enough! Raymond chided himself. Whatever had prompted this feeling was unimportant. He needed to focus on the job at hand, on finding Bryce.

But only minutes later the short, round-faced man returned to the lobby. Now he was accompanied by a bigger, husky man, with a shock of gunmetal-gray hair falling over his forehead. He was handsome in a pleasant way, a man with a good-natured, even-featured face. Raymond had no idea who he was. But as he looked again at the shorter man, he had a shock of recognition. Raymond had supervised the investigation into the bombing at the Peoria train yard and the hunt for the bomber. He looked hard, and he knew: He was staring at the elusive J. W. McGraw.

# TWENTY-TWO

RAYMOND JUMPED UP from his seat by the window and raced to the street. By the time he was outside, McGraw and his friend were already a block ahead and had turned into Illinois Street. Raymond moved quickly, fearful that he had lost them. But as Raymond hurried toward Illinois Street, he saw that the two men had stopped by the Orpheum Theater. They stood talking by the two huge stone pharaohs guarding the entrance. Then they went inside. After a moment Raymond followed.

McGraw and his friend sat up front, close to the screen. Raymond thought about taking a seat behind the two men but decided it would be too risky. His father had standing instructions for shadowing: *Never mind how promising may be the outlook, the shadow must draw off rather than let the subject know he is being followed.* These stern words were echoing in Raymond's ears. He feared McGraw would make him for a detective. If McGraw panicked and ran, he might never be found. It was crucial to keep on him, to track where he went when he left the Orpheum. This time he would not let his father down.

Raymond sat in the rear, too far behind the pair to hear what they were discussing. But from this vantage point, he could keep an eye on the exits. When McGraw left, he'd be able to slip out and follow.

Raymond waited impatiently. He wondered where McGraw would lead him. He was eager to tell his father about what he had discovered. The lights began to dim. All Raymond could do was to wait, and watch the movie.

—————

As it happened, the movie playing that week at the Indianapolis Orpheum was D.W. Griffith's *The Lonedale Operator.* This was the third movie the director had made during his California trip. It was a small story, another melodrama, but it was so expertly done, the suspense so carefully ratcheted up, that Raymond might easily have become caught up in what was happening on the screen. And Raymond might well have noticed the parallels between the heroine who must prove to her father that she can get the job done and his own circumstances.

Blanche Sweet played a young girl who takes over her father's post as a railroad station telegraph operator just as a payroll shipment is due on an arriving train. A pair of hoboes thinks the inexperienced girl will be unable to prevent them from making off with the payroll. However, Blanche rises to the challenge. After failing to summon help, she holds them off. In the final scene the revolver she has been brandishing is revealed to be nothing more than a monkeywrench wrapped in a handkerchief. What father could be prouder of his brave, resourceful daughter?

D.W.'s great power was his ability to tell stories on the screen that would pull at audiences' sympathies and fire their imaginations. Raymond kept a vigilant watch on the exits, but no doubt he was rooting for Blanche, too. He wanted her to triumph, to justify her father's confidence. Just as he was determined to prove to his dad that he was worthy of his respect and his love.

What Raymond could not know or appreciate was all the trouble D.W. had had during the shooting of the movie with Blanche. The attraction that had once existed between the director and his star had disappeared. They no longer felt any ease in each other's presence. She treated D.W. with a feisty belligerence, and the director, with a shrewd resignation, exploited her roiling temperament. He had her play herself. The spunky heroine he captured on the screen was a bristling continuation of her off-camera demeanor. So D.W. was satisfied. He could deal with Blanche to his own advantage.

Linda, however, was proving to be more problematic. She was in the process of filing for separation from D.W., but that did not prevent her from hanging around the set and taking bitter measure of both D.W. and his star. Jealous, she went around the Alex each evening and always managed to share a catty word about the woman she suspected had taken her husband away from her. Years later she would still be seething: "The outdoor life of the West had plumped up the fair Blanche . . . Why wouldn't Blanche have plumped up when she arrived on location with a bag of cream puffs nearly every day and her grandmother got up at odd hours of the night to fry her bacon sandwiches? She soon filled out every wrinkle of the home-made looking tweed suit she had worn on her arrival in Los Angeles."

By the time the movie was in the can, D.W. had no patience for either of them. He had come to California to make movies. He had lots of ideas, and he wasn't going to be sidetracked by a difficult star or a jealous wife. Anyway, there were plenty of other actresses to occupy his thoughts. The crew had even started calling him "Mr. Heinz" when he was out of earshot; D.W. had, they playfully calculated, "57 varieties" of women hanging around on and off the set.

Also unknown to Raymond at the time, the meeting at the movie theater had come about because of woman trouble, too. The man McGraw was with was J.J. McNamara, the secretary-treasurer of the union. And J.J. had fled from his office because he didn't want Mary Dye to see him speaking with McGraw.

Mary was a stenographer for the union, a pretty blue-eyed small-town Ohio girl, and she had fallen hard for J.J. For a while

J.J. had been quite happy with the situation. He had even found Mary a room in the North Street boardinghouse where he lived. Conveniently, a single door separated their two adjoining rooms.

But, life imitating melodrama, complications soon entangled their romance. Mary began to feel unsure of J.J.'s intentions. With her mounting insecurity, she grew possessive. She was not above telling friends that they had sneaked off to Cincinnati and gotten married, or that the baby in a photograph was their son rather than her brother. These fabrications made their way back to J.J., and he fumed.

Yet he knew Mary had reason to doubt him. J.J. had become smitten with their landlady, and she with him. They talked to each other about love and held hands. When union business took him out of Indianapolis, he now wrote ardent, heartfelt letters to his landlady, not to Mary.

Making love to two women living under the same roof was, J.J. realized, a volatile situation. It was as if he were caught up in the complicated plot of a movie showing at the Orpheum—D.W. Griffith had made a film called *The Sorrows of the Unfaithful*. But J.J. quickly came to appreciate that he was facing a larger and very real danger. He worked with Mary. She knew a great deal about what the union was doing. He was not sure about the extent of her knowledge, but a small incident had recently left him rumbling with apprehension. Mary had opened his office mail and found a newspaper clipping about a dynamiting.

"Oh," she said, "what do you think? They have blown up that scab job." She waved the clipping at him.

Was Mary trying to tell him something? J.J. worried. Was she threatening him?

Whatever her ploy, J.J. decided he had had enough. He was determined to end the romance. She would have to leave the boardinghouse. And he would not work in the union office when she was around. McGraw had been scheduled to meet him at the office; it was too late to do anything about that. But he would not speak to him there. Not while Mary was around.

When McGraw appeared, J.J. quickly hustled him off. On the street, his only plan was to lead McGraw away from Mary or anyone else who might be watching. He had no destination in mind. When they turned a corner, he saw the huge stone pharaohs guarding the entrance to the Orpheum. That'd be as good a place as any, he decided at once. They could talk, and in the dark no one would notice them. Besides, he still remembered *A Corner in Wheat* and how much the film had impressed and excited him.

It's doubtful, however, that J.J. found much to enjoy in *The Lonedale Operator*. The unyielding, determined heroine might very well have been too reminiscent of Mary.

When they left the Orpheum, the two men went off in separate directions. Raymond stayed with McGraw. He did not know the identity of the handsome man, but he assumed that could be routinely discovered. Apparently he worked for the union; it wouldn't be hard to connect a name with a face. Raymond wondered what the two had been discussing, but he tried to put that sort of conjecture out of his mind. There would be time to discover that, too. For the present, he had only one task: follow McGraw.

McGraw boarded a train to Chicago, and Raymond found a seat in the same car. When he climbed onto a streetcar outside the Chicago station, Raymond hesitated. Then he hailed a taxi and instructed the driver to follow the streetcar.

McGraw got out at South Sangamon Street, and Raymond watched him walk to a small red painted house, number 414. A woman greeted him at the door, and two small children ran up to him, pulling and hugging. McGraw had come home.

It did not take much detective work for Raymond to discover

that McGraw's real name was Ortie McManigal. He did not know how McManigal fit into the L.A. bombing. Or what role the handsome union man had in all of this. But it was with great pride that he telegraphed all he had learned to his father. As the operator clicked the key, Raymond felt as if each new clipped, staccato burst was building toward his redemption.

# TWENTY-THREE

THEY WAITED, AND they watched. It was tedious work, each day a long, monotonous repeat of the one that had preceded it. Billy had left for Chicago immediately after receiving his son's telegram. Even before he learned about McManigal, he had begun to reconsider the likelihood of finding Caplan and Schmitty in the colony; apparently they had gone to ground, and he now suspected it might be a while before they resurfaced. Nothing would be accomplished by his remaining in Tacoma.

Once in Chicago, Billy took charge of the surveillance operation. It was an odd, troubling case. He did not know if he was following a new trail or turning into another dead end. Never before had he invested so much time and resources into an investigation, only to still be challenged by so many unanswered questions. Caplan and Morris had vanished. Bryce, too, was nowhere to be found. And no less perplexing, Billy had no idea how he fit into the plot. Was Bryce the ringleader? A go-between? A bomber? McManigal was another question mark. He could be traced to Peoria, but there was no evidence he had been in Los Angeles. And what had he been doing in Indianapolis?

His contact there had been identified as J.J. McNamara, the union leader; Billy, being cautious, had ordered that J.J. be tailed, too. It seemed unlikely, though, that McNamara had any involvement in this case. Still, McManigal's meeting up with McNamara struck the detective as curious. Ortie McManigal wasn't a union man; he didn't even have a job, unless showing up at the corner saloon each day could be counted as work. He didn't seem like the sort that J.J.—a lawyer, a literary critic, and even a bit of a poet in addition to being a union officer, Billy had learned—would look to for friendship. What was the connection between the two men? Billy had no answers. All he could do was wait and see where McManigal would lead them.

A week passed, and then Billy got the break he had been hoping for. Of course, at the time he did not know its significance. In fact, he came very close to ignoring it.

William Deane, an agent in the Chicago office, called to report that Subject 1—as the Burns operatives now referred to Ortie McManigal—was on the move. Deane and his partner, Robert Kaiser, had been watching McManigal for the past three days. In that time the subject's only excursions had been his daily stroll to the corner bar. But a little past two that afternoon, he had walked out of his home wearing corduroy trousers, a long black jacket, and a soft black felt hat. In his hand he carried a gun bag; judging by its size and shape, it contained two, possibly three, shotguns.

He's in a real hurry, Deane reported to his boss. Seems to be on his way to the station, probably rushing to catch a train. My guess, he's going hunting. Want us to stick with him?

Billy considered. The last time he had sent his men out into the woods, they had spent months in the Home Colony only to return empty-handed. Odds were that this would play out that way, too. Teams of men, weeks of time, and no results. He also had another concern—money. He was now financing the investigation with borrowed funds, and there was no guarantee of reimbursement. Maybe he should let McManigal go. He'd pick up the surveillance when McManigal returned to Chicago; running the operation in the city would certainly be easier and less expensive.

But what if the hunting trip was a pretense? What if he had

another bomb, not shotguns, in the case? Or perhaps McManigal planned to meet someone. Another contact could mean another lead.

Billy could feel the impatience building at the other end of the telephone line. A decision had to be made, but he would not be rushed. Billy finally instructed, Stick with him. You and Kaiser. Don't lose sight of him, and don't let him get on to you.

Deane stood at one end of the platform, Kaiser at the other. Both men had their eyes on McManigal. When the 3:55 arrived, he didn't board. He waited, head twisting about from time to time, the anxious movements of a man trying to see if he was being watched. Deane nodded in the direction of his partner. It was a signal to step back; the last thing we want is to get made. Kaiser obeyed.

The two detectives, then, were not in a good position to take a close look at the man who got off the train and greeted McManigal. He wore a dark corduroy suit; hunting clothes, they assumed. And he had a lighter-colored corduroy hat pulled down low on his forehead, as if deliberately to obscure his face. The two men shook hands, not formally, but the way old friends greet each other after a long time apart. The new arrival immediately became Subject 2 in the watchers' minds.

It was a hasty reunion. Deane and Kaiser saw their two subjects quickly break off their conversation. Bags in hand, they were now hurrying to catch a train boarding at the other side of the station. The detectives held back for a moment, giving the two hunters a good lead, and then they followed.

Deane and Kaiser found seats two cars down from the subjects. Moments later the train lurched forward. The two operatives had no idea where they were heading, but they also knew it didn't matter. Wherever the two subjects went, they would follow.

When the conductor came by, they bought tickets to the end of the line. Conover, Wisconsin, the conductor announced as he told them the price, and they dug into their pockets. God's country, he added. The last of the great outdoors.

Looking back at the operation, Billy would readily acknowledge the obstacles his men faced. "It would be harder to find more seclusion than in the wilds of the Wisconsin in winter," he observed. Snow dusted the tall evergreens. Deer ran in swift herds through the deep forest. A high winter sun glared down on Pioneer Lake. At night the heavens were a dome of stars. It was the perfect place to hide out.

Subject 1 and Subject 2 made their camp close to the shore of Pioneer Lake, two and a half miles east of the road leading into Conover. The detectives, however, did not rush to begin their surveillance. Burns Agency rules prevailed: Create your cover; get used to the fit; and when you're comfortable with the new role you've invented, then go operational.

So Deane and Kaiser settled in. They bought fur caps, snowshoes, laced boots, and long wool coats. They registered for hunting licenses and considered several rifles until they decided on .303 Savages. A story to explain their continued presence in the Wisconsin woods took shape: They were in the mining business, waiting for some heavy equipment to be shipped from back east. In the meantime, they were killing time by hunting. They rented a cabin in town, close to the general store, so that if they happened to run into the two subjects, it'd be the most natural thing in the world; and it was also near the train station so that no one could arrive or depart without their noticing.

Still, Billy worried. *The task of shadowing men in the camp was not an easy one,* he knew. Deane and Kaiser were also wary. Even the best cover could only stretch so far. If they were spotted too often in the woods surrounding Pioneer Lake, the subjects would certainly grow suspicious. But the way it worked out, the prey came to them.

One afternoon there was a knock on the cabin door. It was McManigal, and he was very upset. His friend, he explained, had wandered off from camp last night. He wondered if they had seen him. Deane and Kaiser hadn't, but they quickly offered to help with the search.

They found Sullivan—the name of Subject 2, the detectives learned—sleeping in a chair in the front room of Steinmetz's boardinghouse. It had been quite a night. Sullivan had already been drinking when he arrived at Steinmetz's, but that didn't stop him from ordering new rounds. He was a mean drunk. A fight broke out with a man named Smiley. Steinmetz tried to stop it and wound up with a cut ear. When Mrs. Steinmetz rushed to her husband, she caught a punch to the jaw. Sullivan had his pistol out and began making threats. But before a bad night could turn worse, Sullivan lay down on the kitchen floor and fell peacefully asleep. By the time McManigal and his two new friends had found him, he had somehow managed to make his way to the chair in the front room.

Deane and Kaiser helped a grateful McManigal get his buddy back to their lakeside camp. Why don't you stay for dinner? McManigal asked. And so, as Billy noted with pride as well as a bit of amazement, "the roping of the two subjects was now well under way. Instead of seeking acquaintance with them they were hunting us up."

It was a dangerous business. Sullivan was a man of skittish, volatile moods. He'd good-naturedly buy drinks for people he fought with the night before, only to wind up brawling with them again. Or he'd be flirting with the Steinmetzes' teenage daughters, taking liberties

with his words and his hands that seemed destined to have unfortunate consequences. Another concern was Sullivan's melancholy. He
confided to Deane and Kaiser that "all I've done for a month is
worry." Half the time, he said, he didn't know what he was worried
about, but still the anxiety was grinding away at him. "I've lost ten
pounds over the past month," he told them. He didn't feel like eating, only drinking. And all that time Deane and Kaiser had to be
alert. A slight suspicion, and things could turn very nasty. The men
they were roping packed rifles and Colt pistols and knew how to
use them. A gun battle with the two subjects would be a fight for
their lives.

But the roping went well. And as the two detectives spent time
at the Pioneer Lake camp, a thought took shape in their minds.
Sullivan had grown a blond mustache and side whiskers and had
lost weight, but he couldn't change his distinctive Roman nose. Or
his height and age. The two men kept looking at him, and they
grew more and more convinced: Sullivan sure fit the description of
J. B. Bryce.

We need a photograph, Billy decided after he received his operatives' report. We need positive identification.

So the two detectives asked their two new friends to pose in
front of Deane's camera; they wanted a souvenir of their time in the
Wisconsin woods. But Sullivan wouldn't cooperate. He hated pho-
tos, he explained. Deane and Kaiser were reluctant to press him; all
they needed was for Sullivan to start thinking about why they
wanted this photo. Suit yourself, he was told.

But after Sullivan shot a stag with a fine set of antlers, they tried
again. This time vanity won out, and he agreed to pose with his
deer. Only as Deane snapped the shutter, Sullivan abruptly moved
his head. When the photograph was developed, his face was a blur.

The fact that Sullivan refused to be photographed only
increased Billy's interest. He was determined to get a photo. It was

too risky, he decided, to try to sneak a shot; if Sullivan caught on, he'd run and they might never find him. Yet there had to be a way to get him to pose.

Resolute, Billy locked himself in his office and began rereading the reports his operatives had filed. He was looking for a clue, something that would help him come up with a ruse. "Sullivan is a great ladies' man and is trying hard to win the two girls here," he read. There were more than two dozen reports, but this was a common theme. Billy thought about it. He realized he had found Sullivan's weakness.

Getting the Steinmetzes' girls to cooperate was the tricky part, but when Deane offered them five dollars to help pull a fast one on Sullivan, they were quick to agree.

I just want something to remember you by, the older girl begged.

Let me sit on your knee, her sister suggested.

And Sullivan was only too glad to pose with them. He had his arm around one girl, the other sister perched on his knee, and a wolfish smile on his face. He was in no hurry. Deane could take all the photographs he wanted, and he did.

Within a week, a photograph of the smiling Sullivan was shown to the salesman at the Giant Powder Works in San Francisco. And to the landlady at the house where Caplan had rented a room. And to Waggoner, the explosives instructor in Seattle. All three agreed: The man in the photograph was J. B. Bryce.

# TWENTY-FOUR

SULLIVAN WAS BRYCE!

The man who had bought the dynamite used in the explosion in Los Angeles was camping in the Wisconsin woods with the man directly tied to the Peoria train yard bombing. At last, Billy rejoiced, the members of the bombing conspiracy were being exposed and identified. The case was finally moving forward.

But who was Bryce/Sullivan? Was he the man giving the orders? From what Billy had read in his operatives' reports, he seemed too skittish, too out of control to be the mastermind of an operation that the detective now knew to be a carefully coordinated and well-financed countrywide terrorist conspiracy. The man in the photograph, Billy had little doubt, was a soldier, not a general. But how could he discover who was in charge, choosing the targets, funding the operation? These were very careful people; they worked hard to cover their tracks. Yet Billy also understood the urgency. Every day he failed to solve the case, the potential danger increased. The last bomb had taken twenty-one lives. How many would die in the next blast?

Anxieties and troubling questions gnawed at Billy. He felt as if he were racing against a ticking clock, only he did not know when the alarm would go off and the next inevitable explosion would erupt. At least, he consoled himself, he knew where the bombers were and he had them under surveillance. As long as they remained holed up deep in the Wisconsin woods, he could be certain they weren't on a mission to plant a new bomb.

Then Billy received a telegram from Deane: "Machinery

moving today." The two subjects had broken camp and were leaving Wisconsin.

What Billy lived, D.W. imagined.

From the early one-reelers, detectives had been characters in movies. An investigator solving a case, putting himself in jeopardy to bring an evildoer to justice, was a familiar cinematic story. Twirled mustaches, menacing snarls, and shocked screams filled the screens. These signals were a visual rhetoric of terror and suspense, and audiences quickly learned to comprehend them.

D.W. did something new. He was able to translate emotions and thoughts into powerful pictures. His audiences didn't merely watch, they felt. They empathized with the detective's predicament. No longer did audiences sit in their seats passively observing the fear or terror on an actor's face. D.W. scared them, too. His audiences experienced the story. It was as if they had stepped into the tale: The danger facing the actor on the screen had become their own. This revolutionary advance in storytelling, this movie magic, was the foundation of D.W.'s powerful genius. And it was the artistry that made everything else that was to come—stars, large stories, big budgets, astounding revenues, an industry—possible.

In *The Fatal Hour* it was as if D.W. had grasped Billy's internalized fear of a ringing alarm clock's detonating another deadly bomb and brought it fully realized to the screen. The plot: A detective trailing white slavers is captured and tied to a chair. The barrel of a revolver points into the detective's face. The gun is rigged to go off in twenty minutes, when the clock strikes twelve. Back and forth, D.W. cuts between the terrorized detective, the police rushing to the rescue, and the relentless progress of the hands of the clock. The situation is excruciating. The detective's fear becomes the audience's.

With a leap of his imagination, D.W. had intuited Billy's ruthless world, the depths of the detective's private fears as he raced against time to build his case. And with another imaginative stroke, D.W. had created a galvanizing screen image that conveyed the tense uncertainty and danger in the detective's life.

Full of canny mischief, D.W. added one further twist to the reality. He made his detective a woman. His camera was attentive to her bondage and the defiance in her struggle. His intent in this casting, the director explained, was to capture the audience's attention and pull even more aggressively at their sympathies. But perhaps his choice was also more personal. In D.W.'s films young pretty women often found themselves in jeopardy, victims of the grotesque.

From Conover, Wisconsin, the two men went their separate ways. McManigal returned to his house on Sangamon Street in Chicago, while Sullivan went on to Indianapolis. The watchers stayed with both of them, but this surveillance brought Billy no comfort. Sullivan, he quickly understood, was up to something.

As soon as he arrived in Indianapolis, Sullivan acted like a man trying to lose a tail. Did he suspect he was being followed? Was this his normal, guarded way? Or—Billy's greatest fear—was this the jumpy behavior of a man preparing to plant a bomb?

Leaving the train, Sullivan had found a streetcar. Then he abruptly switched to another one going in a different direction, up Pennsylvania Avenue. He got off at Market Street and entered the Dennison Hotel. Instead of registering, he hurried out a side entrance and went on foot to the Plaza Hotel. He checked in to room 179 and remained inside for the night.

Early the next morning Sullivan took a train to Cincinnati. He checked his bag at the station and walked to a nearby drugstore. He ordered a cup of coffee and looked at the clock. He finished the coffee and ordered another cup. From time to time, he left the drugstore and returned to the station and studied the schedule. Then he'd go back to the drugstore.

Was Sullivan waiting for a train?

Was he waiting to meet someone?

Every half hour Billy received a telephone report from one of his operatives. If Sullivan made a move, he would know it. In the meantime, he would focus on the weak link in the chain of conspirators. He'd go to work on McManigal.

Now it was Billy's turn to write a script and direct a scene. Raymond had reported that McManigal's wife often went to a local fortune-teller, Madame Q. It was a time when unscrupulous Gypsies were standard movie characters—they were the villains in D.W.'s *Adventures of Dollie*—and perhaps that's what gave Billy the idea to offer Madame Q a bribe. Without preamble, he pulled a fifty-dollar bill from his pocket and asked the fortune-teller if she would cooperate with him. She took the money without either hesitation or questions.

What does Mrs. McManigal want to know? the detective asked.

She's worried about her husband, the fortune-teller said. She has dreams. She dreamed the police were after him. They had him surrounded, and he drew his pistol. In her dream, her husband shot himself.

"She wants me to look into the future and tell her what is going to happen to her husband," Madame Q explained.

Billy considered. In his mind a script was taking shape, but it was not quite there. "Let me devote some thought to this," he decided. "In the meantime, don't tell her anything definite. Just say you're looking into the ball and will let her know when you see something."

"Then there'll be more to this?" Madame Q wondered.

"Yes. And more money for you."

As Billy continued to ponder this scenario, he went to work on another. A surveillance report had revealed that McManigal was as superstitious as his wife. He'd go to the corner saloon and have the barkeep read his fortune from a deck of cards. This information inspired Billy. He had found a way to keep McManigal on edge. An anxious man, after all, was a pliant man.

The detective cast the barkeep as his star, told the man how to play his part, and gave him a new deck—with fifty-two aces of spades. The production began when the unwitting McManigal asked, as he usually did after a few drinks, to have his fortune told.

As Billy had directed, the barkeep shuffled the deck. He handed it to McManigal to cut. And then he matter-of-factly drew the top card.

It was the ace of spades. The dead man's card.

"Maybe your luck will change, Ortie," the bartender suggested, reading from the detective's script. "Take another card."

Once more the deck was shuffled and cut, and McManigal was handed the top card.

It was an ace of spades.

McManigal was reeling. In an instant, all his self-confidence vanished. He felt as if he were doomed. He had never felt as vulnerable. Which was precisely the emotion that Billy, a master director in his own right, had wanted.

In Cincinnati, Sullivan finally paid his check and left the drugstore. He bought a ticket to Northside, a suburb of the city, and waited. At 1:35 the train from Indianapolis pulled in. A big, cheery-faced handsome man, a shock of gunmetal gray hair tumbling over his forehead, got off and gave Sullivan a hug. Two old friends, they went to catch the train to the suburbs.

Malcolm MacLaren had been trailing Sullivan all day. Mac had been brought in from Los Angeles; Billy wanted fresh faces on the surveillance teams. He watched the two men take their seats, and then he found a place in an adjoining car. It wasn't until Mac was seated that he saw someone staring at him. It was Raymond Burns.

What are you doing here? MacLaren asked, genuinely perplexed.

Tailing my man, Raymond explained. I've been on J.J. McNamara since he left Indianapolis.

It was a short ride to Cumminsville, a neighborhood near the city limits. The two operatives were now a team as they descended from the train to follow the two subjects. It was almost rural, hilly country, and the detectives were worried about losing the two men. But they stayed with them. On Quarry Street, Sullivan and McNamara entered a block of four homes. They went to number 4306, a two-story frame house set off from the street by a waist-high iron fence.

By noon the next day, the two men had still not emerged, and Billy was growing concerned. He had tied Sullivan, the man who as Bryce had purchased the dynamite on the West Coast, to J.J. McNamara. But now he wondered if he had lost them. Had they slipped out a back door? He instructed Raymond to find out what was going on.

Raymond played a door-to-door salesman. When he knocked, a sweet-faced old lady, her hair pinned in a neat gray bun, answered. There was a brogue to her voice, and Raymond, his father's son, affected one, too.

No, she said kindly, I don't be needing any new pans. And if you'll be excusing me, young man, I'd like to get back inside.

Raymond smiled at her, full of apology.

But before closing the door she explained: Both my two sons came home yesterday.

# TWENTY-FIVE

---

THERE COMES A time in every investigation, Billy knew from long experience, when a crucial decision must be made: Should you order an arrest, or should you wait, gather more evidence, and build a tighter, more conclusive case? To his great surprise, Billy had established that Subject 2 was neither Bryce nor Sullivan. He was Jim McNamara, the younger brother of the secretary-treasurer of the Structural Iron Workers union. With that discovery, so many questions had immediately been answered in his mind, so many doubts had turned into certainties.

However, Billy also understood that precisely because of J.J.'s prominence as a labor official, the evidence against him would have to be irrefutable. The explosion in Los Angeles had been a national trauma. Twenty-one bodies had been buried, and months later the country was still in mourning. And with grief and anger, suspicions and conspiracies had flourished. Billy felt it was his responsibility to bring comfort to the nation by resolving this case beyond any doubt. Only the unimpeachable truth would put an end to the nation's anxiety. He would expose the "terrorist conspiracy," "the masked war" against "the established form of government in this country." And with the mystery solved and justice swiftly delivered by the courts, America could race forward unencumbered into the new century.

They were large ambitions, Billy knew. But he saw himself as more than a detective. He was, he said, "writing history." And when he looked at the investigation from that lofty perspective, he realized the problems he faced. "We could," he knew, "put the

nippers" on Ortie McManigal and James McNamara. The cases
against them, their roles in the dynamite attacks, had been established. But "we had no real convincing evidence against J.J. McNamara who was directing all the explosions. Nor had we enough
evidence to warrant successful prosecution against . . . other labor
'leaders.' "

So Billy decided to wait. His hope was "to catch J.J. McNamara
in the act of participating in some of the dynamiting schemes." Perhaps there'd be a break and either Caplan or Schmitty would be
found. Perhaps they'd implicate the men who gave the orders.
Patience, he wanted to believe, would bring rewards. He told himself that his decision to delay the arrests until the case against J.J.
could be established was not simply a personal mission, the quest
for another front-page headline. He tried not to think about the
possibility of another bomb's going off because he had chosen to let
the conspirators walk the streets. But it was very difficult.

While he waited, he kept his three subjects under twenty-four-
hour surveillance. His men rented an apartment in Chicago across
from McManigal's home; and there was always an attentive operative perched on a stool in the corner saloon, McManigal's home
away from home. An observation post was established on a hilltop
overlooking Mrs. McNamara's Quarry Street home in Cincinnati;
operatives had a bird's-eye view, although hunters rambling through
the thick brush were a danger. And Raymond had made a long-term
deal to lease the window space he had found in the building across
from the union headquarters in Indianapolis. The teams watched,
and they waited.

Then on April 11 Billy received an excited report from the
Chicago team. McManigal had kissed his wife and children good-
bye and, suitcase in hand, had gone to the La Salle train depot. He
boarded the Lake Shore train.

Billy was pondering the significance of this sudden movement when he received another message. This one was from Cincinnati. Jim McNamara had headed to the train station, too.

This was Billy's worst fear. Both men on the move, heading out across the country. Were they preparing to plant another bomb? Should he grab them now and order their arrests? Or should he wait and see where the subjects would lead him? He was uncertain, his mind leaping between imagined consequences, between success and total failure. "Whatever happens, don't lose them," he instructed his men.

But as soon as he gave the order, Billy worried that waiting was a mistake. Sitting in his office, his uneasy mind transformed every stray noise into an explosion—a disaster caused by his negligence and egotism. What if McManigal and McNamara gave his men the slip?

But the watchers were vigilant. They were right on McManigal when his train arrived in Toledo, Ohio, at 7:40, and they followed him into the station waiting room. Jim was already there. The two subjects sat on a bench, and McManigal unfolded a map. He had a lead pencil in his hand and aimed it like a pointer at the sheet.

Was he indicating a target? the watchers wondered. If only they could get close enough to hear what the two subjects were saying, but that was impossible. If the Burns men were spotted, the chance of catching the conspirators in the act, of dragging down the men in charge, would be lost.

After the map was folded up, the two men left the depot and went up the street to the Meyerhof Hotel. They registered under aliases. That night they left the hotel and went to a movie.

The Burns men, usually so meticulous, kept no record of the film McManigal and McNamara watched. But nevertheless it is significant that on that tense night in Toledo, they decided to go to a movie. The two men were furtively crossing the country, hiding behind aliases, quite possibly intent on planting another bomb, yet they made time to go to see a film.

In the first decade of the century, movies had become integrated into American life, a natural part of the national consciousness. They were "the academy of the working man," a writer observed in 1911. Films offered escape, entertainment, and education. By 1920 half the country's population would be going to movie shows at least once a week.

At that moment, as the two men sat in a Toledo theater, D.W. was working in Los Angeles. He had a new studio on a two-and-a-half-acre lot on Georgia Street and Pico Boulevard. He was earning a remarkable $3,000 a week, an artist proud of his material success and his growing recognition. But even D.W. hadn't yet realized the power in the shadowy mix of beauty and intellect that he had tapped into, and how it would change the way Americans looked at and lived in the world.

Just before five the next morning in Toledo, Raymond arrived to take charge. On his father's instructions, he was accompanied by two Chicago police detective sergeants. The Chicago cops had often worked with the agency in the past; they provided muscle and would, Billy knew from experience, follow Raymond's orders. And while the plan was to avoid arrests, if it became necessary the presence of the officers would make it official.

Raymond had all the exits of the Meyerhof covered, and from a third-floor room in an adjacent hotel his men had a perfect view into the lobby. It would be impossible for the subjects to leave unobserved. He had made that promise to his father, and he was determined to honor it.

At 8:45 that morning the two men wandered down from their rooms and found rockers in the lobby. They sat and talked, their chairs rocking back and forth in a leisurely rhythm. From his post across the street, Raymond studied the two men and felt that his father had exaggerated the danger. McManigal and McNamara acted as if they did not have a single pressing concern. Raymond could imagine the two friends sitting in their rockers, chatting the day away aimlessly. But by ten o'clock they were once again on the move.

They took a train from the Union Depot. McManigal, the watchers noted, had his suitcase. And now McNamara had a valise, too; apparently he had checked it the day before at the station. They arrived in Detroit at 12:52 and registered at the Oxford Hotel, this time using the aliases of Foster and Caldwell.

They did not go immediately up to their rooms. Instead, they left their suitcases with the bellman.

At that moment Raymond knew: They did not want the cases in their rooms, close to them. Because the suitcases contained bombs.

His father's instructions were to avoid arrests if possible. The plan was to let the plotters move forward and implicate themselves more deeply. But Raymond was convinced that two suitcases packed with dynamite were now stored in the lobby of a crowded downtown Detroit hotel. If they exploded—whether by accident or design, the cause did not matter—the destruction would be enormous. And if McManigal and McNamara escaped in the confusion, they might never be caught.

Raymond's mind was set. The two men were at the elevator about to go to their rooms. He signaled to Detective Sergeants Biddinger and Reed. "Let's take 'em down," he ordered.

Raymond had his revolver out as he crossed the lobby. The two men's backs were to him; they stood waiting for the elevator to descend. In a single fluid motion, Raymond jammed the revolver into McManigal's back and at the same time used his free hand to twist him around. The two Chicago officers grabbed McNamara.

"You're under arrest!" Raymond announced as handcuffs were tightened around the two men.

"What for?" Jim McNamara demanded with indignation.

Raymond paused before answering. "Safe blowing. You two pulled a job in Chicago last Saturday night," he lied.

# TWENTY-SIX

I N BILLY'S WORLD, there was no rejoicing. Instead, with the arrests a sense of resignation descended. He did not doubt that Raymond had acted prudently. In fact, when the Detroit police opened the two men's suitcases, they found, along with several guns, twelve clock devices similar to the one that had been recovered in Los Angeles. Nevertheless, Billy could not help but be disappointed that his case had not been allowed to develop further. He now would have to arrest J.J. McNamara before the union leader learned that his brother and McManigal had been grabbed. If Billy delayed, the danger was that J.J. would start destroying evidence or even perhaps go to ground.

Still, when he reviewed the case against J.J., Billy had to concede it came up short. He was certain he had solved "the crime of the century," but he also questioned whether a jury could agree without a reasonable doubt. He blamed himself. If only he had found Caplan and Schmitty. If only he had gotten the two anarchists to confess. He needed eyewitness testimony against J.J. and his union cohorts. It wasn't enough to theorize that they had given the orders, selected the targets, and financed the operation. He needed proof. As soon as the arrests in Detroit became known, a swarm of canny union lawyers would take charge of the defense. They'd make sure that no one would talk. There'd be no possibility of any confessions.

Unless—Billy had a sudden idea.

He would keep the arrests secret. It was Raymond's reluctance to reveal to McManigal and McNamara the true reason for their being picked up that inspired Billy's strategy. The subjects were convinced they were being charged with a safe job, and that the arresting officers believed their names were Foster and Caldwell. They did not know their suitcases had been opened and inventoried. If any inquisitive reporters got hold of the story, they'd write a small article about two fleeing Chicago safecrackers—yeggmen, in common parlance—doggedly tracked down by detectives who had trailed them from the Windy City to Detroit.

As long as the L.A. bombing could not be connected to the arrests of Foster and Caldwell, he had no reason, Billy decided, to rush to arrest J.J. He could continue to work in his methodical, quiet way, hoping to move the case forward on several fronts.

There remained, he told himself, "three vastly important things to be accomplished." First, and most pressing, he would try to obtain a confession from Ortie McManigal; Jim McNamara, he felt, would never cooperate. Second, he'd finally inform Mayor Alexander, get the Los Angeles authorities to issue writs of extradition, and no less essential, keep the existence of the legal papers a secret. And three, he'd need to arrest J.J. McNamara and get him and the two others swiftly to the coast—before any of the states on the way to California could issue habeas corpus writs challenging the extradition.

Of course, Billy understood, to accomplish his three goals, he'd need to manipulate and possibly even disregard habeas corpus, kidnapping, and coercion statutes. The right of habeas corpus was clear: The court had to establish the right to hold a prisoner, or else he must be released from custody. But Billy felt he could act with his own natural authority. His interpretation of the law was not so much broad as it was self-serving: as long as his actions ultimately facilitated justice—*his* concept of justice—then it was proper. The letter of the law was an irrelevance, a nuisance. His only responsibility was to bring to trial the three men whose actions he was certain had resulted in twenty-one deaths.

Secrecy was vital. Billy was determined, as he put it, "not to show my hand." Following his instructions, the Detroit police charged the two men with safecracking. The suspects were told that if they'd sign waivers, they'd be sent back to Chicago to be arraigned. McManigal and McNamara quickly agreed; they didn't want the Detroit police looking into their suitcases and realizing what they really were up to.

On the train, Raymond sat next to Jim McNamara. At first McNamara kept a careful, cautious silence, but as the train picked up speed, his defenses began to fall apart. It was as if the steady clacking of the wheels on the metal rails were also pounding against his confidence, breaking it down. He grew volatile and, as the train neared Chicago, desperate.

"You fellows don't want me for safe blowing," he erupted. "Why, I never cracked a safe in my life. You men are making a mistake."

Raymond tried to draw him out, but McNamara refused to answer his questions. Finally he blurted: "You men have a price. How much do you want?"

McNamara offered $10,000. Then $20,000. And finally $30,000. All the officers had to do was take him and his friend off the train. "If you take me to Chicago it will be too late." He wanted thirty-six hours to contact "the men higher up," and the officers would get the money.

Raymond silently observed that Jim McNamara still hadn't been told that he was going to be charged with the Los Angeles bombing. What, Raymond wondered, would he offer then?

———

Billy was also busy. He sent a wire to Mayor Alexander in Los Angeles: "We have under arrest and hidden away here Bryce and John Doe . . . Have police department proceed immediately to Sacramento, get requisition papers on Illinois, and come here as quick as possible. We won't let arrest be known here until officers arrive with the papers or they would spend a hundred thousand dollars on habeas corpus proceedings, and all sorts of trouble . . . It is of utmost importance you carry out this exactly as I suggest."

By the time the telegram arrived in Los Angeles, the two prisoners had been hidden away. They were not taken to police headquarters or to the Cook County Jail. They were not allowed to contact lawyers. The Chicago district attorney's office did not know about their arrest. In fact, they had not been formally charged with any crime. On Billy's instructions, they had been taken to a house in the suburbs. It was the home of Detective William Reed, one of the Chicago officers sent to Detroit to participate in the arrests. It would be their jail until the Los Angeles extradition papers arrived and could be presented to a Chicago judge. The fact that they were being held in a secret prison without being formally charged with a crime did not concern Billy. The nation, he believed, was "fighting a war against terrorists" who were determined to destroy "the established form of government of this country." The conflict "was masked under the cause of Labor," but the true purpose of "the war with dynamite" was more fundamental. The terrorists wanted to destroy the Republic. To defend the nation, Billy refused to be bound by a squeamish, impractical interpretation of the law. He had no qualms about taking liberties with the Constitution. This was war. And he knew he was on the side of patriotism and justice.

Jim McNamara, however, was led into the house in the Chicago suburbs and quickly saw his predicament from another perspective. "I've been kidnapped," he screamed.

"History repeats itself," Darrow was fond of saying. "That's one of the things that's wrong with history." Four years earlier in the Bill Haywood murder trial, he had fought against the injustice of what he had called "political kidnappings." Pinkerton detectives had grabbed three mine worker union officials—Haywood, Moyer, and Pettibone—at gunpoint in Colorado and then transported them to Idaho to stand trial. Darrow had been enraged. It wasn't just that these three men's constitutional rights had been violated. The state of Idaho, he argued, was establishing a dangerous precedent in allowing citizens to be kidnapped to stand trial by "partisan groups temporarily in charge of the state's legal machinery." Judge James F. Ailshie of the Idaho Supreme Court shot back that Darrow was "an enemy of the people." In his decision, the judge wrote that "the fact that a wrong has been committed against a prisoner . . . can constitute no legal or just reason why he should not answer the charge against him when brought before the proper tribunal."

Darrow saw the events differently. An improper arrest meant that a fair trial was impossible. A "kidnapping" poisoned the entire judicial process. He refused to give up and took the issue to the Supreme Court. The justices, however, voted eight to one that Idaho had acted properly. Justice McKenna, the lone dissenter, sided with Darrow. The Constitution, he agreed, granted every prisoner an irrevocable guarantee of habeas corpus. "But how is it," the justice agonized, "when the law becomes the kidnaper, when the officers of the law . . . become the abductors?"

Darrow did not put much faith in confessions obtained by the police and private detectives. A confession had been central to the Haywood case, too. Harry Orchard had sworn that the three union men had hired him to murder former governor Frank Steunenberg. After Darrow's probing and persistent attack, the jury had seen through Orchard.

But Darrow was also dismissive of even the most heartfelt confessions. It wasn't simply that, as his courtroom experiences had taught him, "the truth" was often deliberately coerced by unscrupulous police or shaped by prosecutors eager for a conviction. Rather, Darrow believed that in criminal cases concepts such as "guilt" and "truth" were imperfect moralistic simplifications of the actual reasons motivating the actions of men. In his assessment, "man is a product of heredity and environment," and as a "biological machine," his actions are often beyond both his self-knowledge and his self-control. Darrow was by nature a cynic, but he could also be compassionate, a man filled with a deep-hearted sympathy for the foibles of his fellow man. How, Darrow ardently challenged, can someone confess his guilt to a crime he could not prevent himself from committing?

But of course, Darrow did not know at the time that William J. Burns had, as the detective would later boast, "Jim McNamara and McManigal safely tucked away in a corner of Chicago's suburbs." Anyway, the lawyer was busy. History might repeat itself, but Darrow had pragmatically moved on. At the time of the arrests, he was in Kankakee, Illinois, defending a manufacturing company accused of fraud.

Billy, meanwhile, focused his attention on Ortie McManigal. The detective had identified him as the weakest link in the chain of conspirators. McManigal was not a committed union man; his allegiance to the McNamaras wouldn't run deep. And he had a wife and children. He certainly had the most to lose. But before Billy confronted him, he decided the time had come to play one of the cards he had been holding.

Billy went to Madame Q, the fortune-teller, and rehearsed a new script he had written. "Tell Mrs. McManigal," he directed, "that your crystal ball shows two men—brothers whose names begin with the letter M—who are in great trouble and who are going to be arrested one of these days. Get her to warn her husband not to trust these brothers. They are plotting against him and are going to throw all the blame on him when they are arrested."

When the detective was satisfied with her performance, he left and contacted Raymond. Tonight, he ordered, McManigal would be allowed to phone his wife.

The next morning Billy arrived at the house in the Chicago suburbs.

Billy stared at Ortie McManigal. He did not speak. His gaze remained fixed and appraising for what must have seemed an eternity to McManigal. He faced, he would say, "a man of medium height, rather dark complexioned, powerfully built and a type of citizen most men would hesitate to anger." But Billy had no intention of provoking McManigal's temper. He wanted to scare him.

"I am not an officer of any kind," Billy began. "Merely a private detective." His tone was polite and conversational. "My name is William J. Burns. I suppose you know who I am."

McManigal did not respond. He tried to be defiant.

Billy ignored the silence and continued. "We expect to put you on trial for murder in the first degree and try you for that," he said.

McManigal betrayed no emotion. Quite possibly he believed the detective was bluffing. The authorities possessed nothing more tangible than suspicions. "You don't know anything about me," McManigal finally shot back.

"Why, I even know where you bought the shoes you've got on," Billy said.

"Where?"

"At No. 117 State Street, Chicago. They are Walkover shoes, and you bought them on April eighth."

All at once McManigal slouched low in his chair; it was as if he were actually deflating, confidence rushing out of him. Billy, however, was relentless.

"I can even tell you what your wife dreamed the night before you left home."

McManigal studied the detective quizzically.

"She dreamed," said Billy, "that the police were after you, that you had drawn your pistol, and that you had shot yourself." He was repeating what Madame Q had told him, but he didn't divulge his source. Instead he acted as if it were simply reasonable and natural that William J. Burns, the great detective, knew someone's dreams.

Billy pulled a chair close to McManigal and sat opposite him. The two men were face to face. In his calm, businesslike way, Billy began to detail the case his men had built. He reviewed McManigal's purchase of the dynamite used in the Peoria train yard. He went through the time McManigal had spent in the Wisconsin woods. He revealed that McManigal had been followed to the Orpheum Theater in Indianapolis and that his house on Sangamon Street was under constant surveillance. He let McManigal understand that the Burns men knew every move that he had made.

McManigal cradled his head in his hands. He was too defeated to fight back. But Billy was not finished. "Perhaps you feel," Billy continued, "that because you did not accompany J.B. McNamara to Los Angeles, you are not responsible for his act?" With a lawyer's ruthless precision, Billy outlined the conspiracy statute. "You will find that you were equally responsible," he said with a certainty that was meant to leave no room for doubt in McManigal's mind.

The hangman's hemp noose might just as well have already been placed around McManigal's neck. Yet Billy, full of Christian kindness, offered him a reprieve. If McManigal felt he wanted to right the wrong he had committed, the detective would be glad to hear his statement.

Without hesitation, McManigal responded. He would be willing to make a full confession.

Still, Billy had the instinct and the discipline to refuse to listen. "Don't answer me offhand," he admonished. "Think it over. It's a serious matter and will be a serious matter to you." Call my office, if you want to talk, he said.

Without another word, Billy rose from his chair and left the room. Returning to his office in Chicago, he wondered if he had overplayed his hand. Billy wanted McManigal to live with the fear that he had planted. He wanted this fear to spread like a virus into the pores of McManigal's entire being. He wanted McManigal to be too desperate, too afraid, to tell anything but the whole and complete story.

But an hour passed, and McManigal had not called. Billy felt like a gambler who had recklessly wagered all his chips on a single roll of the wheel and lost. At last, a telephone message was brought to him: "McManigal wants to see you, and it's very urgent."

Letting the wheel spin again, risking all his hard-fought winnings, Billy ignored the call. With a calm that was all disguise, he waited in his crowded office until three similar messages were received. Then satisfied at last, accompanied by a stenographer, he returned full of confidence to the house in the suburbs.

# TWENTY-SEVEN

T HE THREE OF them—McManigal, Billy, and the stenographer—sat around a table in the kitchen. They might have been friends sharing a pot of coffee. McManigal spoke with a sense of detachment that struck Billy as odd. He seemed to be talking about someone else. But as he went on, the detective realized McManigal *was* talking about another man. With this confession, his life as he had known it was over, and his future was uncertain.

"I was born thirty-seven years ago in Bloomsville, Ohio, near the town of Tiflin," McManigal had begun as if telling a bedtime story. He went on to talk about his service in the Spanish-American War. But after this small sentimental preamble, he quickly got into the heart of the matter.

Nearly two years ago, when he was working on a construction job in Detroit, Herbert Hockin, a member of the executive board of the International Bridge and Structural Iron Workers, had recruited him. McManigal described the terms of the job as though it were a commonplace business transaction: He'd be paid seventy-five dollars to blow up an office building that was being constructed by a nonunion crew. McManigal carried out the assignment successfully and quickly began doing "dynamite jobs" at nonunion sites throughout the Midwest, often several in a single month. Then, in an unrelated matter, he got arrested for stealing tools.

After his release from jail in June 1910 Hockin came by his house to introduce him to a man who had "a new invention." Jim McNamara had wired an alarm clock and battery together so that a circuit could be formed. When the alarm went off, McNamara proudly demonstrated, a spark traveled to the explosive cap, which ignited the dynamite.

A few days after this demonstration McManigal received a telegram instructing him to go to Indianapolis. There he met Jim's brother, J.J., the union's secretary-treasurer. It was J.J. McNamara, he learned and observed, who chose the targets and directed the operation. At this meeting, McManigal was given a raise to two hundred dollars per job and assigned a new target—the Peoria train yard. That was the first time McManigal had used Jim's invention, "the machine, as he called it." He had not participated in the *Los Angeles Times* job. Two anarchists, Caplan and Schmitty, had been recruited in San Francisco to help procure the dynamite and fabricate the bombs, but they never went to Los Angeles. Jim alone had planted that "machine" in the alleyway of the *Times* Building.

The deaths had not been anticipated; they were a shock and a surprise to everyone involved, McManigal explained. Still, the deaths did not put a halt to the operation. J.J. McNamara sent him to the West Coast, and on Christmas Day 1910 he planted the bomb that did $25,000 in damages to the anti-union Llewellyn Iron Works in Los Angeles. Throughout that winter (as his own operatives had been lurking around the Home Colony, Billy sourly noted), McManigal and McNamara had kept busy. They hit targets in the East and the Midwest. During the month of March alone the pair had set off explosions at nonunion sites in Springfield, Illinois; Milwaukee, Wisconsin; French Lick, Indiana; Omaha, Nebraska; and Columbus, Ohio.

Prodded by Billy's questions, McManigal told an impressively detailed and convincing story. He revealed that Jim McNamara had hidden some "soup"—his shorthand for the 80 percent nitro—in a barn on the west side of Indianapolis. There was another reserve of "soup" in J.J. McNamara's safe on the fifth floor of the American Central Life Building. Billy shuddered at the thought of a large quantity of dynamite stored in downtown Indianapolis. But what truly amazed him was the size and scope of the operation McManigal had detailed. Between the summer of 1905 and McManigal's arrest in Detroit, the union had planted, he estimated, more than one hundred bombs. Billy realized that his men would have to investigate each explosion. He would have to build cases against all the union officials involved. It had been, a stunned Billy now understood for the first time, an all-out war. Between three and four hundred quarts of nitroglycerin and more than two thousand pounds of dynamite had been used. The damage had run to well over one million dollars. And twenty-one lives.

McManigal was neither a deep thinker nor a political person, but he had picked up enough from J.J. and the other union officials to offer up a defense for what he had done. The steel magnates, he lectured, had set up the National Erectors' Association (NEA) in 1905 to destroy the union. The NEA insisted that only scabs working for cheap wages be hired for construction projects. The union men, who demanded "a fair day's pay for a fair day's work," were turned away at job sites, unable to feed and clothe their families. They were helpless against the wealth and greed of the capitalists. Morally complacent police dispersed their picket lines. Goon squads of private detectives attacked the protesters. In desperation, the union resorted to terror. The intention was to strike an intimidating blow, to destroy property. It was never to cause physical harm. Terror was a political weapon, a symbol of both the union's frustration and its refusal to yield. Dynamite was the only means the workingman had to fight back against the powerful forces determined to deprive him of his fair, God-given due—the right to work for a decent wage.

Billy heard him out politely, and then moved on. He did not argue, but McManigal's view of the world struck him as too pat and his rationalizations too easy. For the detective, all the political jargon and catechisms could not hold up against a final judgment that was both practical and moral. Billy did not see how killing twenty-one innocent people would help anyone's cause.

McManigal's confession went on for hours, and by the time it was over, Billy felt as if he had joined him on a long, exhausting journey. But Billy also realized that he had reached the end of his own personal mission. It had started six months ago, when he had stood on a street in Los Angeles and looked at the still-smoldering rubble of the *Times* Building. It had taken him to the San Francisco docks, the northwest woods, a Wisconsin camp, an Indianapolis office building, and finally to this kitchen table in the Chicago suburbs. J.J.'s arrest and the task of getting the three conspirators to Los Angeles were still ahead, but Billy at this moment couldn't help looking at all that remained with a sense of anticlimax. He had his confession. Billy Burns had solved the crime of the century.

In the days that followed, McManigal and McNamara remained hidden away while Billy waited with increasing impatience for the extradition writs from Los Angeles. He tried to convince himself that the delay was unimportant; after all, J.J. still did not know that his brother had been arrested for his role in the *Times* explosion. And the union leader certainly had no idea about McManigal's confession. But Billy's artificial calm began to break apart after the Associated Press article appeared.

James Sullivan and Ortie McManigal, the AP reported, had been arrested in Detroit on charges of safe blowing and had then been taken to Chicago. It was only a small story, and fortunately the reporter had not known that "Sullivan" was an alias. Still, it was likely that J.J. McNamara had read the piece with alarm. The union leader had to fear that McManigal would panic and try to work out a deal with the authorities. It wasn't hard for Billy to imagine J.J. deciding to flee while he still had the opportunity. Perhaps, Billy considered, he should forget about the extradition papers. A delay would be foolish. He should make the arrest immediately. But even as he debated, Billy knew that without the proper legal authorization to move the prisoners from Illinois, a shrewd union lawyer could get the entire case dismissed. So, always resourceful, he came up with a new plan—and a new role to play. He rehearsed this new script in his mind and then picked up the phone and called Emma McManigal, Ortie's wife.

"You don't know me," Billy said into the receiver in what he hoped was a suitably gruff, tough guy's voice. "But I have just received a letter from a friend of mine in Detroit."

"Who are you?" Emma demanded.

"I do not care to give my name, but I will read you this letter, and perhaps that will enlighten you," he answered with a sudden formality. "I'm sure it's Greek to me. I don't know anything about it."

"Very well."

" 'Dear Jack,' " he pretended to read. " 'Immediately on receipt of this letter, call up and tell the woman there that her husband and his friend were arrested in Detroit for safe blowing. As nothing could be proved, they were discharged and they are now in Windsor, Canada.' "

"My God, but I'm so glad to hear that. That's splendid news."

"Now listen to the rest of it," Billy interrupted. " 'Tell her to go to a friend of theirs.' Now it doesn't say who the friend is."

"Oh, that's all right. I know who it is."

Billy hid his excitement and continued: " 'Go to a friend of theirs and tell him to give her five hundred dollars, and for her then to return home and await a further message from her husband.' Do you understand that?"

"Yes, perfectly. I will leave tonight."

"All right. Good-bye," Billy said, and then hung up the phone.

The next day the tail he had put on Emma McManigal reported

that she had gone to Indianapolis and met with J.J. McNamara.
Billy congratulated himself. Maybe he really should have been an
actor. His performance had convinced Emma McManigal. Now all
he could do was hope J.J. McNamara had been persuaded, too.

As Billy continued to wait, and as his men continued their uneventful surveillance of the union leader, Los Angeles assistant district attorney Robert Ford arrived in Chicago. He worked swiftly to present the requisition papers to the Illinois authorities. A secret extradition was approved. Billy instructed the men guarding McManigal and Jim McNamara that as soon as he sent word, they should drive the prisoners to Joliet and board the fast train to Los Angeles. Then he went off to Indianapolis to make an arrest.

A light, early spring rain was falling on April 22, 1911, when Billy, accompanied by two local police detectives, went to the Structural Iron Workers offices. An officer rapped at the door. Billy deferentially stood to the side; it was his case, *his* moment of triumph, but he knew he had no legal authority.

A pleasant-looking man with a shock of gray hair that seemed out of place with his youthful face opened the door.

"I want to see J.J. McNamara," the officer announced.

"I'm the man," said McNamara. If he had any suspicion of the reason for the police's arrival, he did not show it.

"Well," said the officer, "the chief would like to see you."

Suddenly J.J. understood, and a rush of panic hit him. Moments before J.J. had been sitting at a long walnut conference table with Frank Ryan, the union's president, and six other members of the executive committee. J.J. now went back to the room and huddled anxiously with Ryan. "They're after me. What had I better do about it?" he whispered.

"You'd better go ahead," Ryan advised.

J.J. considered, then realized he had no choice. "I'll get my hat," he said. But he also made sure to close the union's safe. Trying to regain a bit of his usual breezy manner, he told the executive committee members as he was being led out the door, "I'll be back in time to make the motion for adjournment."

Billy hadn't said a word during the entire arrest. It wasn't necessary. He knew his moment would come. And he knew that if things worked out as he had planned, J.J. McNamara would not be back in the union office, or even in Indianapolis, for a long, long time.

# TWENTY-EIGHT

---

At LAST, TWO very long days later, Billy boarded the *California Limited*. The *Limited* was a wonder, not just the fastest way from the Midwest to the coast but also the most luxurious. The dining car was first-rate, and there was even an onboard barber, a beautician, a steam-operated clothing press, and a shower-bath. And in separate cars, guarded by Winchester-toting police officers, Billy had sequestered the McNamara brothers and McManigal.

The detective was both exhilarated and totally drained. The past days had been a whirlwind. They were filled with moments that were too large, too consequential, to be understood as they happened. But now sitting in a comfortable tufted-red-leather window seat, the countryside outside swiftly changing like successive scenes in a movie, Billy could begin to review the events that had followed the arrest of J.J. McNamara.

Less than an hour after being led from his office, J.J. stood before police court Judge James A. Collins. In a deep booming bass—a voice from Olympus, Billy approvingly decided—Judge Collins had read the extradition papers. Signed by the honorable governors of the states of Illinois and California, John J. McNamara was to be sent to Los Angeles to stand trial for the dynamiting of the *Times* Building and the Llewellyn Iron Works. He was also charged with twenty-one murders.

J.J. paled. Billy watched as the union leader leaned on a chair to steady himself. At that moment the detective tried to feel sympathy, but he could not.

Pointing a long accusatory finger at the union leader, the judge asked, "Are you the man named in the warrant?"

It took J.J. a moment to find the words. Finally: "I admit that I'm the man named in the warrant."

"Very well, then," said the judge, "the only thing left for me to do is to turn you over to the State of California."

Recovering some of his former confidence, J.J. began to protest. "Judge," he insisted, "I do not see how a man can be jerked up from his business when he is committing no wrong and ordered out of the state on five minutes' notice. Are you going to let them take me without giving me a chance to defend myself? I have no attorney and no one to defend me."

The judge cut him off. The man accused of the crime of the century had no rights in his court.

"Take him away," the judge ordered.

Handcuffed to a police officer and accompanied by Billy's hand-picked Chicago police detective, Guy Biddinger, McNamara was led to a waiting seven-passenger Owen motorcar. The officers were armed with rifles and large-caliber revolvers. Two hundred rounds of ammunition were stored by the front passenger seat. Billy instructed Frank Fox, the driver, to go as fast as possible. Don't stop for anything, he warned. No matter what McNamara's friends try, keep going. Billy had a plan, and for it to work they needed to be in Terre Haute, Indiana, not a minute later than 1:45 that morning.

But it was now 6:45 P.M., and Billy's long night was only starting.

Billy returned to the union headquarters in downtown Indianapolis. He was accompanied by an entourage of police, city officials, and reporters. Now that the press had been brought in and the arrests had been announced, Billy made sure it was his show. An instinctive performer, Billy played both to the occasion and to the crowd.

Like a king claiming his throne, Billy sat down in the big

ladderback chair in front of McNamara's roll-top desk. With deliberately elaborate attention, he began examining the union leader's papers. All the while the reporters made note of his every gesture.

"Who are you," Frank Ryan, the outraged union president, demanded, "that you have a right to come in these offices and search these apartments?"

"Burns," the detective answered, full of his own importance and authority. It was only a single one-syllable word, yet he was certain it would carry all the explanation that was necessary.

The room went quiet. Ryan stared at his adversary. Reporters watched, documenting in their notebooks the intensity charging through this small moment of confrontation. "Ah, and who is *Burns*?" Ryan asked disingenuously.

Billy rose from the desk. Insulted and demeaned, it was as if all the frustrations in the long course of his investigation had risen up at once within him. He was looking for a fight.

Ryan did not back down. The union president, a steelworker for years, had traveled his own hard road. He moved toward the detective.

All at once Police Superintendent Hyland stepped between the two men. His bulky presence was an effective obstacle, and the moment passed.

Now ignoring Ryan, Billy headed toward the union's safe. He had found a set of keys on McNamara's desk, but he tried each one only to discover that none of them worked. The safe would have to be drilled. Billy asked the chief of police to get a locksmith. In the meantime, Billy would move on. Like a tour guide, he announced that anyone who wanted to join him was welcome.

It was nearly midnight by the time Billy and his eager troops arrived at the barn on the outskirts of Indianapolis, near Big Eagle Creek. A day's rain had turned the approach to the barn into a sea of mud. Beams from flashlights and torches struggled to light the way through the nearly starless night, and each new step across the oozing, sloshing field was a small battle. In his confession, Ortie McManigal had revealed that a cache of "soup" was hidden in a locked piano box in the barn. Once the box was found, Billy reached into his pockets and took out a set of keys he had confiscated from Jim McNamara. He kept trying keys, until finally one opened the box.

Inside was another locked box. Billy had not expected this. For a moment he seemed to falter. What if McManigal had been lying? Determined not to betray his doubts, he began trying McNamara's keys on the new lock. At last one worked. He had to reach deep into a packing of sawdust until, with a magician's sense of drama, he extracted two quart cans of nitroglycerin and, relishing the moment, fifteen sticks of dynamite.

Billy made sure that each of the reporters had a good look at his discoveries.

An hour and a half later on that same endless night, Billy was back in the downtown union office. The locksmith had still not arrived, but now a janitor approached the famous detective. He, too, wanted to play a role in breaking this momentous case. "Mr. Burns," he suggested, "do you want to search the vault in the cellar?" Billy had not previously known about the vault, but now he hurried to the basement. Full of curiosity, his entourage followed.

Billy inspected the vault and decided that the doors would have to be wrenched off. He instructed the officers to get crowbars and begin. But before the work could start, Leo Rappaport, the union's attorney, arrived. He demanded the officers desist. The court's warrant granted the authorities the right to search only the fifth-floor offices, not the cellar.

Billy's instinct was to ignore the attorney. He'd do what needed

By 1910, Los Angeles had become "the bloodiest arena in the Western world for capital and labor." The editorials in the fiercely anti-union *Los Angeles Times* gleefully fueled the tensions. *Courtesy Brown Brothers USA*

BELOW: "The crime of the century": After midnight on October 1, 1910, a series of explosions thundered through the *Los Angeles Times* Building and left twenty-one dead. *Library of Congress, Prints & Photographs Division, LC-DIG-ggbain-08499*

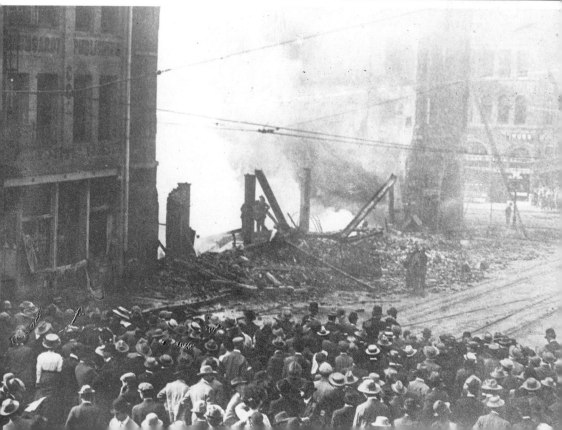

Gen. Harrison Gray Otis, the owner of the *Times*, inspects the ruins of his newspaper's headquarters. "Depraved, corrupt, crooked, and putrescent" was how one labor supporter publicly described Otis. *Los Angeles Times Company Records, The Huntington Library, San Marino, CA*

ABOVE LEFT: Billy Burns, "the American Sherlock Holmes." "The only detective of genius whom the country has produced," gushed a *New York Times* editorial. *Library of Congress, Prints & Photographs Division, LC-USZ62-101093*

ABOVE RIGHT: The Burns Agency threw agents from its offices around the country into the investigation, hoping to solve the mystery behind "the crime of the century."

D.W. Griffith—the man who invented Hollywood, and in the process transformed American life. *Library of Congress, Prints & Photographs Division, LC-DIG-ggbain-34047*

Clarence Darrow, the champion of populist (and often lost) causes was reluctantly recruited to defend the two brothers accused in the *Times* bombing. *Library of Congress, Prints & Photographs Division, LC-DIG-ggbain-06468*

All the rage and anger in the era fed Griffith's imagination and led to his making *A Corner in Wheat*. "No editorial writer . . . could so strongly and effectively present the thoughts conveyed in this picture." *Courtesy of the Paper Print Collection of The Library of Congress*

The ornate Alexandria Hotel was *the* place to stay in Los Angeles at the turn of the century. It was at the Alex, in the aftermath of the bombing, that the unique and complicated lives of Burns, Griffith, and Darrow intersected. *Security Pacific Collection, Los Angeles Public Library*

A cache of "soup"—dynamite—had been hidden by the conspirators in a locked piano box in the Jones barn. Billy Burns, a master showman, led police and reporters on a midnight raid to uncover the evidence. *Library of Congress, Prints & Photographs Division, LC-DIG-ggbain-09156 and 09157*

As the trial approached, the public relations war raged. In this flyer, labor trumpeted Darrow's charge that habeas corpus had been suspended: The McNamaras had been kidnapped by Burns! *Courtesy Archives & Rare Books Library, University of Cincinnati*

The entire case against the McNamara brothers was a "frame-up" insisted Samuel Gompers, the president of the American Federation of Labor. "Burns has lied." (*Left to right:* Jim McNamara, Gompers, J.J. McNamara.) *Courtesy Brown Brothers USA*

Working with D.W., Mary Pickford became the nation's first movie star. She looked young enough to be the director's daughter, but Mary was the embodiment of D.W.'s deeper desires. *Library of Congress, Prints & Photographs Division, LC-USZ62-57952*

ABOVE: Ortie McManigal had been an active participant in the nation-wide terrorists attacks. But after he was caught, he testified against the McNamaras. Here he's explaining to jurors how "the machine" used in more than a hundred bombings, including that of the *Times* Building, worked. *Los Angeles Times Company Records, The Huntington Library, San Marino, CA*

BELOW: Lincoln Steffens, the muckraking journalist, arrived in Los Angeles championing an argument for "justifiable dynamiting." Steffens hoped it would make him "the McNamara of my profession." He'd "blow-up" the trial. *Courtesy Brown Brothers USA*

Juror Robert Bain chases away an inquisitive reporter with a broom. But Bain hadn't run off the member of the Darrow team who had offered him $2,500 to vote for acquittal. He took the money. *Los Angeles Times Company Records, The Huntington Library, San Marino, CA*

# CROWDED COURTROOM WITNESSES DRAMATIC COLLAPSE OF TRIAL

### Accused Brothers Change Their Pleas of "Not Guilty" to "Guilty" With Pale But Calm Faces as Auditors Listen in Amazement to Their Confession.

## PRISON SENTENCES, NOT DEATH, TO BE METED TO THEM TUESDAY

### Sensational End of the Case Is Regarded as a Blow to Both Union Labor and Socialists Who Had Been Defending the Dynamiters of the Los Angeles Times.

Special to The Free Press.

Los Angeles, December 1.—The most sensational criminal trial ever started in America since the trials of the Molly Maguires or the Chicago Haymarket bombthrowers, came to a dramatic end this afternoon when James B. McNamara pleaded guilty to dynamiting on October 1, 1910, the Los Angeles Times building, in which terrible explosion 21 persons lost their lives in flame and agony, and his brother, John J. McNamara, pleaded guilty to dynamiting the Llewellyn Iron Works in Los Angeles a few days later.

### BLOW TO UNIONS AND SOCIALISM.

The accused men had entered pleas of not guilty. They had repeatedly protested to all the world that they were innocent victims of a plot against union labor framed by prominent Los Angeles men and Detective William John Burns and his agents. Union labor leaders all over the United States had rallied to their defense and raised a huge defense fund—$400,000 or more—and some of the ablest lawyers in the west had taken charge of their defense. Socialists in Los Angeles had made their cause their own, awaking popular sympathy to such a degree that election of a Socialist mayor in the municipal election of December 5 had come to be feared by the conservative elements of the city, the candidate being Job Harriman, one of the lawyers for the McNamara defense. So great was local sympathy that bloodshed at the polls was feared. And all over the United States, in every city, Socialists made the McNamara case a text for preachments against the standing order.

So, when this afternoon the brothers changed their pleas voluntarily, though on advice of Clarence S. Darrow and Joseph Scott, two of the ablest of their lawyers, the astonishment was not confined to Los Angeles or the Pacific Slope, but ran with electric flash to the bounds of the nation.

"And this is the truth," Jim McNamara wrote in his confession, ". . . I placed in Ink Alley, a portion of the *Times* Building, a suitcase containing sixteen sticks of 80 per cent dynamite . . ." When the brothers changed their pleas to "guilty," pandemonium filled the courtroom. *Courtesy Archives & Rare Books Library, University of Cincinnati*

Darrow was tried twice for bribing jurors in the McNamara case. He escaped conviction each time. "I know my life," Darrow told the jury in an emotional summation at the first trial. "I know what I have done. My life has not been perfect. It has been human, too human." *Herald Examiner Collection, Los Angeles Public Library*

## WIFE SOBS AS DARROW IS TRIED SECOND TIME

e Arrests
Slayer Hunt

RDINO, Jan. 1.—The
apturing the murderer
x, the Santa Fe oper-
t, is in the accidental
the right man among
cts who are being de-
ountains and on the
sheriffs. As not a
as been found who
a glimpse of the
ly possible means of
pect with the crime
ding of incriminating
n.
has directed his su-
along the railroads to
suspicious character.

Guests
Takes Poison

a party of guests
ring a rarebit at mid-
an Walker, a striking
d to swallow a dose
ght in her apartments
west street, and is alive
hough the presence of

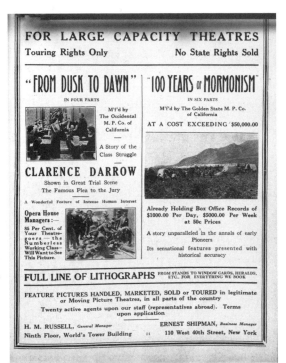

Frank Wolfe, a member of the McNamara defense team and a student of D.W.'s films, directed a commercially successful epic inspired by the case. Darrow, an instinctive actor, played himself—and stole the movie. *The Moving Picture World (20 September 1913: volume 17, issue 12)*

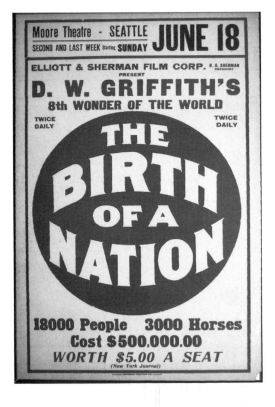

Energized by the politics swirling around him, Griffith looked back into history and created his masterpiece, *The Birth of a Nation. Birth* was history as melodrama, flawed, and yet as Woodrow Wilson observed, "written with lightning."

to be done, and damn the law. But as he was about to give the officers the order to proceed, he stopped himself. Everything that
occurred tonight would have to stand up to a judge's—a
nation's!—scrutiny. Get Mr. Rappaport his warrant, he told the
police superintendent.

And so for over an hour things came to a halt. After all the
charging about, the sudden inactivity seemed strange, even a bit
absurd. But no one left. The crowd remained in the cellar, milling
about in the dim light as if during the intermission of a play. Impatiently, they waited for the next act.

Around two A.M. the superintendent returned with the warrant.
On Billy's command, the heavy vault doors were pried down. The
officers stood back, and Billy stepped into the vault. He shined his
flashlight about the deep dark space and at once felt as elated as any
archaeologist discovering a priceless hidden tomb. Seven packages
of dynamite lay on the shelves—nearly two hundred pounds of
explosives. He also found percussion caps and large coils of fuses.
Even more incriminating, there was a box of fourteen alarm clocks.
The clocks were identical to the ones recovered in Los Angeles and
the Peoria train yard.

But the detective was not finished. As the first light of dawn broke
outside, Billy's relentless search continued into the new day. The
locksmith had arrived. Still accompanied by a tired but not weary
crowd, Billy hurried upstairs to the union offices.

Only now there was a new problem. The locksmith refused to
drill the safe. It was quite possible that there was dynamite inside. If
the drill bit nudged a stick, the explosion would be devastating.

Billy turned to Ryan and demanded the combination.

"McNamara is the only one who knows it," the union president
said. "And you've carried him off, God knows where."

But Billy would not walk away. The night had been filled with too many victories for him to let it end in a defeat. Beside, he still had his audience.

"Well, the safe's got to come open," he announced. "I guess I'll have to tackle it myself."

On his knees in front of the safe, Billy aligned the drill with the lock.

He paused for a moment and looked up to see if the spectators were safely hidden behind a shield of desks and bookcases.

Satisfied, he started. The grinding noise of the drill was the only sound in the room. Each moment was unique, a lifetime. Then Billy stopped. Had his nerve slipped? Or did he feel a tension in the drill? Had it touched something? Billy bit his mustache, and then with a new resolve, he continued.

At last he could hear the tumblers fall back. He rose to his feet. With a single emphatic tug, he opened the safe door.

A tall pile of ledgers was revealed.

Billy nodded, and police officers began to carry away the union books.

"Have we no rights?" Rappaport, the union lawyer shouted.

"Not under the circumstance," Billy shot back.

The lawyer was enraged. He charged at Billy but was blocked by an indignant lawyer from the National Erectors' Association who had been observing the night's activities. Rappaport swung at him, and the other lawyer retaliated with a powerful roundhouse. The two lawyers were still going at it, the police trying with some difficulty to pull them apart, as Billy, taking advantage of the confusion, quietly left the union office.

Billy raced downstairs. Raymond had been waiting in a car outside the American Central Life Building, and as the sun came up, they drove quickly west. If all had gone according to his plan, earlier that morning at 1:45 J.J. McNamara and his armed guards had arrived in Terre Haute. They had boarded the *Pennsylvania Flyer*. In St. Louis, Billy had instructed the guards to lead McNamara off the train.

Let people see what you're up to, the detective had told the guards. Make sure you breakfast in a very public spot. Then make a big production of buying tickets on the Missouri Pacific. Destination—Pueblo, Colorado. We want any union men who might have followed you to know where you're heading.

At least, let 'em think they know, he had continued. They were to sneak back onto the *Pennsylvania Flyer* and get off at Holsington, Kansas. There'd be a car waiting. They'd take a quick ride over rutted dirt roads to Great Bend, Kansas, then a local train to Dodge City. They were to hole up in a hotel until the *California Limited* pulled into town. Then they'd dash on board—guns blazing, if necessary. Jim McNamara and Ortie McManigal, if Billy's plan and luck held, would've gotten on in Joliet, Illinois. And Billy, too, would've caught up with the *Limited* as it crossed Missouri.

It was a complicated plan, filled with many details that could go wrong. A car could get a flat tire or even crash. A train could be delayed. And—Billy's great fear—there could be an attack. Once the press published the news of McManigal's confession, the union, he believed, would be determined to kill the rat. And they'd try at any cost to free the McNamaras. It was crucial, Billy believed, that the union not know the route his three prisoners would take to Los Angeles.

Now the plan was beyond Billy's control. He had given the orders, and all he could do was hope they would be carried out. Raymond drove. Although exhausted to the point of despair, Billy was too tense to sleep. He wanted desperately to know where McManigal and the McNamara brothers were, but communication with his men was impossible. The frantic, high-speed ride could not go fast enough for Billy.

Finally, in Missouri, Raymond caught up with the *Limited*. Waving his derby like a madman, Billy flagged it down. On board Billy was greeted by his men. They led him to Jim McNamara and Ortie McManigal, both shackled and manacled. "This train will either be wrecked or blown up before we reach Los Angeles," Jim snarled at the detective. "I have eluded my captors enough to get word to my friends to see that we do not get to the coast alive."

Billy tried to ignore him. A small army of armed guards roamed the train. Nevertheless the detective could not help worrying that men with rifles would be ineffective if cars were attacked with dynamite. More distressing, he had still not heard from Guy Biddinger, the police officer in charge of transporting J.J. Had they arrived in Dodge City? Or had they been stopped?

As soon as the *Limited* pulled into the Dodge City station, Billy hurried from the train. He looked around the platform, but there was no sign of J.J. McNamara. Then he saw Biddinger. Followed by McNamara. He was handcuffed, but he walked with his head held high. The other officer followed, a rifle cradled in his arms. It was with an immense feeling of relief that Billy joined the small procession and, taking the lead, directed his prisoner up the steps and into the train.

# TWENTY-NINE

A S THE *LIMITED* sped to California, the arrest of the three men and McManigal's confession were announced in banner headlines. The nation was startled.

The *Los Angeles Times*'s front page declared: "Dynamiters of the Times Building Caught. Crimes Traced Directly to High Union Officials. Red-Handed Union Chiefs Implicated in Conspiracy." An editorial congratulated "Detective Burns who has unearthed the most tremendous criminal conspiracy in the history of America."

Eugene Debs rushed to issue a statement: "Sound the alarm to the working class! There is to be a repetition of the Moyer-Haywood-Pettibone outrage upon the labor movement. The secret arrest of John McNamara, by a corporation detective agency, has all the ear-marks of another conspiracy to fasten the crime of murder on the labor union officials to discredit and destroy organized labor in the United States."

Samuel Gompers, head of the conservative American Federation of Labor, sent a telegram to his executive committee: "We know that these men have been arrested on charges that are absolutely false. I have investigated the whole case. Burns has lied!"

The announcement of the arrests had little effect on people's notions of the truth. Facts, an excited America discovered, could be twisted and wedged to fit into any preconceived theory, the intrigue of any conspiracy.

On board the *Limited* the mood was tense. At each new town crowds gathered to catch a glimpse of the prisoners. They were charged with committing the crime of the century—but notoriety, the nation also discovered, carried its own intractable celebrity. In other circumstances Billy would have appreciated the attention, but now he could only worry. He scanned the faces lining the tracks looking for a sign, a telltale gesture, a warning that a bomb was about to be hurled, the train suddenly stormed.

As a precaution, McManigal and Jim were kept in one car, J.J. in another. The brothers, in fact, did not even know that they were traveling on the same train.

The trip seemed to calm J.J. His dress remained that of a gentlemen—black derby, brown suit, black shoes, wing collar, and a well-pressed white shirt. Guy Biddinger remained at his side, and despite all his instincts, his admiration for the union man grew throughout the journey. "He was a model prisoner," Biddinger said. "And it would have been hard to find a better companion."

Billy, mindful both of the nation's curiosity about the accused and of the opportunity to get his own name into the papers, had shrewdly agreed to allow one reporter onto the *Limited*. The *Los Angeles Examiner*'s John Alexander Gray was picked, and he turned out candid portraits, compelling in their contrasts, of the two brothers.

J.J., the reporter wrote about the union official, "may be the most amazing criminal of the age, or a just and unjustly accused man. He has a splendid, upright physique and a clarity of complexion that indicate perfect health and habits that know no excess."

He found the younger brother, Jim, an entirely different and far less attractive sort. He was gaunt, a dingy, anemic-looking man whose fingertips were singed yellow by cigarette smoke. His eyes glared at his interviewer with "a light of amusement mixed with insolence." Only twenty-nine, he appeared downtrodden, and at least a hard-lived decade older.

Throughout the interview Jim lay stretched out on his seat, a deck of cards nearby. He had been playing solitaire.

The reporter asked, "Can you beat it?"

"No," said Jim flatly. "It's been my experience that you can't beat any game in this life."

For three days the train continued west, crossing America. Billy stared out the window as the *Limited*'s big iron wheels clanked against tracks laid over prairies, deserts, and mountain passes. At night, unable to sleep, still on guard, Billy imagined the locomotive's front light shining into the darkness like a beacon lighting the way to the Pacific. He felt deep in his heart that he was a passenger on a remarkable journey. With the arrival of the *Limited* in California, a new chapter in the nation's history would be written. His manhunt had put an end to the terrorists' war.

But even as the train rumbled into California, the detective was still careful. Precautions, he insisted, must be observed. It had been announced that the train would arrive in Los Angeles with the prisoners at three o'clock on the afternoon of April 25. But all along Billy had been making other plans.

When the *Limited* stopped at Pasadena at 2:05, two of Billy's men hurried McManigal to a car parked by the station. Moments later guards emerged with Jim McNamara. Another car was waiting, but they did not rush him. Oddly, they seemed to be taking their time. It was as if they were parading him along the station platform.

Which was precisely what Billy had instructed. Seated in a sheriff's car parked adjacent to the platform was a woman, her face covered by a long veil. As an unsuspecting Jim approached, she abruptly lifted her veil. She took a long look at the prisoner.

"That's Bryce!" shouted Lena Ingersoll. She was the owner of the San Francisco boardinghouse where, using the alias J. B. Bryce, Jim had finalized the plans with Caplan and Schmitty.

Instinctively Jim turned when he heard her shout. His recognition was immediate, too. He covered his face with his hands and hurried to the car that would take him to Los Angeles.

J.J., with little formal ceremony or even precaution, came off the train a stop later accompanied by Raymond. Reporter John Gray was an awed witness: "His manner was so dignified and impressive that the officers were at pain to assure him that the exigencies of the situation compelled the sort of treatment they were giving him. Nothing more strange, more amazing has ever been known since there was law and the ability of the law to conjure force to execute its dictates, for here, practically unguarded and treated with all courtesy, was the man accused of having told his brother to bomb the Los Angeles *Times*."

By five that afternoon, all three of the men were in separate cells in the Los Angeles County Jail.

PART III

---

## "THE LAST BIG FIGHT"

# THIRTY

BILLY'S BOLD PLAN had worked. He had succeeded in making his way across the country without incident. He had feared writs and ambushes, but now his three prisoners were safely locked in the Los Angeles County Jail. His job was finished. His pride of accomplishment swelled further when he found waiting for him at the Alexandria Hotel a wire from former president Theodore Roosevelt: ALL GOOD AMERICAN CITIZENS FEEL THAT THEY OWE YOU A DEBT OF GRATITUDE FOR YOUR SIGNAL SERVICE TO AMERICAN CITIZENSHIP. He went to his room looking forward to a night's sleep in a comfortable bed rather than a narrow, rolling train berth and, in the new morning, a leisurely breakfast in the Alex's dining room. It would take a few days to tie up the bureaucratic loose ends necessary to collect the much-needed reward money; then he'd be on his way back to Chicago. And on to his next investigation.

But the reward money was not forthcoming, and even his victory was short-lived. In the clutter of the days that followed, any sense of having come to the conclusion of his efforts, any lightness of heart, any swagger, quickly vanished. Billy realized that the case had entered a new, more combative stage. The arrests had not resolved the mystery but rather had provided two living symbols to polarize the nation further; doubts and suspicions about the circumstances that had led to the apprehension of the McNamara brothers now dueled with the incriminating logic of their guilt. A courtroom in Los Angeles would be the republic's next—possibly final—battleground in the fierce war between labor and capital.

And after all the front-page headlines, the dramatic accounts of his uncovering caches of dynamite and the furtive train journey, Billy, too, had become a symbol. When Ortie McManigal's confession was published in a pamphlet as a first-person account of "the national dynamite plot," it was a stern photograph of Billy, not the narrator, that greeted the readers. The detective had become as famous as the mystery he had solved.

For labor and its supporters, Billy replaced Otis as the personification of the enemy. They had no doubts about why he had been hired. The cocky, publicity-seeking detective was the unscrupulous agent of the deep-pocketed capitalists. In the Haywood case, the ruthless Pinkertons had manufactured evidence and kidnapped union officials. Four years later the McNamaras were the unfortunate victims of another corrupt private detective, another bought-and-paid-for thug willing to do whatever his masters ordered to help destroy the labor movement.

For Billy, prideful and vain, the personal attacks were a torment. He could not find the coldbloodedness to ignore the impugning of his honor, to dismiss the wild slurs as simply a strategy. He had spent seven difficult months building his case, painstakingly collecting his evidence. It had been a time of hardship and sacrifice. How could anyone believe that the results—*his triumph*—were a fabrication? Each new accusation about his conduct served only to solidify his determination to see the McNamaras hanged. Their execution would be his own vindication. He made up his mind to do whatever was necessary to ensure their convictions. A battler, Billy closed his heavy fists, dropped his shoulders, and prepared to fight back.

The reality, he silently complained, was that by both instinct and principle, he had always been sympathetic to organized labor. The immigrant tailor's son still believed that unions offered workers their best chance to achieve a fair wage. He was a detective for hire, but he was no toady of the rich and powerful. Hadn't he proved that in the Oregon land graft investigation and in the San Francisco corruption cases? Each new charge that he was antilabor was mystifying and tapped at the same sore spot. His resentment hardened.

The threats were another matter: a real danger. Bags of letters, signed and anonymous, postmarked from cities all over the country, arrived at his office in the months after the arrests. Most contained pledges to kill the man who had framed the McNamaras. He tried to ignore them, but then the police discovered a plot to place a suitcase filled with nitro in the room next to his at the Alex. And when Billy read that labor leaders in San Francisco routinely told crowds that "only the withdrawal of Burns could save the accused men," he had no doubts. Their words might just as well have been a command: Get rid of Burns. He knew he had to respond.

Billy sent his men to San Francisco to deliver a message to the union heads: *If anything happens to Burns, then the same thing will happen to you.*

"But my God!" protested one of the union men. "Some crank might kill him! I would not be responsible."

When this response was reported to Billy, he hesitated for only a moment. Then he sent his operative back to San Francisco with another message.

"Mr. Burns asks me to tell you," the detective matter-of-factly explained, "that if he is killed by a crank, another crank will kill you."

After that, Billy noted with a measure of relief, there was no more fiery talk at rallies about the benefits of the detective's sudden "withdrawal" from the case.

Still, Billy understood that he couldn't be too careful. As a precaution, he had duplicates made of all the McNamara files, all the investigators' surveillance and evidence reports, and he arranged for them to be delivered in secret to an address in Pueblo, Colorado. Frank Heney, the prosecutor who had been shot in the San Francisco courtroom, had retired to a ranch in that mountain town. Heney was instructed that should Billy die, whether by assassination or as the result of an accident or an illness, he was immediately to bring the files to the Los Angeles district attorney. The case against the McNamaras, Billy made certain, would continue even if he was no longer alive.

So in the months before trial Billy labored on. With a measure of resignation, he came to accept that only "the detective story of fiction would end with the arrests of the guilty men in the case." Instead, Billy entered what was, he would decide, "the hardest stretch."

It was a busy time. Billy was determined to bolster the prosecutors' case against the McNamaras. And he also had a new agenda. McManigal's confession had left him stunned. He had not previously grasped either the number or the scope of the dynamite attacks. This was not, he now understood, a "one-man conspiracy." There had been more than one hundred bombings at nonunion sites on both coasts and throughout the Midwest. It was inconceivable that J.J. McNamara could have single-handedly conceived, financed, and orchestrated such a long-running nationwide campaign. Union officials from across the country had undoubtedly suggested targets, and then given their approval to the strategy of terror. To Billy's mind, they were all culpable. They all must be brought to justice. A search warrant was secured, and his operatives swarmed through the McNamara house on Quarry Street in Cincinnati. In a dresser drawer a pile of letters was discovered. Written by J.J. to his brother Jim, they were handwritten orders to attack sites throughout the nation. Many of the letters also contained thinly veiled references to the union's executive committee. Billy saw this as proof the union officials were intricately involved in the plot. The union's record books taken on the night of the arrests also confirmed their complicity: The executive committee had approved J.J.'s receiving a thousand dollars each month to finance the bombing campaign.

Billy made sure copies of the letters and the union ledgers were sent on to Los Angeles; that evidence would solidify the city's case against the McNamaras. And Billy also had copies of the documents delivered to federal prosecutors in Indianapolis, where the Structural Iron Workers union had its headquarters. The explosion at the *Times* was only one of hundreds of bombings throughout the country, he lectured the government lawyers, yet only two men would be on trial in Los Angeles. Act boldly, Billy urged the Indianapolis U.S. attorney. The entire union leadership must be indicted.

Money, meanwhile, remained a problem. Billy had come to accept that the reward would not be paid until the McNamaras were convicted. But a courtroom victory would be problematic unless Billy could keep his small, expensive army of operatives digging into the case; dozens of leads in McManigal's lengthy confession alone needed to be explored. So Billy improvised.

In Muncie, Indiana, for example, his men went to a house rented by the union that, according to McManigal, had been used to store nitroglycerin. The cans of the explosive were gone; apparently they had been used in bombings. However, the pile of leaking nitro cans had left a pattern of deep, clearly identifiable stains on the wooden floor. Here was evidence, Billy realized, that would support the veracity of McManigal's confession and would also implicate the union officials who had rented the property. He needed that floor.

The house, however, was about to be sold. Billy's first instinct was to offer a higher bid and buy the property. Except he couldn't afford it. He was already in debt, and he had no immediate prospect of new funds. His only alternative was, as he put it, "to dicker." Improvising, he offered the owner a new floor if he could have the old stained one. Why not? decided the bemused owner. So each incriminating floorboard was photographed, numbered, carefully removed, and then sent on to Los Angeles—a new series of exhibits to be used at the trial.

Unfortunately, not all of Billy's efforts were so productive. A team of his investigators went to a vacant lot on the corner of Morgan and Van Buren streets in Chicago to dig for a cache of explosives that McManigal claimed to have buried. It was slow, tense work. Each time a shovel was thrust into the ground, there was the genuine fear it would set off a thunderous explosion. Yet they kept at it for hours. Finally, with a metallic echo, the tip of a shovel nudged an iron box. They had located the cache. Elated, an agent ran to a telephone to inform the Chicago office. Raymond ordered the detectives not remove anything until he arrived. He wanted to witness the discovery and then be the one to report the details to his father.

A half hour later Raymond arrived. Under his supervision, the dense brown earth was cleared with great care from around the box. Two detectives lifted the box with slow precision from its underground hiding place. Open it, Raymond instructed.

The crowd of men stood back. A detective pushed open a latch and gingerly lifted the top.

Inside was a dead dog.

After that the prospect of continuing to dig for the dynamite seemed too daunting. No one wanted to go through a repetition of similar unnerving moments. The detectives decided to move on to other matters. There still remained, after all, a good deal for them to do.


And all the while, as his operatives kept adding to the already impressive collection of evidence against the brothers, the attacks on Billy continued. *Appeal to Reason,* the weekly paper of Eugene Debs's Socialist Party, had a 400,000 circulation and vowed to throw "all its resources into the fight for the Iron Workers arrested on palpably trumped up charges." The McNamara case was, Debs told his readers, "the last big fight." The cause of the explosion at the *Times,* an investigation by the paper revealed, was gas, not dynamite. The two accused brothers were "as innocent as new-born babes."

Samuel Gompers, the head of the nationwide American Federation of Labor, in the past had often been a conciliatory, pragmatic voice in the disputes between labor and capital. He appreciated that it was businessmen who employed the workers; for practical reasons an accord between the two factions was a necessity. He also had grown uncomfortable with the radical excesses, both real and imagined, of the Socialists. He feared they ultimately wanted to replace traditional family life with more open and experimental unions. As a matter of principle, he publicly dissociated himself from the party: "I want to tell you Socialists that I am entirely at variance with your philosophy . . . Economically, you are unsound; socially, you are wrong; industrially, you are an impossibility." Yet like Debs, he, too, realized that the McNamara trial would be labor's "last big fight." So he put aside his misgivings and stood side by side with the Socialists in Los Angeles. And with unwavering fury and conviction, he tore into Billy.

"Burns has lied," he announced. The entire case was a "frame-up." Billy had "planted" the dynamite he had recovered from the barn and the union vault. Gompers had no doubts. His certainty was unshakable. He insisted that Billy "is well known to have no hesitancy or scruples in manufacturing evidence." He was confident the McNamaras were victims and that their innocence would be established by the courts.

Billy raged. Gompers's words, he felt, were not just a slander but also a threat. They were "calculated to inflame the minds of some irresponsible persons who might seek to revenge themselves on me personally." Full of self-protective anger, he shot back to a hastily convened assembly of reporters, "What has become of Gompers's conscience? We've got the goods on the prisoners, and

Gompers knows so better than anyone else." Billy could not understand how a reasonable person could reach any conclusion other than that the McNamaras were murderers.

And there was a further annoyance. Billy soon noticed that the man wearing the distinctive brown fedora was once again trailing him about Los Angeles. This was the final straw, and Billy, eager for a showdown, set a trap. He led his tail away from the Alexandria Hotel, turned a quick corner, and then lay in wait. When his shadow followed, Billy pounced. One punch, and the man went down. Billy hoped he'd get up and fight. The detective was ready to give somebody a beating. But the man produced a badge. He had been assigned by the district attorney to keep tabs on the detective.

Embarrassed, feeling besieged on all sides, Billy skulked off.

But all the personal attacks were, Billy was soon to find, simply a small nasty introduction to larger, more consequential intrigues. As the McNamaras moved closer to trial, the accusations became more vituperative, and the machinations more underhanded. The stakes in the outcome had intensified. Everything changed once Clarence Darrow agreed to represent the two brothers.

# THIRTY-ONE

SOMETHING WAS WRONG. Darrow knew it the moment he walked into the apartment and saw the troubled look on his wife's face.

What? he asked.

Ruby responded with a heavy, accusatory silence.

At last she pointed toward the library. You have a visitor, she explained tersely. Without another word, she headed off in an angry march toward the bedroom, her heels clicking against the wooden floor with a martial intensity. Darrow walked up the long hallway toward the sunlit red room, curious about whom he would find. Who, he wondered, could have provoked such an intense reaction from his wife?

Standing by the fireplace was a short, squat man dressed in a mournful black suit. He had impressively broad shoulders and held himself very erect, as if to compensate for his diminutive stature. A thin cover of graying hair was combed over the dome of a large noble head. Through wire-rimmed glasses, dark determined eyes glowed at Darrow.

"Hello, Clarence," said Sam Gompers.

At once the lawyer understood the reason for Ruby's agitated mood. And why Gompers had come to see him.

"No!" said Darrow.

For the past week Darrow had been defending the board of directors of the Kankakee Manufacturing Company in suburban Chicago. Charles Myerhoff, an elderly Civil War veteran, had lost the bulk of his life savings by investing in the company and had sued for fraud. Myerhoff contended that Kankakee's brochures and advertisements were filled with deliberately false statements to attract investors. Darrow did not attempt to defend the rosy promises made by the board. His strategy was to attack the naïveté of the nearly bankrupt old man. Myerhoff, he declared with as much indignation as he could summon, had a legal responsibility to research the company's claims. His clients could not be blamed for Myerhoff's imprudent failure to perform the necessary due diligence.

The logic, cruel and specious, would have left even many Wall Street attorneys uneasy. Once "the people's champion," Darrow felt demeaned, his energies and talents misplaced. Yet he carried on, resolute in his defense. He had, he constantly reminded himself, made a vow.

Darrow had sworn first to Ruby, and then with equal conviction to himself, that he would no longer fill his life with causes. The many battles had taken their toll—on his health, on his finances, and on his will. At fifty-four, he was weary. All he now wanted from the law was to be able to earn sufficient money to remove the burden of his debts and then save enough to retire. He looked forward to spending his unencumbered days in his book-lined library writing the novel that had taken shape in his mind over too many harried decades. If this case, with its contrived defense, its tacit endorsement of the bilking of elderly veterans, was what his life by necessity had become, Darrow, with a listless philosophical shrug, accepted its terms.

But although he had made up his mind to move away from all that he once was, it was, of course, impossible to prevent the past— his proud legacy—from intruding. He had read the headlines about the arrests of the McNamara brothers and the sly dash across state lines to California. The parallels to the Haywood case were clear and distinct. But so, too, were the memories of how the trial had left him drained. At its end, exhausted, despairing, wracked with an intolerable physical pain, he had escaped to Los Angeles—only to settle into a lingering sickness that had seemed a certain prelude to death. Fate, however, had intervened to save him; and now he looked back at his earlier days with a critical detachment that left him astonished by the bravado of his crusades. He was glad the McNamaras were not his concern. Wars, he had learned through hard experience, should be fought by the young and the strong. He was neither. Besides, he would never return to Los Angeles. The city held too many memories of a time when he had inhabited his own internal hell. All things considered, Darrow decided, Kankakee, Illinois, suited him just fine.

If he felt the necessity to champion a cause, Darrow reminded himself, his pen still had bite and power. Just months before the explosion at the *Times* Building, he had written "The Open Shop." This carefully crafted essay had stated that "in reality the open shop only means the open door through which the union man goes out and the non-union man comes in to take his place . . . The closed shops are the only sure protection for the trade agreements and the defense of the individual." For Darrow, this argument, a nonnegotiable belief that only union members should be employed in the workplace, was at the crux of the bitter dispute between capital and labor. With this pamphlet he had shown what side he was on. "The Open Shop" had been widely circulated throughout the country; 20,000 copies, in fact, had been distributed in Los Angeles. He didn't need to go into the courtroom to make his case.

Still, it was not unexpected when, only days after the McNamaras' arrest, a telegram from Gompers arrived at Darrow's Chicago office: "There is no other advocate in the whole United States who holds such a commanding post before the people and in whom labor has such confidence. You owe it to yourself and to the cause of labor to appear as the advocate of these men so unjustly accused."

Darrow ignored the telegram. He refused to think about what, if anything, he "owed" labor. He remained focused instead on what he owed his wife and himself. He had made a promise, and he was determined to keep it. Besides, protecting the board of the Kanka-kee Manufacturing Company from the consequences of their bla-tantly deceptive advertisements was enough of a challenge.

Still, Darrow could not deny that he was surprised to find Gom-pers in his apartment. And flattered, too.

Darrow sank wearily into the wicker chair by the fireplace, while Gompers paced and talked. The labor leader seemed unable to stop moving about the room, unsettled by nervous energy. And who could blame him? Gompers understood his predicament. He needed to persuade an attorney whose skill in convincing skeptical juries had made him famous. Darrow was shrewd; he wouldn't be suscep-tible to any verbal tricks. But Gompers also knew that he had made his own reputation as a pugnacious union negotiator. His tenacity was legendary. "My legs are so short I can never run away from a fight," he often boasted. Gompers told himself that he could win Darrow over.

He tried flattery. From all over the country, Gompers began, his voice at rally pitch, union men had sent letters and telegrams to the AFL urging that Darrow, and Darrow alone, handle the defense. Only the man who had saved Bill Haywood from the hangman's noose could rescue the McNamaras from a similarly unjust end. Only Darrow could expose the high-powered conspiracy that had manufactured evidence and coerced a confession. Only Darrow could prevent the inevitable triumph of the open shop if the McNa-maras were convicted. "No force except you, Clarence," Gompers insisted, nearly begging.

Darrow remained collapsed in his wicker chair, mute and full of a sullen indifference.

So Gompers tried money. The AFL would guarantee his fee. They would go to their two million members and raise whatever was necessary to defend the McNamaras.

"No!" said Darrow. He did not want to leave his home, his orderly life. There were twenty-one counts in the indictment. Each would have to be defended. He'd be in Los Angeles for a year, perhaps longer. A decade ago that would not have mattered. He would have seized the opportunity. He would have relished the challenges, the national forum. But he could no longer find in his heart the wild force that in the face of reason still makes daring and momentous decisions. "No!" he repeated.

For a week Darrow sulked, but he did not waver. Ruby told him he had acted wisely; it'd be suicidal to return to Los Angeles. His law partners, Masters and Wilson, agreed that he had made the correct choice. Their practice was finally succeeding; if Darrow left for a year or longer, all they had struggled so conscientiously to build up would fall into ruin. And when Ernest Stout, a reporter from the United Press, cornered him and asked about the rumor that he would be taking charge of the McNamaras' case, Darrow did not equivocate. He would not be involved in the brothers' defense, Darrow stated emphatically. He had turned the unions down.

But on Sunday afternoon Gompers returned to Darrow's apartment. And—a canny touch—he brought a crowd of labor leaders with him.

This time Gompers tried another tack: he threatened. "You will go down in history as a traitor to the great cause you have so faithfully championed and defended if now, in their greatest hour of need, you refuse to take charge of the McNamara case," he said.

Ed Nockles, a Chicago union official who over the years had

been side by side with Darrow in some rough situations, plowed another tract. "The whole world is expecting you to defend the boys," he said. "If you refuse, you convict them before they come to trial."

The two men had spoken evenly, no raised voices, no snarling bitterness. But Darrow could not fail to recognize the warning beneath their apparent calm. They were telling him that it wasn't only the McNamaras who had something to lose. At stake was Darrow's most valued possession: his carefully groomed reputation. If he did not come to labor's aid, he would forever be inscribed in history as a traitor to the cause. He would be remembered as the man who had condemned the McNamaras to death. And as the man who had destroyed trade unionism in America.

Darrow sighed. He had been in enough courtrooms and grappled with enough prosecutors to realize that he had been outmaneuvered. He had no choice. Either he could lose the only reward he had reaped from a grueling life's work, or he could reclaim center stage to serve as the voice of the defense in the trial of the century.

"There is no way to try this case with a chance of winning without a great deal of money," he finally told Gompers.

At that moment Gompers realized a shift had taken place in Darrow's mind. Darrow would take the case. Nevertheless Gompers did not press things to the inevitable conclusion. He allowed the discussion to meander on for hours. He wanted Darrow to feel he was in control, that he had not been coerced. Pride, Gompers knew, must be respected.

He listened patiently to Darrow's demands. The attorney insisted on a $200,000 defense fund, money to be spent as he alone determined. He would choose his co-counsels, and he would set the legal strategy. His fee, after expenses, would be $50,000. Many of the labor leaders felt this was outrageous, Darrow was asking for a fortune. Gompers did not disagree. But he needed Darrow. With only a small hesitation, he accepted the terms.

Yet still Darrow did not sign on. It was as if he were trying to delay the concluding formalities for as long as possible. Perhaps he also hoped the exasperated union men would decide that they no longer wanted to deal with him.

At last, a beaten man, Darrow asked Gompers and the others to excuse him. If they would be kind enough to wait in the library, he hoped to return shortly with his decision. But first he needed to talk to his wife.

With great trepidation Darrow went to the bedroom in the rear of the apartment to confront Ruby. She was seated on the bed, and he sat down next to her. He took her hand and with infinite sadness looked into her eyes.

He waited a moment; the man whose speeches had stirred crowds and juries was reduced in his own bedroom to someone struggling to find the proper words. Then he asked her for permission to break his pledge. He told her the men in the front room had said he would go down in history as a traitor to the cause if he did not defend the McNamaras.

Come with me to Los Angeles, he begged.

Ruby understood how difficult this decision had been for her husband. She knew he had been manipulated. She understood he had little choice. She worried about him, his health, his peace of mind. And she loved him.

"If you think it best," she agreed.

Darrow returned to the library and shook hands with Gompers. He would take the case.

"It was with heavy hearts that Mrs. Darrow and I drove to the Chicago and North Western stations and boarded the train for Los

Angeles," Darrow would write about the morning nearly three weeks later, in May 1911, when he had headed west.

Ruby, too, recalled that they had departed filled with "dread and distress."

Despite his misgivings Darrow had already been busy shaping the defense. A case of this magnitude, he realized, must be tried both in and *out* of the courtroom. He needed to take attention away from the piles of damning evidence and focus it instead on something else. He wanted the newspapers to move on from their teary-eyed accounts of the twenty-one dead. He had to shape the way people thought about the McNamaras. Before a jury could believe the brothers were not guilty, the nation had to believe they were victims. So just as he had done in the Kankakee Manufacturing case, he created an ancillary issue, a contrivance designed to distract attention from the damning charges in the indictment.

The law, Darrow had defiantly announced to the swarm of reporters who now flocked around him each day, was quite clear. Since J.J. McNamara had not been in California when the explosion occurred, he could not be extradited. "He was," Darrow boomed, "kidnapped!"

It was a masterstroke. Headlines dutifully repeated the charge. Across the country people began wearing buttons showing J.J.'s handsome, sincere face with a single word emblazoned like a lightning bolt across his granite jaw—"Kidnapped!" And Darrow kept trumpeting the charge with mischievous delight. He was determined not to stop until Burns was indicted for his excesses.

But another motive was also driving Darrow's strategy. After only a cursory look at the evidence against the two brothers, he had reached a conclusion. He had not shared it with Gompers or any of the union men. But as he rode the train out west, Darrow found himself wondering if his only victories would be in the court of public opinion. He had little doubt that the McNamaras were guilty. They would hang.

Already haunted by old ghosts—Gompers, Haywood, Los Angeles—Darrow soon saw another surface. Full of excitement, Mary Field had written to him to share the news that *American Magazine* had asked her to cover the trial.

Do not come to Los Angeles, Darrow immediately wrote back. He told her he would be watched by detectives. Her presence would "expose or divert" him. He would not be able to spend time with her. "*Any*, even purely friendly intercourse of a formal nature would be out of the question." Don't come, he reiterated.

# THIRTY-TWO

IT WAS GOMPERS'S idea, or so he would later claim. And he had indeed authorized the AFL's McNamara Legal Defense Committee to pay $2,577 to the W.H. Seeley Company of Dayton, Ohio. But even Gompers had to concede that he had drawn the inspiration for his breakthrough concept from others.

From Darrow, for one. The term *public relations* had been coyly bandied about since before the turn of the century. In 1897, to cite one early example, the anonymous writers of the *Year Book of Railway Literature* had decided on that euphemistic term to describe the railroads' cutthroat campaign to pressure municipalities and state legislatures to let them bully their way into new territories. But it was Darrow, Gompers recognized, who had first thought to bring the manipulative gimmickry of public relations to the McNamara case.

From the outset Darrow had grasped that the arguments should not be made only in the courthouse. Justice, he liked to say, was one thing, but a trial was something else entirely. It was a drama, and the accused were the principal players, its stars. No happy ending in the final act was possible unless the audience—the jury—genuinely cared about the unfortunate victims standing in the dock.

Yes, Gompers found himself agreeing. The McNamara trial would be a bit of theater—with the whole nation watching. And with the future of labor riding on the reviews.

Darrow also emphasized that the cost of the trial would be enormous. "The other side is spending in every direction," the attorney reminded in what had become a thudding and constant refrain. "Then they have all the organized channels of society, the state's attorney, grand jury, police force, mayor, manufacturers' association . . . No one will do anything without money and I want you to understand it."

Gompers understood too well. "The great need of the hour is money," he told his flock. "In the name of justice and humanity," he appealed to them "to contribute as liberally as their abilities will permit." The AFL had nearly 2.3 million members. If each man contributed a quarter, he reasoned, the defense's war chest would be bulging; it would certainly be sufficient to match the prosecution dollar for dollar. Yes, the mathematics was reassuring, even providential—if Gompers could find a way to entice his workingman membership to part with their quarters.

Burns was another inspiration. With rare objectivity, Gompers sourly credited his adversary for helping to focus in his mind the need for public relations. Every day, or so it seemed to him, the Hearst and Pulitzer papers, as well as Otis's always vitriolic *Times*, would carry another story portraying the McNamaras as low and evil—terrorists, high-living philanderers, or even socialists and anarchists. All the "scoops" had been eagerly provided to the reporters by the same nimble and persistent polemicist—William J. Burns.

"My purpose," Billy would too glibly explain, "was to leave nothing of their lives covered." The more complicated truth was that like Darrow, he understood the value of a pretrial public relations strategy. So he set out to demonize the two brothers, to disclose "step by step, the downward career of each."

His portrait of Jim was dismal and unforgiving: "Physically he was weak and of the tubercular type. He could not stand dissipation and went down under it, lower and lower . . . Immediately following the destruction of the *Times* Building and the killing of the twenty-one people who perished through his act, he left Los Angeles for San Francisco and celebrated his terrible act by scattering money about in the lowest of drinking dives, spending it on women of the streets, negro singers, and café musicians. He had no conscience, no trace of it."

Billy's portrait of J.J. was no less venomous: "The brains of the dynamiting crew . . . might have led a useful life." Instead, he "managed to fatten on the hard-earned money of those structural ironworkers who did the actual work." Worse, according to the grumbling, moralistic tales Billy spun, there was a "list of women on whom he spent good money of the union." J.J., he claimed, had taken up with "Katherine Kent who was not only a courtesan, but also turned out to be crooked in other ways, and left Indianapolis after being charged with robbing one of her male admirers."

J.J. had then moved on to another "very interesting creature of the gentle sex"; she was "Katherine II," as Billy, with gentlemanly discretion, identified her. It wasn't just that she "had no visible means of support," was "full of life and vim," and wantonly "made a number of trips around the country with McNamara." With only scraps of evidence, and those of obscure provenance at best, Billy further charged that "McNamara was putting her to good use in the masked warfare, for she could get information at times without creating any suspicion where a man would have had no chance at all."

Billy also gave a damning twist to the story of J.J.'s doomed relationship with Mary Dye, the union's stenographer. "The heartbreaking dynamiter," as Billy relished calling J.J., had grown frightened that Mary, full of fury because another woman was "hanging at his heels," would reveal the union's illegal activities. "There was only one safe way," according to the fanciful story Billy rushed to share, "and that was to kill her." Therefore, "McNamara gave her the Christmas week holiday and then tried to get his brother . . . to put a bomb under her seat in the train and blow her to fragments." The bomb was never planted, nor was there ever any convincing proof that such a plot had been contemplated. But that did not stop the story, Gompers noted with glum exasperation, from exploding across the country. He needed a way to set the nation straight.

And finally, although certainly not least, Gompers paid close attention to another voice—D.W. Griffith's.

The labor leader had noted the lure that the new moving pictures had on his constituency. The nickel price of admission—the cost of a glass of beer—was naturally part of the appeal. And your nickel got you a seat anywhere in the house. There was none of the undemocratic division between cheap and expensive seats that was the elitist practice in vaudeville houses and burlesque shows. Canny old Edison, Gompers fully agreed, had been on to something when he dubbed moving pictures "the entertainment of the working man."

By watching D.W. Griffith's Biograph one-reelers, an excited Gompers began to understand what films could do. Gompers had been thirteen when his family immigrated to America. He had grown up in a crowded tenement on New York's Lower East Side. There was a slaughterhouse next door, and he had to live with the squeal of animals and the reek of death. As a young man, he had written a series of articles in the *New Yorker Volks-Zeitung* exposing how cigars were manufactured in the tenements. For the workers, it was a brutally hard life: "little children with old-young faces and work-weary figures." He became active in the union because he thought it gave workingmen the collective power to effect change in their lives, to improve the conditions in which they had been forced to live and work. And now in Griffith's films he was convinced he had found a fellow reformer exposing the grinding and heartless injustices of urban capitalist life.

Inspired by the era's celebrated muckrakers, D.W. had refused to stay sequestered with his crew in the brownstone on Fourteenth Street. Time after time he left the film studio, headed downtown, and with a crusader's zeal aimed his camera at the crowds and tumult of the tenement streets. "Rivington Street," the director would explain, "never appeared as a melting pot to me, but more like a boiling pot."

*A Child of the Ghetto* and *Simple Charity* were melodramas, but they also might have been documentaries, so vividly did the shots reveal the harshness of life in the city. *The Lily of the Tenements* as well as *A Corner in Wheat* were plaintive editorials calling for fairer prices and better working conditions. *One Is Business, the Other Crime* challenged American justice: one set of laws for the rich, and another far less equitable or objective for the poor. And in the union leader's favorite film, the 1908 *The Song of the Shirt*, Griffith had made a call to join labor's battles against unjust management.

The plot in *Song*, Gompers could only shrug in uncritical agreement, was nothing more than a heart-tugging melodrama. A sweet-looking sewing machine girl conscientiously works to buy food and medicine for her bed-ridden sister. A small imperfection, however, is found in one of the shirts she has sewn. The factory owner and the manager ignore her pleas. They refuse to pay for work that they capriciously decide is slipshod. So the girl trudges home. And her sister, without the life-saving medicine, dies.

But despite the dank predictability of its narrative, Griffith's artistry gave the film a power of advocacy that Gompers couldn't help but admire. The director had repeatedly cut back and forth between scenes of management and labor, and each of the contrasts fell like an indictment. The seamstress hovers over her sick sister's bed, while the factory owner menaces his underlings; the factory owner frolics with a showgirl in a restaurant, while the seamstress dutifully sews in her wretched apartment and her sister writhes in pain; the factory owner drinks champagne, dances, and kisses showgirls, while in the seamstress's arms, the sister dies a wrenching painful death. It was all there in pictures on the screen, Gompers rejoiced. It was what the struggle was all about.

And so it came to him, with Darrow, Burns, and Griffith all helpfully nudging the idea along. It would rally people to labor's side; trump the malicious stories the opposition was gleefully spreading; and get workers to reach readily into their pockets to contribute to the cause. Gompers decided to have a film made about J.J. McNamara.

It was called *A Martyr to His Cause,* and it began like a fairy tale. Which was appropriate since it had just as much relation to reality.

Once upon a time a boyishly handsome seventeen-year-old J.J. left his doting parents' loving home to go out into the world. He promises, the opening title card reports, "to be a good boy and to play fair in all that he does." He finds a job as an ironworker, and we see actual footage—the impressive documentary touch inspired by the realism in D.W.'s films—of men fearlessly balanced on beams hanging high in the sky and matter-of-factly passing red-hot rivets to one another. J.J.'s remarkable journey continues, and "through his industry and sobriety," another title card explains, he is promoted to foreman and is subsequently elected secretary of the union.

Then disaster strikes. Management declares war against the unions. The courts and police join in, acting, a new card states, "contrary to the laws and traditions of our republic."

The film makes no mention of the *Times* bombing. As if he were simply the victim of cruel fate, J.J. becomes a blameless casualty of the unprovoked warfare. A rotund, striped-pants capitalist orders a hulking, snarling Burns to steal union property and then kidnap J.J. to stand trial. Burns obeys his master's command and happily gives J.J. a ferocious beating in the process.

The final scene is a tearjerker. The saintly gray-haired mum sits alone, weeping the tears of immense sorrow as she reads the letter her son has sent from his prison cell. "I am innocent of any infraction of the law," J.J. insists with steely defiance. He asks that his mother and the rest of the nation refrain from passing judgment "until a fair and full defense has been afforded."

The two-reel film, produced by the W.H. Seeley Company, was advertised as "The Greatest Moving Picture of the Twentieth Century." Still, Frank Morrison, the AFL secretary, felt compelled to admit to Darrow in a letter that "the story of the picture as it is ready for exhibition, and the story from which it is taken, very often differ materially."

But Darrow did not mind. The film opened in Cincinnati, and in its first week 50,000 people went to see it. Then it moved on to play to crowds all across the country. The hope was that the film would earn $100,000 for the defense fund, perhaps more. Either way, it would be a shrewd return on the $2,577 that the union had paid for the twenty-scene film.

The film made Billy livid. He hated the way he was depicted. A fearsome bruiser? A torturer? How could anyone twist the truth with such guiltless agility? he wondered with the facile innocence of the self-righteous. But Billy was also astute. His first meeting with D.W. Griffith had been prompted by his recognition of the affecting power that a film could have on a murderer's shaky mind. Now he began to consider other possibilities for the moving pictures. *Martyr* showed him that a film could persuade. And what had worked for labor would work for capital, too. So he suggested to his biggest client, the American Bankers Association, that they commission a film to counter labor's griping about low wages. It took some persuading, but the bankers eventually grasped the wisdom of Billy's advice. For a moment they even discussed approaching the great D.W. Griffith to direct their film, but when they learned that the director was under exclusive contract to Biograph, they quickly dropped the idea.

*The Rewards of Thrift* told the happy story of a conscientious worker who saved his money, avoided the temptation of alcohol, and was able to afford to buy his own home.

The bankers were very pleased with the result and quickly made plans to commission more films. The fact that they stood to make a sizable profit from the production, the bankers agreed, was only further proof of the fundamental rightness of its message.

# THIRTY-THREE

B ACK IN NEW YORK CITY that same May, a riot erupted in a Brooklyn movie theater. D.W. had just returned from his long winter's shooting in L.A., and when he read the story in the *New York Call*, it jolted him. It was as if he understood for the first time the potential in the flow of energy that was on the screen. He now knew: At his command was "a new force in the intellectual world as revolutionary as electricity."

Ironically, the film that had been shown at the Folly Theater in Williamsburg, Brooklyn, was not one of his. But given the audience's negative reaction, D.W. quickly reminded himself, perhaps that was just as well. *The Strike at the Mines* was an Edison production. It had been advertised as an account of the famous coal strike in Westmoreland County, Pennsylvania. More than ten thousand men, women, and children had marched on the picket lines in often punishing weather and had stood up to the owners' truncheon-waving goons. Week after week for nearly a year the bitter confrontation had dragged on. To workers across America, the strikers' resolve was heroic. Yet the movie told a different story. On the screen hordes of thuggish union men go on a rampage, attacking defenseless scabs and then demolishing the mining compound with joyful abandon. When the film's hero, an orphaned worker, atones for his brutal behavior and pleads with a kind-hearted mine manager to take him back, the audience in Brooklyn had seen enough.

"Lies," people shouted. "Lies." Seats were broken apart and the pieces hurled in protest at the screen. As if one, the audience stood and stomped their feet in unison. A large angry noise thundered through the theater. It kept building until the projectionist, perhaps fearful for his own safety, stopped the film.

When D.W. read this account, his heart leaped, and he might just as well have stomped his feet, too. His reaction, though, wasn't prompted by an urge to show solidarity with the protesters. True, this was a film he would never have made. His sympathies were with the poor and the working class, and he turned out movies that, as much by instinct as design, condemned the greedy clique that he felt controlled America. But he was a storyteller, not an activist. It would be several years before he would be emboldened to write an article for the *Los Angeles Citizen* entitled "Motion Pictures Can Be Made to Help and Hearten Labor." Nevertheless, he took great satisfaction in the audience's uproar at the Folly Theater. It had crystallized his thoughts and at the same time reassured his nagging doubts about the importance of his new profession.

For he had had doubts. Only "a matter of dumb luck," D.W. knew only too well, had taken him on his rapid journey from the stage to the moving pictures. But after spending the three years exploring the new world where fate had landed him, D.W. had finally come to appreciate its richness. "Now he has a vision," his friend Lionel Barrymore, the actor, recognized. "He really believes we're pioneering in a new art—a medium that can cross barriers of language and culture."

D.W.'s commitment to this vision ran deep. In one of his rare bursts of temper, the director had lashed out at a Biograph ingenue whom he had overheard talking about the "flickers." He reprimanded, "Never let me hear that word in this studio. Just remember," he continued to lecture, "you're no longer working in some second-rate theatrical company. What we do here will be seen tomorrow by people all over America—people all over the world. Just remember that the next time you go before a camera."

With a convert's fervor, D.W. had come to believe that movies could do "more than entertain." They were "a moral and educational force," a way "to bring out the truth about unjust social and economic conditions." What was on the screen could make people laugh or cry or even think. The tumult at the Folly Theater had proven to D.W. that a film had the strength to reach out and literally pull people to their feet. Had any storyteller in history, he wondered with pride and gratitude, ever been able to harness his muse to such a power?

Yet even as a fortified D.W. charged toward new creative battles, he found himself, not unlike Darrow, facing old ones. Mary Pickford had returned. And with her arrival, the old torments and insecurities resurfaced.

Mary's marriage had been a mistake; "five years of despair," she called it. Her brief contracts with IMP and then Majestic Pictures had also been unsatisfactory interludes. So she went to the Biograph Studio, and D.W., with no apparent hesitation or resentment, signed her up.

Mary was twenty-one. Her bundle of curls was still golden, and the passing of the years had blessed her face with a chameleon beauty. She could glisten with a coquette's bright charm in one take; in the next, her big demon eyes would be fired up with a sharp womanly wisdom. And from the start Mary and D.W.—or "His Majesty," as she now dubbed him—were once again locked in to their strained and disquieting relationship. He was obsessed by her, yet at the same time he knew Mary's stiff-backed reserve made her ultimately unattainable. She resented the power D.W. had over her career, yet at the same time she knew his director's skills enhanced her natural talent. And so he pushed and she pulled—until it was her turn to push, and his to pull.

D.W. tried to make Mary jealous, or maybe he simply needed the comfort that comes with reciprocated affection. What is certain is that D.W. sent a telegram and a prepaid ticket to Mae Marsh in California. He wanted her to come to New York and appear in his films.

Mae was just seventeen, the younger sister of the glamorous titian-haired Margaret Loveridge, who had joined the company the past winter in California. Mae had been hanging around the set, fascinated by her big sister's intriguing world, when she caught the director's eye.

As it happened, Linda, recently separated from D.W. (their legal divorce would drag on for rancorous decades), witnessed this moment. Years later the scene continued to play out acidly in her memory: "Little sister was a mite: most pathetic and half-starved she looked in her wispy clothes, with stockings sort of falling down over her shoe-tops. No one paid a particle of attention to the child. But Mr. Griffith popped up from somewhere and spied her, and gave her a smile. The frail, appealing look of her struck him. So he said, 'How'd *you* like to work in a picture?' "

And so Mae's moving picture career began; and in due course, so did her off-screen relationship with the director. She was young, vulnerable, and fatherless—all traits that pulled D.W. to her as though they were magnets. There was something else, too. "Your talking and giggling make me forget my worries for a time," he confided to her.

As soon as Mae arrived in New York, D.W. set to work playing her against Mary. The director was preparing to shoot *Man's Genesis,* a story set in prehistoric times. Full of mischief, he offered Mary the female lead. With great indignation, she refused. As D.W. knew she would.

Mary was too proper to wear the grass skirt that the role

required. "I'm sorry, Mr. Griffith," she told him, "but the part calls for bare legs and feet."

Mae, however, was untroubled. She possessed none of Mary's icy demure. She took the part and had a good time showing off her shapely legs in the process.

When the camera stopped rolling, D.W. assembled the company and made an announcement: "I should like to say for the benefit of those who may be interested that as a reward for her graciousness Miss Marsh will also receive the role of the heroine in *The Sands of Dee.*"

*Sands* was Biograph's important "literary" production of the season, an adaptation of a Charles Kingsley poem. The role of the girl who breaks with her father over her love for a painter had been coveted by all the company's actresses.

The director's announcement left Mary, she freely admitted, "thunderstruck." As D.W. knew she would be.

Mary fumed. "Only a short while before Miss Marsh had given up a job at the lining counter of Bullock's Department Store and had come without any previous training in the theater to Biograph." Even Mary's mother complained to D.W. about his poor judgment.

Mary, however, was practical as well as ambitious. And she knew precisely how to get back at her nemesis.

At the screening of *Sands,* she was the first to applaud Mae's performance. But she also shared a "sudden" realization with the director: "If a little girl fresh from the department store could give a performance as good or better than any of us who had spent years mastering our techniques, then pictures were not for me." She coolly announced that she wanted to return to the theater, "where years of study were a safeguard against the encroachments of amateurs." Delivering another blow, she haughtily waved about a letter that the playwright William DeMille had written on her behalf to David Belasco, the celebrated man of the theater. "There will never be any real money in these galloping tintypes," DeMille had pontificated. "And certainly no one can expect them to develop into anything which could, by the wildest stretch of the imagination, be called art."

D.W. was left reeling. As Mary knew he would be. All his previous uncertainties, all his insecurities about his achievement, rose up. He found himself forced to confront a harsh and self-incriminating memory: If he had succeeded in making a career for himself in the theater, he would never have become involved in the movies.

Yet he remained on the surface a model of calm and politeness. He asked Mary to complete one final film, please, and then she could go to Belasco and Broadway. She graciously agreed.

Once again caught up in his work, in the weeks before the filming of *The New York Hat* D.W.'s doubts gradually receded, and a new understanding took hold. The New York cultural scions would always look down their noses at the moving-picture business. The city belonged to the theater and the Belascos. If he were ever going to make the sort of large, transcendent films that were taking shape in his mind, if he were going to unleash the still-untapped power in his "new force," he would have to leave New York. His future was in Los Angeles.

# THIRTY-FOUR

DARROW'S DESTINATION WAS the Los Angeles County Jail, a dull gray box of a building next to the Lincoln Heights police station. He sent Ruby on to the Alexandria Hotel, but he hurried to the prison directly from the train station. During the long, introspective trip from Chicago, the challenges he faced had grown larger and his responsibilities more daunting. And as soon as he arrived in Los Angeles, Darrow felt an urgent need to take measure of the two men whose lives, against all odds, he had been hired to save. Darrow needed to be reassured of the necessity of his unwanted and doubtful mission.

His meeting that morning with his clients was brief, and Darrow carefully controlled the agenda. J.J. wore a gray suit for the occasion and struck Darrow as self-assured and full of open charm. His younger brother did not bother to shave and offered only curt, oddly defensive responses to the lawyer's discursive and chatty questions.

It was Darrow's practice never to ask if his clients were guilty. Once he had taken a case, the only relevant question was how he would guide the defense. In fact, Darrow brought up nothing substantive at this first meeting, and the McNamaras, for their part, made no attempt either to explain or to dismiss any of the mountain of evidence the prosecution had piled up against them. Nevertheless, Darrow walked out of the prison satisfied. He had shaken hands with the two brothers, touched his flesh to theirs, and looked them straight in the eye. Seated across from them, hearing the sound of their voices, they were no longer the anointed symbols of millions of workers' hopes and struggles. They were two living, breathing, mortal souls. He knew he could not allow the state of California to take their lives.

But that same afternoon Darrow found he suddenly needed to go to the site of the crime. Perhaps, he would suggest later, he had been testing himself, gauging his own resolve. He stood in Ink Alley at the precise spot where the prosecution charged the bomb had been planted. The site of the *Times* Building was now a vacant lot. He stared into a terrible stillness, and his imagination filled in the empty space. Summoned, the tragic night took shape in his mind, and it was as if he were reliving the memory of a horrible dream. Only he knew it had been all too real. What must it have been like, the inescapable flames, the choking smoke? Abruptly Darrow willed himself to stop. Nothing could bring back the twenty-one dead. And nothing could convince him that any version of justice would be served by adding two more victims to the already sorrowful total.

When he returned to the Alex that evening, a reporter was waiting. Otheman Stevens from the *Examiner* asked, "Do you believe the men you will defend are innocent?"

"I always believe in the innocence of the men I defend," Darrow parried. But he might as well have added that he also tried not to think about their guilt.

Work, Darrow hoped, would steady his seesawing thoughts and refocus his mind. Nearly an entire floor of offices had been rented in the Higgins Building on Second and Main, and Darrow, swift, purposeful, and with a surprising pragmatism, began selecting his defense team. They were an eclectic group, each man chosen with a knowing nod for the unique qualities he'd bring to the fray.

Co-counsel LeCompte Davis carried himself with the gilded bearing of the Kentucky gentleman he had been before tuberculosis had forced him to seek the healing California sun. As an assistant district attorney, Davis had not hesitated to prosecute labor. But he had gone on to earn a reputation as a skilled criminal attorney, and no less valuable given Darrow's despairing assessment of the case, he was an expert in the complex laws of California. If the facts gave little comfort, then legal nuances, Darrow tried to hope, would come to the rescue of his clients.

Joseph Scott, another co-counsel, was chosen for strategic reasons that trumped any mere legal expertise. A former president of the Los Angeles school board, he had long been a vocal leader of the city's Irish Catholic community. Put the well-known, ruddy-faced Scott at the defense table, and maybe the jury would think the McNamaras were cut from the same sort of solid, devout Irish stock.

Cyrus McNutt, a former Indiana Supreme Court justice, was selected primarily because he was a legendary champion of labor. The AFL was paying the bills; it didn't hurt, Darrow knew, to give them a co-counsel with whom they'd feel comfortable.

Still, Darrow knew he wouldn't be wrangling with just John Fredericks, the relentless L.A. district attorney, and his crew of ambitious assistants. Outside the courtroom he'd have to deal with the sly Burns and the detective's own legion of diligent operatives. He'd need people who wouldn't hesitate to trade punches or, even better, strike the first low blow. Two lives hung in the balance; it was a time for bare knuckles, not squeamishness. So Darrow recruited his own squad of practical and stubbornly aggressive tough-guy investigators.

The head of this unruly team was John Harrington, an old friend of Darrow's. The two men had worked together on several cases in Chicago, and the attorney was convinced he was "the best evidence gatherer I have ever seen." Harrington had lost his previous job as an investigator for the Chicago Surface Lines because of "insubordination," but Darrow was not concerned. He was looking for someone who wouldn't pay too much attention either to rules or to authority.

Bert Franklin, a former head of the L.A. sheriff's office of criminal investigations, possessed both a veteran cop's bulldog cunning and an alcoholic's familiarity with deceit. For someone whose job it was to conduct background checks of potential jurors, these were prized qualities.

Larry Sullivan, however, was the bruiser in the crew, a broad-shouldered giant who could give shivers with just a long, solid look. He had been a famous exhibition fighter, going ninety-nine rounds in one river-barge bout. Now retired from the ring, he still lumbered about as if looking for an excuse to come out swinging. Sullivan came to Darrow with a warning about his "reckless unscrupulousness." The attorney, though, did not think this caveat was any cause for concern at all.

In addition, Darrow had to find a way to counter the daily thumping that the brothers would undoubtedly get in the press once the trial began. Otis and the other sniping news barons would demand an incriminating tone. Darrow's only hope, and a small one at that, was to reach out directly to the crowd of reporters who'd be covering the case. Perhaps some level of objectivity was possible in a few of the dispatches. To handle this task—decades later it would be given the lofty title of "media relations"—Darrow settled on an inspired choice, Frank E. Wolfe.

What made Wolfe so effective? What was his great gift? In part, he had earned the respect of his fellow journalists. He had been a reporter and then editor at the Associated Press, but he had made his mark as managing editor of the *Los Angeles Daily Herald*: Wolfe transformed a moribund daily into a influential muckraking journal with a galloping circulation. Then, too, there was his easy conviviality. Wolfe was no backslapper, but people liked him, and he also enjoyed their company. He'd happily sit drinking with his fellow newshounds until the last round was called. But most of all Wolfe was admired for his crusader's passion. He had quit school at fourteen and found work on flatboats, then the railroad, and later as a telegraph operator. These hard-lived experiences had left him with a deep belief not just in trade unionism but in socialism as the necessary alternative to the injustices of capitalism. He was a true believer, unencumbered by doubts, and even many of those who disagreed with him found themselves respecting the integrity of his commitment.

But the real treasure on Darrow's team was Job Harriman, the lawyer who had single-handedly been directing the McNamaras' defense before Darrow arrived in the city. Harriman, nearly fifty, had a presence; he was the sort of rakishly handsome man—arresting blue eyes, a mane of coal-black hair—upon whom all eyes fixed when he strode into a room. He was an affecting orator, good at getting cheers from a crowd, and by all accounts he was a steady and competent lawyer.

But his great, invaluable gift to the defense was his well-known tie to the Socialist Party. In 1900 he had been Eugene Debs's vice-presidential running mate on the Socialist ticket in the national election. And more important to the fate of the McNamaras, he had for years taken an outspoken—and controversial—public stand in Los Angeles. Labor and socialism, he insisted with conviction, were brothers in a common struggle. "Whenever there is a labor movement in the field," Harrington had declared, "we should support it."

# THIRTY-FIVE

I N 1911 ALL across the country Socialists were packing meeting halls and winning elections. Voters in New York, Massachusetts, Pennsylvania, Minnesota, and Rhode Island had put Socialists into the state legislatures. Socialist mayors had triumphed in Milwaukee and Schenectady. And now in Los Angeles the Socialist ticket seemed poised for victory, too.

In 1909, when a special election had been held to replace the Democratic mayor who had resigned in disgrace, the Socialists had come tantalizingly close. A progressive "Good Government" coalition—popularly, and a bit derisively, known as the Goo Goos—had nominated George Alexander, a former city supervisor. "Honest Uncle George" campaigned dressed up as Uncle Sam on a moralistic reform platform that promised to rid the freewheeling city of gamblers, prostitutes, and even the bewilderingly popular blind pig races. Fred Wheeler, the Socialist candidate, had been a longtime labor organizer, and most observers did not give him much of a chance. But on election day Wheeler succeeded in getting a large turnout in the previously untapped working-class wards. He lost by only about sixteen hundred votes, a margin that was both unexpectedly narrow and dramatic.

And now two years later in the mayoral election scheduled for the fall of 1911, the Socialists—as well as their anxious opponents—were convinced that their victory would be an inevitability. Shrewdly, the party focused on two issues that it hoped would enlarge its solid worker base to include an increasingly angry and exasperated middle class.

One: Los Angeles was a city teetering. Another disruptive shove, and it could tumble into chaos. The high pitch of conflict between labor and capital, the stream of vituperative strikes, the tense picket lines—on any day an all-out class war could erupt that would have consequences for the entire city. Workers *and* the middle class. Yet, the Socialists were quick to point out, the Alexander administration had deliberately exacerbated these tensions. The Goo Goos had refused to appoint representatives of labor to city policy committees and mayoral posts. And without even a public debate, Mayor Alexander and his city council had approved a heavy-handed anti-picketing ordinance that had been drafted by the Merchants and Manufacturers Association and that had left the jails filled with grumbling workers.

Second: The Owens Valley aqueduct project was a dishonest, avaricious scheme shamelessly endorsed by the Alexander administration. It would make the city's political elite richer—and middle-class taxes would provide the money to finance the entire enterprise. This multimillion-dollar aqueduct, the Socialists raged in rallies and broadsheets, was not simply corrupt. It was further proof of the deep class struggle in the city. It was another demonstration of the greedy rich covertly conspiring to exploit both the workers and the middle class in order to line their already-bulging pockets.

Both these issues were the matches that ignited the Socialist campaign, and support spread like a raging fire throughout the city. Then in early August the Socialists further improved their chances for victory in the October primary. They selected Job Harriman as their mayoral candidate and Frank Wolfe for the city council.

With the selection of these highly visible members of the McNamara defense team, the Socialists tacitly articulated another issue in the election. They were clearly identifying their ticket with the fate of the McNamaras.

J.J. quickly spoke up from his jail cell, endorsing Harriman: "There is but one way for the working class to get justice. Elect its own representatives to office." Bill Haywood came to the city and urged a wildly cheering crowd to elect Harriman, "candidate of the people." Gompers spoke at an overflowing rally in the Shrine Auditorium. "Let your watchword be 'Harriman and Labor,' " he shouted. A vote for socialism would be a vote to acquit the two brothers. In fact, after the election the trial would no doubt come to a halt. Mayor Job Harriman, it was generally agreed, would dismiss the charges against the McNamaras.

As the intensity of the campaign built, Frank Wolfe, Socialist candidate and trial publicist, had an idea. He had seen many of D.W. Griffith's films, and the director's stories about the poor and the workers had stayed strong in his mind. Then the release of *A Martyr to His Cause* gave his thoughts a further clarity and momentum. And now he conceived a plan that would encourage "workers to use your nickels as your weapon."

"Socialist propagandists who have seen the maze of people flocking to the nickel pantomime shows and who have later gone into sparsely peopled halls to deliver the message of Socialism have asked me for the answer to the situation," he would explain. "I think I have found it."

Wolfe decided to "take Socialism before the people of the world on the rising tide of movie popularity."

In September he joined with a group of promoters to open the Socialist Movie Theater on Fifth Street in downtown Los Angeles. It would show only films "depicting the real life and ideals of the working class."

The theater was an immediate success. And as it turned out, it was only Wolfe's first small step into the moving-picture business.

On another front, although the trial and the election were both still
months away, Darrow's aggressive give-as-good-as-you-get strategy
had already reaped one reward. On June 16 an Indianapolis grand
jury indicted William J. Burns. The charge—kidnapping J.J. McNamara. Billy was furious as he scrambled to raise the money to cover
the $10,000 bond. Then he took off to Europe on a business trip.
With the arrest of the McNamaras, the detective had become an
international celebrity. If there was an unsolvable mystery anywhere
in the world, the cry went out, Get Burns!

So it happened that three weeks later Billy was in Paris. He
spent the evening dining with an old friend, the journalist Lincoln
Steffens. Steffens had years earlier filed several admiring reports on
Billy's successful work in the San Francisco corruption cases. But
tonight in Paris all Steffens seemed to want to talk about was the
McNamaras. He didn't doubt their guilt, but at the same time he
argued that Billy didn't appreciate the circumstances that had
prompted their actions. Billy listened politely, then told Steffens that
he didn't feel like arguing. Why ruin a delicious meal? If Steffens
wanted, he could come by Billy's hotel any afternoon this week
when, without the distractions of food or bottles of wine, the detective would lay out all the condemning evidence against the two
heartless brothers. Agreed, said Steffens, as the sommelier was summoned and another bottle ordered.

But that evening when Billy returned to his hotel, he found a
telegram waiting for him. It was from Raymond. His son wrote
that he had to return to Indianapolis immediately to deal with the
kidnapping charge. If Billy didn't, the $10,000 bond would be
forfeited.

By the time Steffens came by the hotel later in the week, Billy
had checked out. Steffens was sorry he had missed him, but he also
suspected he would soon be seeing the detective again. His dinner

with Billy had gotten him thinking. Steffens had made up his mind to come to Los Angeles. He would cover the trial of the McNamara brothers.

Mary Field was another journalist determined to report on the trial. She ignored all of Darrow's harsh letters to stay in New York. Instead, she came to Los Angeles.

Darrow took Mary out to dinner the night she arrived. He sat across the table from her and reached for her hand. He said he was glad she had not paid any attention to his foolish advice. He was happy to see her.

I never expected you'd change your mind, she lied convincingly.

But she had a difficult time trying to act surprised when he insisted on walking her back to the apartment she had rented. Or when he asked if he could come upstairs for a cup of coffee.

# THIRTY-SIX

---

T HE DICTAPHONE HAD, for all practical purposes, been invented in 1881. Alexander Graham Bell, his cousin, and another scientist had been working on the problem of recording telephone conversations. They came up with a device with a steel stylus that etched sounds as grooves onto a wax-coated rotating cylinder. It wasn't until 1907, when Bell sold his patent to the American Graphophone Company, that the machine began to be widely manufactured for business recordings and the name *Dictaphone* was trademarked. But it was Billy who hit upon another use for the device. He invented the first "bug."

Simply, quite effectively, and without any moral or legal quibbles, Billy had bugged the Los Angeles County Jail. A metal "ear"—the Dictaphone's rudimentary, shell-shaped microphone—was hidden in the attorneys' conference room. Every discussion by the McNamara defense team was picked up by this "ear," then traveled through an artfully concealed, snaking rubber hose to the Dictaphone in the adjoining room. Within hours of Darrow's jailhouse strategy sessions with his clients, a typed transcript of the entire discussion would be prepared for Billy's attentive reading.

Another "ear" was planted in Ortie McManigal's cell. This time a lengthier coil of rubber hose was required. It ran out the narrow window of the third-floor cell, then crawled up the side of the prison and into a fourth-floor room where it connected to the Dictaphone. It, too, worked perfectly. The machine recorded every word.

As the trial approached, both the prosecution and the defense were struggling to find an advantage. Theirs was a dirty little war. And it was fought on many fronts.

Ortie McManigal was the object of much intrigue. In Chicago, Billy had gotten the detailed confession that was central to the prosecution's case. And in return for turning state's evidence, McManigal had received a generous deal: He would escape prosecution. But Darrow was undeterred. If he could get McManigal to recant, to say that the confession had been coerced by Burns and his thugs, the case against the McNamaras would crumble. So with well-practiced cunning, Darrow went to work.

Billy had expected the attorney to try to undermine McManigal's confession; that tactic, after all, had succeeded in the Haywood case. But still Billy was fooled. Emma McManigal, he was forced to admit, "trimmed us and trimmed her husband."

Billy had previously used a fortune-teller to manipulate the unsuspecting and vulnerable Emma. But now it was Emma's turn for mischief. With a cool nerve, she set in motion her plan to play the famous detective. First she went to the Burns office in Chicago and asked for a fifty-dollar ticket to Los Angeles so that she and her two children could visit her husband in jail. Burns readily agreed. His operative Malcolm MacLaren, who on Billy's instructions had been visiting McManigal daily, had passed on reports about the "half crazy" letters that the prisoner was writing to his wife, desperate appeals to see her and the children. Billy reasoned that fifty dollars was a small sum to pay to win the gratitude of the McManigal family. But when Emma arrived on the West Coast, she was met by Job Harriman, just as had been arranged from the start. When the two waiting Burns detectives approached, Emma pointedly refused to speak to them. She went directly to a rooming house owned by Harriman.

The next day she arrived at the jail and set to work on the second part of her—and Darrow's—plan. "Mrs. McManigal," Billy fumed, "managed to get into her husband's cell with him alone and begin her task of winning him away from us."

She did not hesitate. One small kiss of greeting for her husband, and then she announced, "I want you to sign a note to Clarence Darrow. Place yourself in the hands of the union's attorneys."

She followed this up with, first, the enticing carrot: The lawyer had promised to provide for the whole family for life. There would be a cash gift, and McManigal would also get a lucrative job once he was freed.

Then she swung the heavy stick: If he didn't sign a note requesting that Darrow represent him, he'd never see her again.

McManigal, already driven to despair by his predicament, was now pushed into an even deeper hopelessness. Desperate, he attempted to explain what would happen if he were convicted.

Emma put her fingers in her ears.

"Please," her husband begged.

"Shut up," she ordered.

And finally, McManigal, sobbing, signed the note.


"Things looked very bad," Billy conceded. "His wife, it seemed, had done the work she was sent to do." But Billy, who loved a good fight, refused to give up. He ordered MacLaren to come down hard on the prisoner.

Mac, dour and officious, did. It no longer matters if you recant, the operative warned McManigal. Burns himself has gathered the evidence to substantiate every bombing. At the trial you'll be the fall guy. The defense will put all the blame on you. You'll hang.

Emma played tough, too. One day she would refuse to visit her husband; the next she would hurl threats about losing her and the children unless he cooperated with Darrow. She continued to reiterate how prosperous the family would become once the trial was over.

Of course, Billy knew what was said during her visits. The

Dictaphone recorded every harsh word. And Billy used this intelligence to bolster the sting of Mac's rebuttals.

The needling went on until McManigal, pulled in opposite
directions by his two unyielding opponents, finally broke apart.
Day after day he sat hunched in his cell moaning and sobbing.

In the end Billy won. McManigal would listen to MacLaren's
solemn warnings, and after each new lecture he could imagine himself being led one step closer to the gallows. McManigal signed a
note repudiating the earlier one. He would not work with the
defense.

The wife had failed. So, gamely, Darrow turned to the uncle.
Throughout McManigal's lonely childhood, his uncle, George
Behm, was the one person who had offered him any affection.
When Darrow discovered this, he quickly brought Behm across the
continent to Los Angeles.

McManigal cheered up when he learned Uncle George was
coming to visit him. For days he looked forward to the occasion.
But the reunion, he quickly discovered, was only one more attempt
to persuade him to change sides and sit with the defense. Feeling
betrayed and exploited, McManigal sank even lower.

This was the point when the real torture began. It was "worse
than any third degree," said Billy with the authority of a man who
had witnessed his share of brass-knuckled persuasion in the back
rooms of police stations.

Uncle George took to parading along the street outside the jail.
He knew his nephew, who liked to peer out his cell window, would
be sure to see him. Pounding on the window's wire screen,
McManigal would shout hysterically, "Oh, Uncle George, here I
am. Oh come up and see me, Uncle George." Behm just kept on
walking.

Some days Behm would have his nephew's five-year-old son

accompany him on this stroll. "Hey," McManigal yelled, "Uncle George! Bring the boy over and let me see him." Behm held the boy's hand tight and walked on in stony silence.

Afterward Behm reported to Darrow, "I didn't take the boy over. I didn't pay any attention to the hollering."

Darrow congratulated Behm on his resolve. "That's right, god-dammit," said the attorney. "Tease him, and he will come across."

But McManigal didn't come across. MacLaren told Billy that "Ortie is in a very nervous condition bordering on collapse." Despite the pressures, though, McManigal grasped the grim, intractable logic in Billy's argument. If he turned and went with the defense, the jury's verdict could be easily predicted: death by hanging.

In August both Emma and Uncle George realized the futility of any further attempts. Resigned and disconsolate, they took a train together back to Chicago.

But there were other witnesses for Darrow to have a go at, and he sent his men off in pursuit. Larry Sullivan, the former prizefighter, and John Harrington, the defense's chief investigator, headed up to San Francisco. Their target: George Phillips, a clerk at the Giant Powder Works, who had sold Jim McNamara—using the alias Bryce—the dynamite for the *Times* bombing. Phillips had announced he was prepared to identify Jim in court.

The approach to Phillips was weirdly oblique. Using the cover name of Kelly, Sullivan went to Michael Gilmore, another clerk at Giant Powder, with a letter purportedly written by a priest. The letter, though, was succinct and compelling:

"My dear Michael:

"I wish you would assist this man in the information which he will need. Help him in every way you can. Mr. L. M. Kelly will explain when he sees you."

Sullivan—posing as Kelly—gruffly provided the promised

explanation. Gilmore must urge his friend Phillips to change his testimony in the McNamara case. The man who bought the dynamite,
Phillips should suddenly remember, was someone else. A man missing an index finger.

If he shared this newly recalled memory at the trial, "Phillips
can name his own price." However, if he pointed to Jim, "he will
not die a natural death."

But Billy also had men keeping a conscientious watch on
Phillips, and when he learned of the threat, he hurried to San Francisco. "I'm going to stand pat," Phillips told the detective. He was
nervous, but he "would not permit anybody to frighten me out of
doing my duty as a good citizen."

Inwardly, Billy rejoiced, and at the same time the detective
earnestly promised Phillips he didn't need to worry. He would make
sure no one harmed him or his family. From that day, a contingent
of guards, sober men in topcoats and derbys, surrounded the modest Phillips house in Oakland.

Still, the Darrow team kept hammering away, determined to create
a crack in the prosecution's case. Lena Ingersoll owned the San
Francisco boardinghouse where Jim (giving his name once again as
Bryce) had stayed. Watching from the sheriff's car as McNamara
was led off the train in Pasadena two months ago, she had confirmed his identity. And she had agreed to repeat the identification
at the trial. Sullivan met with her husband at a San Francisco hotel
and, dispensing with any preliminaries, made a blunt offer: It would
be worth $5,000 to the couple if they'd stay out of Los Angeles dur-
ing the trial.

Kurt Diekelman was another potential star witness. He was a
Los Angeles hotel clerk who could establish that Jim (once again
posing as Bryce) had been in the city at the time of the explosion.

Diekelman had moved to Albuquerque to run a restaurant, but Darrow's investigators tracked him down.

This time the Darrow team decided that the courting would require more finesse than menace. A special emissary was sent to Albuquerque.

A man introducing himself as Bert Higgins, a member of the McNamara defense team, arrived at Diekelman's Fashion Café.

"We are trying our best to save that man," Higgins began. "He is innocent."

"I don't think there is any doubt," said Diekelman.

Encouraged, Higgins continued. "Now you are a valuable witness to us, and whatever your price is, we will give it to you."

With that bald opening, the negotiations started. Restaurant jobs in Chicago were offered, then simply cash. Finally Diekelman agreed to accept a ticket on the *Sante Fe Limited* to Chicago and a hundred dollars for expenses. Once in Chicago, the discussion would continue until terms could be established that would guarantee Diekelman's refusal to identify McNamara.

On his first morning in Chicago, Diekelman went, as instructed, to Darrow's law office. Waiting for him was Ed Nockles, a local labor leader, and Higgins.

"My name is not Higgins," the man who had come to Albuquerque announced dramatically. "My name is Hammerstrom. I am Mr. Darrow's brother-in-law."

With that revelation, the talks began again.

But Darrow had not been the only one looking for Diekelman. Burns, too, had been on his trail. And when it was discovered that the witness had left for Chicago, Guy Biddinger was sent after him.

Biddinger was a confident, genial former cop who had been present at Jim's arrest, then was part of the contingent of Burns guards who had traveled on the train to Los Angeles with the prisoners. Biddinger's great talent, Billy knew, was that at any sudden moment he could drop his easy friendliness, let his dark eyes narrow into two slits like gun holes, and turn mean. He was the perfect man to persuade Diekelman that it would be in his best interest to leave Chicago, return to his restaurant, and wait to be called to Los Angeles to testify. And after listening to Biddinger, a subdued Diekelman took the next train back to Albuquerque.

Yet even as the two sides jockeyed for the allegiances of the witnesses, they also pursued a subtler covert strategy. Darrow conspired to place moles—informants—in the prosecution's team. Billy, for his part, tried to identify the co-opted agents and turn them. He hoped to send them back as doubles, operatives spying on the men who had recruited them. For both camps, it was a tense, tricky game.

First, Billy learned that Olaf Tveitmoe, the San Francisco labor leader, was trying to recruit a spy from among the Burns men. So Billy provided him with one—investigator Ed McKeown. In a series of meetings McKeown gave Tveitmoe's people carefully expurgated lists of prosecution witnesses and invented summaries of the district attorney's strategy sessions. And while delivering this disinformation, McKeown picked up all he could about what the Darrow team was planning—a gold mine of intelligence delivered to Billy for his plundering.

Darrow, meanwhile, was boldly directing his own operation to land a valuable deep penetration asset. He personally orchestrated the recruitment of Guy Biddinger.

William Turner, a former Chicago detective who had worked for Darrow, was the go-between. He met with Biddinger and explained, one ex-cop to another, that Darrow had paid out big money, as much as $15,000, to informants during the Haywood case. Biddinger listened attentively. It was a lot of money, he agreed. Sure, he said at last, he'd talk to Darrow.

The meeting between one of the top Burns operatives and the renowned leader of the McNamara defense team played out like a coy first date. Darrow threw out the suggestion that $5,000 could possibly be paid for information. Who knows, said Biddinger with an equally contrived aloofness, he might be able to pass on a morsel someday.

For two tentative months Darrow and Biddinger continued their flirtation. Then Biddinger called the attorney: He had something to deal. He had documents that established that J.J. had orchestrated the bombings. Darrow suggested a meeting at eight the next morning in the bar of the Alexandria Hotel.

At the Alex, Biddinger spotted a *Times* reporter and immediately turned antsy.

"I have got that money for you," Darrow said, trying to coax some calm into Biddinger's jumpy mood.

"I don't want to take it here. We may be watched."

"Do it here, open and aboveboard," said Darrow. This was the experienced professional giving a lesson to the novice agent: A bold move often attracts less attention than a surreptitious one.

Biddinger, however, insisted that they conduct their business in the privacy of the mezzanine.

By the elevator, Darrow handed Biddinger $500 in cash.

"I thought you were going to bring a thousand." Biddinger was upset.

Once again Darrow worked to calm him. "Money isn't rolling in," he explained. "Give me a little time."

At last Biddinger pocketed the money; and Darrow relaxed. He knew he had bought his mole. He immediately gave Biddinger his first assignment.

"There is some man in the Iron Workers organization who is

tipping everything off to Burns," Darrow said. "I would like to find out who it is."

Biddinger suggested the leak came from Gene Clancy, the top Iron Workers official on the West Coast.

Darrow was stunned—and grateful. This was troubling but valuable news.

Over the following months, Biddinger continued to supply Darrow with names and information—all of it as deliberately false as the revelation of Clancy's name had been. From the start, Biddinger had been loyally working for Billy, helping him to spread disinformation and dissension to the enemy.

And so the intrigues continued throughout the summer and early fall. Then it was announced that "the greatest trial of the century" would begin on October 11.

D.W., as it happened, was also busy dealing with a spy in his camp. The Biograph studio heads had assigned an accountant to monitor and then report on the director's excesses as his productions became more elaborate.

Johannes Charlemagne Epping looked as if the studio casting director had picked him for this accountant's role. He was a short, meek, bespectacled man. But with D.W.'s masterly direction, Epping was soon playing a new, more forceful part—a double agent.

The director had confided to Epping that he realized his days working for Biograph would soon come to an end. He envisioned making more technically ambitious and expensive films than the ones the studio would want. And, D.W. also revealed, he had come to appreciate that his annual winter sojourns to Los Angeles were no longer sufficient. He wanted to make all his movies in California.

When D.W. made his break, he'd need a financial officer. Was Epping interested? Epping decided he was. With that agreement, the alerts that the studio had been receiving about unanticipated costs in the Griffith productions abruptly stopped.

Before D.W. and his designated financial director left Biograph, however, the company made one last winter's trip to Los Angeles.

# THIRTY-SEVEN

AN EXACTING SMALL-SCALE model of the downtown block where the *Times* Building had stood had been built with great care, at great expense, and with great expectations. A row of miniature streetlamps lined the sidewalk. A side of the newspaper building had been left open to reveal five floors filled with tiny desks, printing presses, and linotype machines. Little doors swung open with the pull of minute metal handles. It was a beautiful piece of craftsmanship. And Darrow couldn't wait to blow it up.

The attorney was hoping to prove that a gas leak had caused the fateful explosion. Articles had reported that for weeks *Times* employees had been complaining of the smell of escaping gas. His investigators had contacted union supporters at the paper who said they would swear to this in court. If Darrow's technicians were able to reinforce this testimony by demonstrating that gas, not dynamite, was the catalyst, then the McNamaras had a chance.

On Darrow's command, a gas charge was set off, and the model erupted into flames.

The fire burned high and bright, but there was only localized damage.

Try it again, Darrow ordered.

The model was repaired, and this time a larger amount of gas was used. The results were also disappointing.

Again, Darrow ordered.

The technicians kept at it, restoring the model and igniting gas charges. But the fundamental conclusion did not vary: Gas could not have caused the catastrophic explosion that rocked the *Times*

Building. Only dynamite could have set off such devastating and rolling waves of destruction.

With this knowledge, Darrow lost all confidence in his case. His mood blackened. He sat slumped over his desk in the Higgins Building, a man overwhelmed. He was reminded of the last time he was in Los Angeles. Once again he was living with another devastating illness. Only this time the sickness, he knew with a total and resigned certainty, would end in death. The case would be lost, and the two brothers would be executed.

For the moment it was beyond him to focus on a new strategy. When it got like this, Darrow had to escape.

It was only a two-room apartment. Thirty-five dollars a month, including the Murphy bed that folded up into the wall. But 1110 Ingraham Street offered Darrow a freedom that was liberation. He was able to ease the weight of "the trial of the century" off his stooped shoulders and enjoy small moments with his Mary. They talked about the articles Mary wrote for Dreiser's *Delineator* and for the *American Magazine*. Darrow read poetry out loud in his perfect voice. And when it was time, the Murphy bed would be pulled down from the wall.

Ruby knew. Darrow was away so many nights, it became impossible for him to continue to invent plausible excuses.

Billy knew, too. The Burns men kept Darrow under constant surveillance. But Billy said nothing to the press or the district attorney. It was a piece of intelligence that Billy parsimoniously filed away. Capital, the self-made man knew, should not be drawn on unless it was a necessity.

With an infinite resignation, Darrow assumed that both his wife and his enemies knew the risks he was taking. But it was not only his marriage and his reputation that were in jeopardy. In Los Angeles it was against the law—a statutory crime—to be in a bedroom with a woman who was not your wife. If he was charged, the McNamara jury would turn against him—and no doubt also against his clients. But Darrow was beyond caring. Desperate men act recklessly. As do, it would soon become evident, desperate attorneys.

George Monroe, the Los Angeles court clerk, gave the wheel a spin. Twirling about inside were slips of paper with the names of sixteen hundred potential jurors. When the wheel came to a stop, he opened a small hatch, reached inside, and began to withdraw 125 slips. It was Friday morning, September 29, 1911, and Monroe was selecting the jury pool for the McNamara trial.

The trial was expected to last three months, possibly longer. Not every juror could accommodate such an extended absence from his work or was sufficiently healthy to endure months in a courtroom. Judge Walter Bordwell met with the candidates and within days reduced the list to forty-three men.

This new list of names was given to the county clerk. And he promptly passed it on to Bert Franklin, one of Darrow's investigators.

Officially, Franklin's job for the defense was "to find out the apparent age, religion, nationality, of every prospective juror, what their feelings were to union labor, their feelings and opinions regarding the *Times* explosion, their opinion as to whether the McNamaras were guilty or not guilty of the crime with which they were charged, their financial condition, their property, the bank at which they did business."

Unofficially, Franklin's duties went further. He was to make sure that at least two members of the jury would, regardless of the evidence, vote for acquittal.

Although he was a native of Iowa, Franklin had spent enough years in the L.A. sheriff's office and then as a deputy U.S. marshal to have a wide network of acquaintances throughout the region. Still, it was a matter of luck that Robert Bain, an elderly carpenter whom he had known for going on twenty years, was one of the forty-three potential jurors. On October 6 he paid his old friend a visit.

Bain wasn't around, but his wife Dora was. This was the first time Franklin had been to their new home, and he told Dora it was lovely. "What do you owe on it?" he then blurted out.

Dora was shocked by his impertinence and told him so. But Franklin would rub people the wrong way, and he didn't seem to care. He was a short, dapper man with a mustache that he clearly put a lot of effort into trimming until it was just right. Take me or leave me was his attitude. He was more than satisfied with himself.

For that matter, Dora's attitude changed as Franklin breezily continued. He suggested to her that there was a way they could pay off their mortgage. "I would like to have Bob on the McNamara jury. I'm in a position to pay him five hundred dollars down. Four thousand total when he had voted for an acquittal for McNamara."

"Well, Bob is a very honest man . . ."

Franklin listened patiently.

"—But that sounds good to me. I would like to have Bob consider it."

He did. Particularly after Dora (as she would later remember with regret) "begged piteously." When Franklin showed up that evening, Bain accepted $400 in twenties. The remaining $3,600 would be paid when he voted not guilty.

But only hours later Bain was filled with a tremendous self-loathing. "My honor is gone," he told his wife.

Franklin passed the word to Darrow that if Bain were chosen, there would be one vote for acquittal.

But two sure votes would be even better. And as it happened, there was another name among the potential jurors that Franklin recognized. In fact, he had once worked with George Lockwood in the sheriff's office. Now that was promising, Franklin decided. There was a bond between cops, and on the job you learn not to be too squeamish. It wouldn't take much persuasion, Franklin was confident, to get Lockwood onboard.

Franklin went to the small alfalfa ranch outside Covina where Lockwood, semiretired, was living. Once again he was direct.

"George, I have a proposition to make to you. You can make some money and be of material assistance to myself at the same time."

Lockwood was also a direct man. "Bert, spit it out," he said.

"Did you know that your name was on a prospective list of jurors?"

"No, I didn't."

"In case you are drawn, would you vote for a verdict of acquittal in the McNamara case?"

Lockwood didn't answer. "Well, I don't know," he said after some thought.

Franklin offered $500 in cash right away and an additional $3,500 at the end of the case.

Lockwood paced back and forth. The money would certainly come in handy. Still . . .

"Bert, this is a matter I would want to think over."

And that was how it was left, for now.


On October 11 the trial began. There were more than a thousand people crowding the street outside the courthouse trying to get in, pushing and shoving in the uncommonly warm early morning autumn heat. Reporters had arrived from all over the country. Mary, with press credentials from *American Magazine,* sat between the men from Pulitzer's *New York World* and Hearst's *San Francisco Examiner.* Like everyone else, she had come to see Clarence Darrow perform.

The first order of business was to pick a jury. It loomed as a long, contentious process. John Fredericks, the district attorney, interrogated each of the candidates with stern precision. Darrow was more garrulous and often witty, playing both to the press and to the judge. When a candidate tried to disqualify himself because his property was under his wife's name, a grinning Darrow taunted, "Most workingmen's property is in their employer's name." And he reassured another prospective juror who complained about his finances, "You know, every man is a capitalist in Los Angeles who doesn't sleep in a disappearing bed or eat at a cafeteria."

But even at this preliminary stage of the proceedings, Darrow was determined to articulate what he hoped to make the central issue in the case. "I presume you have heard of the bitter war that is going on in this country between capital and labor?" he challenged the first juror to take the stand. The prosecution objected, but by then it was too late. Darrow had let the potential jurors know that at stake in this courtroom was not simply the fate of two brothers but the future of the nation.

After two weeks of battling, both sides had so far only agreed on one juror. He was an elderly retired carpenter who sported a flower in his buttonhole. His name was Robert Bain.

As the jury selection continued, Lincoln Steffens arrived to cover the trial. He was Billy's old friend and Darrow's, too. But he saw himself as working independently of the two adversaries. His role—and he was as cocky and self-assured as both the detective and the attorney—was, he boasted, to "be the McNamara of my profession." He had his own theory about crime and punishment, and he came to Los Angeles determined to use his explosive ideas not to cover the trial but to blow it up.

# THIRTY-EIGHT

**D**. W. HAD ALSO turned his mind and his camera to thoughts about crime and punishment. He was never a big thinker, more the sort of curious man who traveled along latching on to bits and pieces in the flow of circulating ideas. So from the police gazettes that were popularizing Billy's detective exploits, he began to focus on the realization that gangsters were never boring. Audiences would flock to see a crime story. And from the writings of men like Steffens and Darrow, he began to give some thought to the reformers' argument that criminals were made, not born. Put anybody into their ill-fitting shoes, and the odds were that they'd cross the line, too.

But D.W. was an innovator. He could take elements from a clutter of ideas and bring them to the screen with a clarity that was pure power. His *Musketeers of Pig Alley* was a small masterpiece, a melodrama from the sidewalks of New York that Billy had policed. And it was a wonderfully visual essay about the shaping of the criminal mind that either Darrow or Steffens might have used to bolster his argument in defense of the unfortunate McNamara brothers. How can you be truly guilty, D.W. was suggesting to his audiences, if you never had the opportunity to be innocent?

*Musketeers* tells a sappy, wildly improbable story. A young couple, a struggling musician and his seamstress fiancée, take an unanticipated detour into gangland. The Snapper Kid, a gang leader, is both villain and hero. He steals the musician's wallet but then prevents the seamstress from swallowing the doped drink offered to her at a dance hall by a rival hood. This act of gallantry provokes a gang war, a brutal and mesmerizing cinematic jumble of tense close-ups, shifting eyes, and jumping guns. In the end the wallet is recovered, the seamstress and her musician are reunited, and the young girl helps the Snapper Kid escape from the police, a repayment for his kindness.

But there was a genuine and unique achievement in this sixteen-minute film. D.W. had once again led his cameraman Billy Bitzer into the slums and streets of New York. Scene after scene pounds with the crowded tumult of the Lower East Side. There is a remarkable energy in the dense montages of immigrant faces—Italian, Irish, Jewish—leaning out of tenement windows, restless children perched on fire escapes, and the vast caravan of people weaving through narrow streets lined with hustling vendors and bubbling food stalls.

These pictures are an education. Like the photographs of D.W.'s contemporary Jacob Riis, they are documents that reveal a hard, mean foreign land in our own cities, a breeding ground for crime and criminals. What choice did the Snapper Kid have? D.W.'s camera was asking. Snapper was a fundamentally good man, a noble soul, brought down by the unavoidable circumstances of his life.

It was a logic—reason as well as rationalization—whose principles would find their way into the trial in Los Angeles. And with dramatic results.

# THIRTY-NINE

---

J ustifiable dynamiting," Steffens announced.

It was his first day in Los Angeles, and it had been a busy one. He had breakfasted at the Alex; made an appearance at the trial, explaining to Judge Bordwell without irony that he had come "to try the case"; and then had quickly decided watching the duel over the jurors was not big enough sport for a journalist of his renown. He had a mission and was eager to get under way. He asked Darrow to have him admitted into the jail so that he could meet with the two brothers. The attorney promptly made the arrangements. But then, Darrow had no idea what Steffens was going to propose to his clients.

Steffens marched like a toy soldier into the jailhouse conference room, and the brothers stared with open fascination. He was a fastidious little man with a tightly cut little three-piece suit, a little dark mustache, and a little goatee. A curtain of brown hair fell down over his little forehead. His blue eyes shone as if to signal his own importance and natural authority. He was the man who had alerted the nation with his 1904 book *The Shame of the Cities,* and now, eager to regain the spotlight, he was going to change the course of the McNamara trial.

"Justifiable Dynamiting," he repeated with evident pride. That was the title of the article he wanted to write. He explained that he assumed that organized labor had committed the dynamiting. But he wanted to raise the question: Why? Why did the labor leaders feel so hateful they had to kill? He wanted to educate people about how a conspiracy of capital had forced them into violence.

The brothers listened in stunned silence.

"It's a doubtful experiment and risk for you," Steffens continued on merrily, "but it's got to be done sometime. Why not now?" He added, "I might be able to show why you turned to dynamite."

This odd little man had finally come and said it! the brothers realized. Steffens was asking them to admit their guilt! He was asking them to put the hangman's noose around their own necks.

The McNamaras attacked with a wail of objections.

No, no, Steffens demurred. It would never come to something so dire. His article would establish the guilt of *both* labor and capital. Judge Bordwell would certainly appreciate that the ultimate blame for the bombing was shared. He'd probably pardon them "as political prisoners."

The little man's naïveté was breathtaking, the brothers decided.

"Have you seen Darrow about this?" an exasperated J.J. managed to ask at last.

No! said Darrow to Steffens later that evening in the office in the Higgins Building. Impossible. He did not even want to discuss the possibility of the brothers' admitting their guilt.

But it was a discussion that Steffens was determined to have. His article depended upon their admission; it was the fulcrum upon which his theory of equal culpability teetered. And so he engineered invitations for both Darrow and him to spend Sunday, November 19, at Miramar.

Rolling through the lush foothills of La Jolla, a shimmering slice of the blue Pacific in the distance, the air ripe with the scent of oranges and the perfume of bougainvillea, Miramar was a two-thousand-acre paradise. It was also the home of E. W. Scripps, the liberal-thinking newspaper publisher and proudly self-described "old crank."

Scripps enjoyed his wealth. His house was a sprawling hacienda.

He had his own speedway with a fleet of fast cars to race around in. He had built a biological laboratory near his estate and staffed it with researchers. But his greatest passion was ideas. He collected ideas the way other very rich men collect pictures or sculptures. So when Steffens had telephoned and suggested that perhaps Darrow and he could come down for a day to escape the pressures in Los Angeles, Scripps eagerly assented. The McNamara case had been very much on his mind, too.

But throughout the day at Miramar, Darrow had been uncharacteristically taciturn. To Scripps's eyes he seemed morose, like a man mourning an irreplaceable loss. It wasn't until they were sitting on the patio in the starry evening, coaxed by the warming comfort of the brandy and the pull of Scripps's hand-rolled Key West cigars, that Darrow opened up.

As if he could no longer bear the pain in silence, Darrow suddenly blurted it out. The evidence against the brothers was devastating. J.J. could somehow perhaps hope to get off. But Jim's conviction was inevitable. It was "a dead cinch." "The boy will be hanged."

Steffens had been waiting for his moment all day. Now he seized it.

Their deaths could serve a purpose, he suggested with a helpfulness that struck Darrow as simply cruel. But Steffens did not notice the reaction, or possibly he didn't care. He simply continued: The nation will realize the necessity to resolve the differences between capital and labor. Think of it! The end to a war.

Darrow's thoughts, however, remained focused on the two men. "I can't stand it to have a man I am defending hanged." The words rushed out in a thin, weak moan. "I can't stand it."

With that admission, the conversation stalled. But Scripps had heard enough. Like Steffens, he had been waiting for his moment. He rose and said he had written an article for his papers. He wanted to share it with his two guests.

Scripps went into the house and unlocked a black steel box. Inside was a manuscript. He removed the sheaf of pages and returned to the patio. Handing the article to Darrow, he asked the attorney to read it aloud.

" 'Belligerent Rights,' " Darrow began, reciting the title. What followed was a passionate, idealistic, yet often cogently reasoned argument declaring that the McNamara brothers were soldiers in a war—the conflict between capital and labor. Darrow read:

" 'These men that were killed should be considered what they really were—soldiers enlisted under a capitalist employer whose main purpose in life was warfare against the unions.

" 'If belligerent rights were accorded to the two parties in this war, then McNamara was guilty of no greater offense than would be the officer of any band, large or small, of soldiers who ordered his men to fire upon an enemy and killed a great number of them . . .

" 'Workingmen should have the same belligerent rights in labor controversies that nations have in warfare . . . The war is over now; the defeated side should be granted the rights of a belligerent under international law.' "

When Darrow finished reading, he bowed his head and held it in his two hands as if he were supporting a heavy weight. He knew that all was lost.

Slowly he raised his head and stared up into the clear starry night as if searching for an inspiration. But he found only the counterfeit comfort of wishful thinking.

"I just wish they would see that it's in the best interest of the community to settle the case without shedding any human blood," he told the two men.

A moment; and then even this small hope slipped away. "But they never will," he said.

On the sleeper that night returning to Los Angeles, Steffens lay in his bunk and replayed the after-dinner conversation back in his mind. Steffens made his living and his reputation with words. He understood their power. Darrow, he realized with excitement, had spoken what had previously been unspeakable. However tentatively, however abstractly, the attorney had indicated that he would like to settle the case.

Over an early breakfast at the Van Nuys Hotel near the train station, Steffens pounced. "Did you really mean it when you said you wanted to make a settlement?" he asked.

"Yes," Darrow agreed with little conviction. "But it's impossible, of course. The feeling is too bitter. The people are not in a reasonable state of mind."

"But why not try it?" urged Steffens. And with an egotist's unwavering certainty, he declared, "I think I can convince the businessmen of Los Angeles that it would be better all around to avoid the passion of a trial."

Darrow smirked at this absurdity. Otis and the M&M wanted a trial. They wanted a very public victory. And they wanted to claim their spoils—the corpses of the McNamara brothers.

But Steffens's belief in his own power was boundless. He kept pressing the attorney. And Darrow no longer had either the calm or the will to hold up against such a persistent assault.

"I am perfectly willing," Darrow finally agreed. Steffens could meet with "your crowd," as Darrow sneeringly referred to the journalist's contacts in the business community. He could raise the possibility of a settlement.

But the attorney insisted that two nonnegotiable conditions must be attached to his surrender. One, all charges against J.J. must be dropped. And two, Jim must not be hanged.

Suddenly Darrow paled. It was as if the significance of what he was conceding, of what he was embarking on, had now become real. He started to shake. With great emotion, he begged Steffens to proceed as if he had not discussed the proposal with anyone in the defense. The journalist should present it as his own idea. "If it should get out to the community that we are making overtures it will make it that much more difficult to defend the men and save their lives," Darrow warned.

"Any proposition will come *to* you, not *from* you," Steffens promised.

And so it began. What once had seemed utterly impossible now struggled to become a reality. A settlement in the case against the two brothers accused of "the crime of the century" was under discussion.

Steffens started by approaching Meyer Lissner, a prosperous lawyer and businessman. Lissner knew all the town leaders. Even better, they saw him as one of their own. But Steffens's own friendship with Lissner had revealed him to be a reasonable man, more civic-minded and generous of spirit than the vengeful M&M ideologues. Lissner listened to Steffens and, with an insider's shrewd knowledge, suggested they bring Tom Gibbon into the discussion. If this was going to work, Lissner explained, the *Times* ownership would need to endorse the plan. And Tommy was Harry Chandler's buddy; he could bring any proposal directly to the man who was not only the paper's assistant publisher but also, no less significantly, Otis's son-in-law.

When Gibbon arrived, he needed to hear only the opening of Steffens's argument before he interrupted. I agree, he said. How can I be of assistance?

Steffens explained. Eager to move his plan forward, he dictated a memo, and Lissner's secretary typed it:

"Party on trial"—the case against Jim was to be prosecuted first—"to plead guilty and receive such sentence as the court might administer (except capital punishment). All other prosecutions with the affair to be dropped."

Gibbon took a copy of the memo and hurried off to deliver it to Harry Chandler. Hours later Gibbon reported back to an anxious Steffens and Lissner.

Chandler had agreed, Gibbon revealed. He'd support the settlement as it was outlined.

Steffens was elated. He had done it! His impossible plan was going to succeed! He would broker the peace between capital and labor!

The talks had been secret, but secrets involving many people rarely remain so for long. When Darrow's co-counsel LeCompte Davis walked into the courtroom the next morning, District Attorney Fredericks charged toward him.

"Why don't you get those boys to plead guilty and quit your horseplay?" thundered Fredericks.

Davis was taken aback. What was the district attorney talking about?

"You know you're going to do it," Fredericks stormed on. "A committee has been consulted about it, and I have been approached." He found Davis's disingenuousness infuriating.

But Davis had not been acting. He had no idea that a settlement had been discussed. Furious, he went off to confront Darrow.

The two men were friends as well as partners, and as they talked, rage turned into resignation. They both agreed that the two brothers had no chance. Quickly they decided what needed to be done, and then with a lawyerly pragmatism they went about doing it.

Darrow wired Fremont Older, the crusading editor of the *San*

*Francisco Bulletin,* and asked him to come "to an important conference at Hotel Alexandria here tomorrow."

Over lunch at the hotel, Darrow asked for the editor's help in
persuading labor leaders to accept a settlement.

A settlement? Fremont was astonished. But after listening to
Darrow's pained recitation of the evidence Burns had collected, he
came around. "I'll do what I can to make them understand," he said
without enthusiasm.

Next, Darrow sent a wire to Gompers. He needed to speak with
someone in authority in the AFL's heirarchy. The union was paying
his fee, bankrolling the defense. It was only proper that he inform
them of his intentions. But the union was conducting its annual
meeting in Atlanta; and the telegram, if it ever found its way to
Gompers, was ignored.

Regardless, the time had come for Darrow to speak to his two
clients. It was a very difficult meeting. But Darrow knew from long
experience that hedging would not dull the blow; and swiftness had
its own mercy. So he came out with it: He wanted Jim to plead
guilty.

Without waiting for a response, Darrow plowed on. He wanted
the brothers to appreciate what they'd be getting—winning!—if
Jim admitted his guilt. He recited a carefully rehearsed list: Jim
would escape the hangman; he'd avoid having to make the sort of
detailed confession that would implicate other union leaders; the
state could be convinced, Darrow felt assured, to give up its pursuit
of the two anarchists still at large, Caplan and Schmitty; and J.J.,
after pleading guilty, would probably receive only a light sentence.

Jim interrupted: J.J. would also have to plead guilty?

Yes, said Darrow.

And serve some time? Jim asked.

Perhaps, Darrow conceded.

Then no deal, said Jim with authority.

At the same time as Darrow's meeting with the two brothers was collapsing, LeCompte Davis was sitting down with Harrison Otis. Otis was an unpleasant mountain of a man, by nature and habit both rude and aggressive. But Davis paid no attention, or he was too much a southern gentleman and too good a lawyer to show his dismay. Which was why, of course, he rather than Darrow had been chosen for this delicate mission.

"Take the bird while you've got it in your hand, General," he told the *Times* owner. "By his plea of guilty McNamara will give you a complete victory and prove that everything you have been claiming is right."

Otis stared at Davis with a stony belligerence. It was as if he wanted to reach across the table and wring the audacious lawyer's neck.

But Davis simply continued on with a smooth cordiality. "If you take a chance and force them into trial," he blithely suggested, "lightning might strike . . . An accident might happen. They might get off."

Otis had heard enough. "I want those sons of bitches to hang!" he bellowed.

And with that declaration, the possibility for a settlement was smashed into pieces. But then again, after Jim rejected Darrow's terms, there really hadn't been much of a chance left anyway.

Billy knew nothing about these talks. If he had, it's doubtful that he would have let them play out even as far as they went.

On the day that Darrow met with the McNamaras, Billy was in New Orleans. He had come to the city to make a speech about the case, and he delivered it with such heated passion that he might as well have been preaching from an evangelical pulpit.

"I will tell you," the detective roared to the overflowing crowd, "they have the money and have endeavored to buy our witness. They have offered some of the prosecution witnesses their own price. And when these witnesses refused to accept the offers, they have been threatened with death."

It would've been impossible for Billy to support a settlement. In fact, after the way the defense had been skulking about, he didn't just want the two brothers executed. He wanted to see their lawyers hanging from ropes, too.

# FORTY

Y ET JUST WHEN it seemed a settlement of the case was an impossibility, three unexpected and seemingly unrelated events conspired to move the discussions rapidly forward. The first was an attempt on the president's life.

There are many rolling rivers and rushing streams in southern California, clear fresh water perfect for trout fishing, swimming, or simply skimming stones on a pleasant day. The El Capitan Creek did not suggest this sort of diversion. It was a flat brown muddy stream that twisted through the countryside near Santa Barbara. Its only significance was that it lay directly in the coastal route that the Southern Pacific Railroad had staked out. So the railroad engineers had constructed a sturdy gray steel bridge across the forlorn creek.

On the morning of October 16, 1911, a railroad watchman was out walking across the El Capitan Bridge, on duty, eyes alert. In the bright sunshine, something caught his attention. A brown package stood near the base of a heavy steel girder. He hurried over to inspect.

It was not a package. It was a bomb. Thirty-nine sticks of dynamite, fuses attached, had been tied into a bundle.

The watchman's instinct was to run, but he restrained himself. He knew he had to work quickly. There was not much time. In his mind he was already hearing the tooting whistle of the approaching Southern Pacific. With great caution and a silent prayer, he began to detach the fuses from the explosives. The work was agonizing. But he managed to get it done.

Not long after that the train carrying President William Howard Taft crossed the El Capitan Bridge, then continued on without incident toward Los Angeles.

It was never determined who had planted the dynamite. Was it the work of anarchists? Perhaps embittered railroad workers hoping to dramatize their grievances? Some even speculated that capitalist goons had left the device: The death of a president would be a small sacrifice for a grieving nation's unrestrained backlash against labor.

But although the identity of the would-be assassins remained unknown, the consequences of the dynamite plot to kill the president were both swift and definitive. The next day an angry President Taft conferred with Attorney General George Wickersham and issued an order: The federal government would join the legal fight against the Structural Iron Workers union. Two weeks later an Indianapolis federal criminal grand jury began to investigate the charge that officials connected to the union had unlawfully conspired to transport dynamite across state lines. The evidence that Billy had gathered against the leadership would finally be put to use.

While in Los Angeles, there was a growing anxiety. If forces lurking nearby were prepared to initiate a dynamite attack on the President of the United States, it seemed only a matter of time before they would target the McNamara trial. Perhaps a bomb would go off on the day a key prosecution witness was scheduled to testify. Or maybe a slew of bombs, a tattoo of fiery explosions, would detonate if there was a guilty verdict, the resulting deaths dwarfing the *Times* Building disaster.

Either way many people throughout the city—largely the middle class and the rich; they had the most to lose—found themselves coming to the earnest conclusion that the bitter war between capital and labor in Los Angeles had to end. Now that the U.S. government was going after the Structural Iron Workers, the bombing of the *Times* Building would be avenged, and the city of Los Angeles should discreetly remove itself from the line of fire.

The second mobilizing event was no less influential to the course of the settlement and in its public way was even more dramatic. It began, however, with a small moment. After still another group of potential jurors failed to satisfy either Darrow or the district attorney, the court clerk went down his list and matter-of-factly began filling in the names on service papers for new jury candidates. One of the names he wrote that Friday, November 24, was George Lockwood.

Two days later Bert Franklin showed up at Lockwood's ranch. Now that Lockwood had been selected as a jury candidate, Franklin told his old friend, he needed an answer: Would he accept the $4,000 and vote for acquittal?

The wind was howling, and Lockwood suggested they could talk more easily in the barn. He led the way, the unanswered question still a wall between them. When Lockwood closed the door, the two men stood facing each other in nearly total darkness.

This could go either way, Franklin realized. But all he could do was wait.

"If I go into this, I want no mistake about the money," Lockwood said firmly at last. "I want to be sure of it."

Franklin ignored the challenge in the old cop's voice and instead celebrated with a silent cheer. Lockwood was hooked. He would be another vote for acquittal.

But there were still the details to agree on, and Franklin had already given them some thought. He proposed to pay $500 down. The remaining $3,500 would be held by Captain White, a county jailer they both knew from their days in the sheriff's office. After the verdict was announced, Lockwood could collect the money from the captain.

Lockwood didn't object, and the next afternoon the two friends talked again to finalize the arrangements. They would meet at nine on Tuesday morning on the corner of Third and Los Angeles Street. Captain White would be there, too. The captain would give Lockwood his $500 down payment and a look at the roll of bills he'd be holding until the trial's end.

On Tuesday, Lockwood took a streetcar into town and arrived promptly at nine at the rendezvous. Captain White was waiting for him. Franklin, though, had gone into a nearby saloon; he needed a shot to wash down his breakfast. And in position on the streets surrounding the busy downtown intersection were six Los Angeles police detectives.

It was a trap. After Franklin's first visit to his ranch, an indignant Lockwood had rushed to the district attorney's office. He had been cooperating with them ever since, coolly stringing Franklin along. And now they were going to catch one of Darrow's men in the act of bribing a potential juror.

Only there was a problem. "Where's Franklin?" Lockwood asked the captain. He didn't want to take the money until Franklin was present. He needed the detectives to be able to testify that they had witnessed Darrow's investigator taking part in the scheme. Lockwood realized that his only hope was to buy time. He didn't know how long he could delay without the captain growing suspicious. But he was determined to try.

He improvised with frantic invention. First, he insisted the captain re-count the money in the thick roll. Then once he was satisfied the $4,000 was all there, Lockwood began complaining about the denominations of the bills. "It should have been in twos and fives," he argued. He'd attract too much attention spending big bills. Could the money be exchanged?

The captain had heard enough. He peeled $500 from the roll and handed it to Lockwood.

And as Lockwood took the money, Franklin strolled out of the saloon, walking in a happy tipsy strut toward him.

When he got closer, Franklin was seized with a sudden panic. He had glanced up the block and recognized LAPD Detective George Home. "The sons of bitches," he cursed. "Let's get out of here," he told Lockwood.

Setting a quick pace, he led Lockwood down Third Street, away from the officer.

And straight into Clarence Darrow. The head of the McNamara defense team was walking toward them.

"Wait a minute," Franklin told Lockwood. "I want to speak to this man."

He never got the chance. Detective Home rammed his automatic into Franklin's side and ordered, "Keep your hands in your pockets." Across the street another detective arrested Captain White.

Darrow stood mute, stunned into silence. His investigator had just been arrested after passing a bribe to a potential juror. And the police had witnessed that he was there, too.

That afternoon extras hit the stands, headlines shouting "Jury Bribery Charged in McNamara Trial." None of the first stories reported that Darrow had been present when the bribe occurred.

But the attorney knew it would not be long before this became a story. He might even be charged. He now had more reason than ever to push for a settlement. A bribed juror wouldn't help his clients' case at all. Nor, for that matter, would the suspicion that the McNamaras' lead counsel had been part of the scheme.

But it was still another arguably even more memorable occurrence that was to bring the most recalcitrant opponents of a settlement rushing back into the discussion. On October 31—Halloween—the L.A. mayoral primary election was held. Socialist candidate Job

Harriman had polled 20,183 votes to 16,790 for the incumbent Alexander and an additional 8,191 for the independent Mushet. The plurality was insufficient to avoid a runoff election. But it was, as the *Los Angeles Citizen* rejoiced, "a momentous spectacle." And on December 5—just five short weeks—the runoff would be held between Harriman and Alexander. Los Angeles, it was expected, would soon elect a Socialist mayor.

Many powerful people in the city anticipated Harriman's victory with genuine fear. "Protect Los Angeles Homes!" shouted the *Times*. "Socialism in the saddle will mean less civic and private credit, less building, less industry, and thereby less work and wages."

Los Angeles had been growing at a gallop, but businessmen worried that Harriman's election would put a sudden end to the city's hope to become a metropolis. "Can Los Angeles sell $17,000,000 of its bonds in the next year if Harriman is elected mayor?" the *Times* wondered doubtfully. "If Los Angeles fails to sell bonds in that sum it cannot carry on the great undertakings on the success of which its continued growth and prosperity alike depend. *Failure in those undertakings means municipal disaster!*"

But another clique of influential citizens was concerned not just about the effects of Harriman's election on the city. They knew his victory would cost them millions, perhaps even wipe them out.

For years they had nurtured their scheme. It had been a masterpiece of patience and deliberate misdirection. They had moved to control the water in Owens Valley. They had audaciously persuaded the city taxpayers to build a $23 million aqueduct to bring the water to Los Angeles. They had purchased tens of thousands of seemingly worthless acres in the bleak desert of San Fernando Valley. Now with the completion of the aqueduct, they would siphon off the surplus water and irrigate the valley. A desert would be reclaimed, miraculously transformed into a green suburban paradise. The Los Angeles Suburban Home Company—and its principals, Otis, Chandler, and their circle of wealthy friends—would start building and selling subdivisions. And at last reaping their pile of millions.

But if Harriman was elected, if the Socialists were in control, the scheme would fall apart. The Socialists would insist that city water belonged to the city. They would not allow it to be sold to the Suburban Home Company.

Harriman must not be elected on December 5.

Otis, Chandler, and the other businessmen understood this. Their own fortunes were at stake.

And the only way to put a certain stop to Harriman was to end any talk of vengeance, any talk of a war between capital and labor. The time had come to deal rationally and reasonably, like businessmen, with the fate of the McNamaras.

Darrow had thought it a shrewdness to entwine his defense so tightly with the Socialist candidates. Their popularity, he had reasoned with sly delight, would reflect on his clients. But the attorney had never given any thought to the converse: If the McNamaras went down in defeat, so would the Socialists.

Otis, however, grasped this negative logic. He realized with total certainty that if the McNamaras pleaded guilty, the Socialists would be tarred, too. Harriman would never be elected.

At the start of his investigation, Billy had followed the money, and it had led him to a motive. He had been wrong. Still, his detective's intuition had perceptively focused on the conspiracy that would ultimately play a role in determining the course of the case.

The McNamara trial had to be settled, Otis decided. It would have been a blessing to see the brothers hang. But business was business, after all.

———

And so, the product of these different events and sentiments, a firm desire for a settlement took hold. But it was also a race. Everything had to be efficiently resolved before the election on December 5. Or else there might as well be a hanging.

# FORTY-ONE

ISTRICT ATTORNEY JOHN FREDERICKS liked to think of himself as a military man. He had commanded a cavalry troop during the Spanish-American War and had led gallant charges. In civilian life a hard-driving martial spirit continued to infuse all his activities. His hobbies were no exception. He rode with abandon, tearing over the steeplechase and galloping toward every jump. On the golf course—his other passion—he was no less of a phenomenon. Making towering drives at every hole and brisk, mechanical putts, he'd routinely charge through the eighteen holes in a flash.

But today—November 30, 1911, Thanksgiving Day—Fredericks played the course with leisure. For once he was in no rush. He wanted to walk the fairways for hours; and he wanted to be unreachable. He did not want to offer the defense any opportunity to open up new negotiations. He had told Darrow to telephone his home by three. Either the attorney had obtained an acceptable agreement from his clients for a settlement by then, or they had nothing to discuss. The trial would proceed. And in five days so would the election.

As Fredericks enjoyed his day of golf, Darrow and his co-counsels were at the county jail meeting with the McNamaras. The discussion was a misery, both for the brothers and for their lawyers.

Jim was full of calm resolve. "I am willing to go before the court and take the blame. I will plead guilty," he said.

However, he would not allow J.J. to do the same. In a steady voice he told the lawyers, "I am willing to save my brother for he knew nothing of this, and is as guiltless as you are."

Joe Scott, the co-counsel who had been brought into the case because of his ties to the Catholic community, interrupted him. "But when J.J. pleads guilty, it may save you from the gallows."

Jim was unpersuaded. He no longer cared if he died. All he cared about was protecting his older brother's reputation. He would not cooperate if J.J. had to plead guilty. There were principles worth dying for, he told Darrow.

With the voice of an old man, the lawyer answered, "I understand."

LeCompte Davis made the three o'clock call to the district attorney.

"The big man" cannot be convinced, he said referring to Jim. Could he call back at nine?

"If you get the consent of both men," Fredericks insisted. "If you do not, don't call me up. It is useless to waste time under any circumstances."

There had been a break for a Thanksgiving meal, but the food brought Darrow no enjoyment. He ate listlessly, as if each swallow were a concession. He returned to the prison but could barely find the strength to talk to his clients. He knew they were making a mistake, yet he respected Jim's resolve. Tomorrow the trial would resume, and he could not bear the prospect. Or the inevitability of its conclusion.

As Darrow brooded, Davis had a go at persuading the brothers. Reason had failed, so he tried psychology.

"Jim," he began, "I think you're right, and we've been wrong. It's best that you hang. It'll be better for labor."

Jim did not respond. Perhaps he agreed, or perhaps he was simply beyond listening to further arguments.

But Davis would not stop. "It's better your brother hangs too," he said. "Then labor will have two martyrs."

Suddenly Jim was incredulous. "They'll hang him, too?"

"That's the way it looks to me," said Davis evenly.

The words slammed into Jim. He fell facedown onto his cot as if poleaxed and began to sob.

Darrow looked away, but still the wild animal sound of Jim's desperate tears filled the small cell.

At last Jim raised his head. "All right. I'm licked."

Darrow quietly told Davis to call the district attorney.

The next morning when court convened, Fredericks acted with coy drama. The bewildered reporters listened as he requested a continuance until after lunch. There were, he said portentously, "certain grave matters to be considered."

Like most grave matters, they were played out behind closed doors.

First, Darrow and Davis met with Judge Bordwell. The McNamaras had agreed to the district attorney's terms, Darrow announced. Both would plead guilty. Jim would receive a life sentence. J.J. would do ten years.

"Ten years isn't enough for John J. McNamara," ruled the judge. "He'll have to take fifteen."

It was not the deal that had been negotiated, but J.J. did not argue. Things had gotten to the hopeless point where an additional five years in prison loomed as just one more vindictive lash of the whip; there was no choice but to suffer.

After that, Jim wrote his confession. He sat down in his bunk, as both Darrow and Fredericks stood like silent sentinels above him:

"And this is the truth, on the night of September 30, 1910, at 5:45 P.M. I placed in Ink Alley, a portion of the *Times* Building, a suitcase containing sixteen sticks of 80 per cent dynamite, set to explode at one o'clock the next morning. It was my intention to injure the building and scare the owners. I did not intend to take the life of anyone."

And suddenly it was two P.M.

The afternoon sunlight streamed radiantly through the courtroom windows. With a sense of appropriateness, a bailiff drew the heavy brown curtains. The brothers entered a lugubrious room.

Jim went first, walking briskly like a man in a hurry. J.J. followed. He was as neatly dressed as someone going to church.

Fredericks rose from his seat. "J.B. McNamara," he said in a booming voice, "you have withdrawn your plea of not guilty. Do you wish to plead at this time?"

Jim somehow couldn't find the words. Davis spoke for him. "Yes, sir."

"To this indictment, charging you with the crime of murder, do you plead guilty or not guilty?"

"Guilty," said Jim. A single word, and it was over.

J.J. was told to come forward to the defense table. Fredericks asked his question, and the entire room waited for J.J.'s response.

"Guilty," J.J. said in a loud, clear voice.

The moment was too large, too inconceivable to be fully grasped by those caught up in it. Pandemonium filled the courtroom. Reporters raced to file stories. Tears of utter disbelief fell. Shouts erupted that labor had been hoodwinked, betrayed. And all the while Darrow remained slumped in his seat, old and ruined. Another victim.

Job Harriman was a co-counsel on the defense team. Still, he learned about the settlement for the first time that afternoon when he heard a newsboy hawking, EXTRA! MCNAMARAS PLEAD GUILTY.

The words reverberated through his head with a funereal cadence.

He had been betrayed by Darrow.

The election would be lost.

And Otis had triumphed.

The next morning street sweepers gathered up thousands and thousands of McNamara buttons that had been tossed away like so many bad memories. It was difficult not to feel deceived. By the cause. And by the two brothers who had sworn they were innocent.

On election day Alexander defeated Harriman 85,739 votes to 51,796.

Steffens was a hero. He was the one, he was quick to point out, who had initiated the settlement talks. "I'm famous again," he boasted to his sister. "I'll use it to make people think. They'll listen again now."

Billy, in his self-involved way, saw the settlement of the case as "a great personal vindication." He railed at all the union officials who had criticized him. But he saved his sharpest knives for Gompers, that "discredited leader," that "shifty, false-hearted demagogue."

Gompers, for his part, was hurt and embarrassed. Like a jilted lover, he whined, "We have been cruelly deceived."

As for Darrow, he was a beaten man. "I am very tired. I am very worn out and very sorrowful," he admitted to a reporter.

And he might have added that he was very worried. He suspected that Fredericks, always the crusader, would decide to prosecute him on the bribery charge. He had survived "the trial of the century." He had saved his clients' lives. But he feared that the next time he was in a courtroom, it would be to defend his own soiled reputation.

———

Meanwhile in New York D.W. read the news. Out of curiosity, he had seen *A Martyr to His Cause* and had dismissed it as tripe. Now that the brothers had pleaded guilty, he thought even less of the film. He did, however, find the news reports about the Los Angeles aqueduct project to be of particular interest. For he, too, knew there was money to be made from water. With his cousin Woodson Oglesby, he had recently purchased a controlling interest in the Cascadian Spring Water Company. He had high hopes for the venture. But at the same time he knew his opportunity for genuine wealth and success would lie in California. And fortunately in just weeks he would be back at the Alexandria Hotel.

# PART IV

---

# REVOLVERS

# FORTY-TWO

----

**D**ARROW TOOK THE revolver from his raincoat pocket and set it down on the kitchen table next to the bottle of whiskey.

It was late on a rainy night in December 1911, and Darrow had appeared without warning at the Ingraham Street apartment. He knew Mary would be leaving in the morning for San Francisco; days ago she had finally ended their affair. Still, he had to see her one last time. She was the only person in whom he could confide.

"I'm going to kill myself," he told Mary.

They were sitting opposite each other at the table, and Mary had no doubt he was serious. He spoke with the flat conviction of a resigned man.

"They're going to indict me for bribing the McNamara jury. I can't stand the disgrace."

Tears fell from his eyes. He could not find a hope to latch on to. Reason, too, was beyond his grasp. His only possession was a vast sadness.

Mary tried to offer him something else. She talked of God, of his reputation, of his legacy. But her words could not reach him, for he had moved on to a distant, inhospitable place. From there all he could see was the splendid comfort in escape.

Yet the hours passed.

And with time, and soothed by the tenderness of Mary's words, the prospect of a new reality started to take hold over Darrow's mind. Despite his deep shame, he was beginning to find intimations of the will to fight back. There were other, more prideful choices he could make than surrender.

"Maybe you're right," he said to Mary.

He rose from the chair. In one pocket of his raincoat, he shoved the nearly drained whiskey bottle. In the other he hid the revolver.

Outside it was still raining, but he trudged along oblivious. He was locked deep into the intensity of his own new thoughts. His mind was reengaged, alert, and once more combative.

Billy, too, had taken to carrying a revolver in his suit pocket. He also carried a cane that, with a twist of the silver handle and a quick pull, revealed a sword. He suspected his enemies would be coming after him, and he was prepared to fight back.

After the guilty pleas were announced, the New York Times published an applauding editorial entitled "Apologies Due a Detective":

"Among the minor but highly satisfactory and far from unimportant consequences of the McNamara confessions is the brilliant vindication they give to William J. Burns . . . who for months was violently assailed as conspirator, who, for hire, had manufactured an elaborate case against innocent men."

But encomiums from the press were only small and fleeting balms. Labor could never forgive Billy. And a drumbeat of newly perceived outrages would not allow his enemies to forget.

The federal grand jury in Indianapolis had used the cartons of evidence that Billy had painstakingly gathered to indict forty-five leaders of the Structural Iron Workers union both from that city and from the West Coast. Nearly the entire executive committee faced long jail sentences for their complicity in planning the dynamite attacks. They blamed Billy.

No less disconcerting, in the winter of 1912 Billy found himself once again preparing to head for Los Angeles. He was to fight a new vituperative battle in, irony of sad ironies, a war he already fought and had convincingly won. On January 29, 1912, Clarence Darrow was indicted for bribing a juror. In his defense, Billy was certain that the entire McNamara case would be replayed. Darrow would deny, deny—and when that failed, he would argue that he had had no choice. He had been up against the unscrupulous Burns and his minions. In fact, the entire bribery scheme, Billy was certain the defense would disingenuously contend, had been invented by Burns to embarrass Darrow and to undermine labor.

Billy had been subpoenaed and was looking with anticipation to taking the stand. He never had his moment during the McNamara trial; the courtroom spectacle had abruptly ended with the settlement. But now he would have his chance to testify in public.

Billy had entered the McNamara case not simply to solve a mystery. From the start, he had viewed his role as more than that of an intrepid detective. He had hunted for clues, followed a meandering trial across the country, and made the arrests, driven by a larger motivation. Beliefs had driven America to violence. But Billy hoped that with the apprehension and conviction of the criminal plotters, the nation could move on from the dangerous idea that dynamiting was a valid form of political expression. The real value of solving the crime of the century was ultimately not to identify the conspirators or even to get a measure of retribution for the twenty-one deaths. Rather, it was to put a declarative end to a savage and outmoded way of thinking and at last propel the country forward into the complexities and challenges of the twentieth century. With Darrow's trial, the past, Billy realized, could finally be made past. With this final validation, with Justice's victory, America's great new era could truly begin.

But Billy also knew this last confrontation would be the most dangerous one. His enemies were desperate. He arrived in Los Angeles and went directly to the Alexandria Hotel, a gun in his pocket, a cane with an ominous silver handle clutched in his hand.

D.W. also had a revolver. And now he suddenly pulled the gun from his pocket, waved the weapon with a frantic menace at the teenage

sisters, and began firing. It was madness, and yet it had begun inno-
cently enough.

The troupe had only recently returned from Los Angeles, and
on this humid summer's morning the two Gish sisters, Lillian, fifteen, and Dorothy, fourteen, had arrived at the Fourteenth Street
brownstone for a surprise reunion with Mary Pickford. The three
girls had often appeared on stage together before Mary had gone off
to work in the movies. But now the sisters were in between stage
engagements and were hoping their old friend would be able to help
them get interim work at Biograph.

Mary approached, and the girls rushed to her with hugs. Mary,
too, was glad to see her old friends and did not hesitate to offer her
assistance. In fact, she said she would introduce them to her director.

At that moment, like a king strolling with regal authority
through his domain, D.W. appeared. A wide-brimmed straw hat on
his head, he had been absently singing a bit of opera in his clear
baritone, but he stopped when Mary called to him. He turned
toward her and saw the two sisters.

D.W. found himself staring; a disquieting intensity of feeling
rose up within him. "Suddenly," he would later recall, "all the
gloom seemed to disappear. The change of atmosphere was caused
by the presence of two young girls sitting side by side on a half
bench. They were blondish and were sitting affectionately close
together. I am certain I have never seen a prettier picture."

"Aren't you afraid to bring such pretty girls to the studio?"
D.W. baited Mary.

Mary, playing out their feisty dialectic, bit right back: If they
could win her job, well then, she didn't deserve it.

But today D.W. paid Mary no mind. He was captivated by the
two young girls. Without allowing them a chance to refuse, he
insisted on giving them a screen test.

Have Lionel Barrymore and Elmer Booth come upstairs

immediately! he yelled to no one in particular as he led the startled youngsters to the upstairs studio. The two actors quickly appeared, and D.W. started barking instructions. First, he ordered the bewildered girls to remove their black hair bows. To replace them, he gave a blue bow to Dorothy, a red one to Lillian. He couldn't be bothered remembering their names; Blue and Red would have to do.

Then he sketched the scene that had come into his director's mind:

"We will rehearse the story of two girls trapped in an isolated house while thieves are trying to get in and rob the safe . . . Now, Red, you hear a strange noise. Run to your sister. Blue, you're seated, too . . .

"Show your fear. You're two frightened children trapped in a lonely house by these brutes. They're in the next room."

"Elmer," he ordered the actor, "pry open a window. Climb into the house. Kick down the door to the room that holds the safe. You are mean!

"Blue, you hear the door breaking. You run in a panic to bolt it—"

Lillian was confused. She didn't understand. "What door?" she nearly screamed.

D.W.'s voice was stern, insistent, demanding. "Right in front of you! I know there's no door, but pretend there is. Run to the telephone. Start to use it. No one answers. You realize the wires have been cut. Tell the camera what you feel. Fear—more fear! Look into the lens! Now you see a gun come through the hole as he knocks the stovepipe to the floor. Look scared, I tell you!"

The girls were squirming, trembling. Their victimization seemed very real to them. The director was pushing them beyond acting. Their terror was genuine. They were quivering. And still unsatisfied, D.W. could not stop.

"No, that's not enough! Girls, hold each other. Cower in the corner."

That was when D.W., as if in a frenzy, pulled the gun from his pocket. Whipping the gun about in the air, he jumped on the set and began chasing the girls. They were crying, screaming, and all the while he raced after them shooting blanks up into the ceiling. Each shot was a loud, violent explosion, but it could not cover up the wild, full-throated yelps of their panic.

When D.W. finally put the gun back into his pocket, he was smiling.

"You have expressive bodies. I can use you," he said. "Do you want to work for me? Would you like to make the picture we just rehearsed?"

*The Unseen Enemy* was shot a few weeks later. And when the troupe went to California, the Gishes came along, too. As the company left Fourteenth Street that winter, they knew they would not be returning. A new studio was being built on 174th Street in the Bronx, modern, more functional. A structure specifically designed for making moving pictures. A home for the art and industry that D.W., almost single-handedly, had created. For many in the company, leaving the brownstone was like moving on from a childhood home. But D.W. had no time for nostalgia. He looked forward. His spirits were soaring. New, large ideas were taking hold in his imagination; and his reckless attachment to young Lillian was so irrepressible that it filled him with a genuine happiness.

And so all three men—Darrow, Billy, D.W.—found themselves in California fortified by an intuitive awareness that they were playing out a last act, and that the future was only just beyond their knowing and extended grasp.

# FORTY-THREE

T HOSE WERE DIFFICULT days," Darrow would concede. "But I settled down . . . to fight." And as if to demonstrate his newfound stoicism, he quickly made a decision that was as curious as it was unexpected. Darrow hired Earl Rogers to lead his defense.

Rogers was the enemy. After the bombing at the *Times,* Otis and the M&M had chosen him to represent their interests in the investigation. And following the arrests, he was appointed special prosecutor. It was Rogers who had crafted and presented to the grand jury the fierce twenty-one-count indictment demanding the execution of the two brothers.

Rogers was also a very different sort of man and lawyer from his client. In the courtroom Rogers was a preening, bombastic, and archly clever showman. Marching up to prosecution witnesses in his cutaway coats with their braided edges, his spats and gaudy waistcoats, bristling with a self-satisfied intelligence, Rogers would humillate and destroy. Lofty causes, courtroom ethics, the guilt or innocence of his many gangster and pimp clients—all were extraneous concerns in his narrow world. He had little philosophy, and his only loyalty was to his own ambition. Another complication: Alcohol had a relentless grip on his life. When the cravings took hold, he had no choice but to surrender; and as a consequence he was a man of racing and unpredictable moods.

None of this was lost on the homespun yet certainly no less shrewd Darrow. He could not help but find Rogers's lack of idealism, his routine advocacy of detestable clients, to be proof of the man's soiled character. Rogers would never be solid enough to be his friend. Yet Darrow also appreciated how far his own life had fallen; and it was an understanding that tempered his judgmental strain and made accommodation possible. There was also Rogers's achievement to consider: He was a remarkably effective criminal lawyer. When Darrow, accompanied by Ruby, went to Hanford, California, to watch Rogers try a case, he found the performance mesmerizing. Rogers strutted, barked, charged, obfuscated—all the time working, Darrow recognized, from a carefully prepared strategy. It wasn't lawyerly or tasteful, but the performance shook up the courtroom and took the focus off a flawed client. Rogers, Darrow conceded to himself with a shudder of regret, was just the man he needed.

And, Darrow mischievously predicted, Rogers's feud with Burns could work to his benefit, too. It was well known that the detective and Rogers detested each other with the long-standing ill will that only the self-absorbed can find the patience to sustain. The bitterness had its roots in the cutthroat San Francisco corruption investigation where Rogers had represented the men Billy believed were trying to assassinate him. It was given another mean twist after Mayor Alexander had granted the detective independent authority to conduct the *Times* case, but then quickly bowed to Otis's volcanic will and announced that Rogers was coming on board, too. Things turned even nastier when the investigation dragged on and Rogers, out for fresh blood, urged the city to stop paying the apparently unproductive detective. And more recently the dispute had heated up to a boil again when Rogers, with giddy malevolence, announced that in his view as special prosecutor, Burns was not entitled to the reward Los Angeles had promised to pay for the arrest and conviction of the men responsible for the *Times* explosion.

Darrow knew a large part of his case would be to convince the jury that the manipulative Burns had masterminded the circumstances leading to the bribery indictment. The spectacle of the arrogant detective in the witness stand going head to head with the flamboyant Rogers was sure to be combustible. It would give the jury plenty to think and talk about. And caught up in the diversion, they wouldn't bother to spend much time wondering why Darrow had also been at the scene of the crime. Or so he hoped.

The case was officially *The People vs. Clarence Darrow,* but it was Rogers who did most of the attacking. He went after George Lockwood.

"You deliberately tried to trap Darrow, didn't you?" Rogers challenged. The attorney bellowed that Lockwood's meeting with Captain White was "a performance," a "frame-up."

He went after John Harrington, after Darrow's chief investigator decided to work with the district attorney.

"You mean to say Mr. Darrow showed you a roll of bills and told you he was going to bribe jurors with it?" Rogers, sneering with a theatrical incredulity, asked during his cross-examination.

"He didn't use the word 'bribe,' he used the word 'reach,' " Harrington shot back unflustered.

He went after Bert Franklin, who had already pleaded guilty to the charge of bribing a juror and testified, with the hope of having his sentence reduced.

"You told Mr. Darrow that if he had not showed up on the scene at that unfortunate moment that you would have pulled off your stunt of turning Lockwood over to the police and charging him with extortion, did you not?" Rogers tried.

"I did not say that," Franklin answered firmly.

"What did you say?"

"I didn't say anything about a stunt."

Rogers kept on tearing into the prosecution's witnesses, hoping to throw out a provocative word or a loaded phrase that would lodge in a juror's mind. It was busy, promiscuous work. But for all Rogers's tricks, evasions, and distractions, it was apparent to everyone in the courtroom that the defense was stymied. Despite the audacious self-confidence in his performance, Rogers kept running into an unyielding wall of irrefutable facts.

And so Darrow's case seemed already lost when Billy took the stand.

"I've waited a long time for Mr. Burns to walk into my parlor," Rogers boasted to the press the day before the detective took the stand. Billy felt vengeful, too. They had scores to settle. And within moments of Billy's stepping into the witness box, the people in the courtroom could only watch with fascination as the case against Darrow became irrelevant and the two adversaries went to war.

Rogers came out swinging—literally. He wore a lorgnette on a long black ribbon, and he used it to jab at Billy. He shot out his questions in a rapid, staccato rhythm, and at the same time he kept flicking the lorgnette closer and closer to Billy's face.

The attack seemed small and ludicrous to a man who had known real menace. Billy smirked. And playing to the jury, the old actor raised his hands in mock horror. It was a facetious performance—and very effective. The jury applauded with their laughter.

Rogers seethed. He had been demeaned, and that was unforgivable. He tried to recover, insisting that it was Billy who was more likely to assault someone; after all, it was the detective who was armed with a revolver and a cane that turned into a sword. But the testimony about the weapons only inflated Billy's presence. The detective was a man who lived a dangerous life.

So Rogers went looking elsewhere. Abruptly, he turned the questioning to the reward money. Poke this raw wound, and he was confident the detective would cry out.

"There is a reward in the McNamara case, I believe?" Rogers began. "You intend to claim this money?"

"I do."

"You think that you alone caught the McNamaras . . . ?"

Billy was taken aback. His great accomplishment was being publicly impugned. A further rub, Billy needed the reward to repay the money he had borrowed to finance the investigation. At last he exploded. The roar that he let out was ferocious.

"Rogers, you've been getting off a lot of bunk. I've heard something of your claim. It's a lot of rot."

The prosecution objected. Darrow shuddered. Rogers was out of control. It served no tactical purpose to raise the issue of the McNamara reward money. And Rogers and Billy kept up their venomous exchange until the frustrated judge fined each of them twenty-five dollars and ordered a recess.

In the corridor outside the courtroom, the press flocked to Billy. A reporter asked if he felt Rogers had been trying to "bully" him. Billy, as always, enjoyed the attention. With an impish smile on his face, he called Rogers "a well-bred hoodlum."

The reporters laughed as they wrote it down.

And the sounds of their amusement, derisive and humiliating, reached down the hallway to where Rogers was standing. He charged toward Billy.

"Did you call me a son of a bitch, Mr. Burns?" he barked. He loomed over the short, squat detective.

But Billy was in a reckless mood. And he never backed down from a fight. He did not answer. He simply stared back in challenge, a man fortified by a decisive patience.

Rogers did not possess the detective's discipline. He threw a furious punch at Billy.

Billy managed to take a small step to the side, so the blow

landed with a thud against his shoulder. Then, responding both with instinct and a methodical anger, Billy went at him. He wanted to do harm. He threw one punch, and another, his short arms shooting out like pistons. Both blows landed with firm accuracy on the attorney's chin. Rogers went down. He lay on his back, the tails of his dark cutaway coat splayed out against the white marble floor like a fan.

Billy looked down at Rogers: a beaten man. At that moment Billy knew that his work was finally completed. He had solved the crime of the century. He had put an end to the national campaign of terror. It was time for him—and the nation—to move on. Without a further word, he turned his back on Rogers and the reporters, walked down the long flight of stairs, and out of the courthouse.

# FORTY-FOUR

---

RUBY SURRENDERED.

It was apparent to her that the case was lost. Rogers's crude the-atrics and his rude interrogations were only an embarrassment. He brought no honor to her husband's defense. In the courtroom she looked pale and fragile, busily cooling herself with her fan in the futile hope that it would bring a measure of relief. At night she relived the day and worried about the future. Sleep was impossible. It all weighed on her until she could not bear it anymore. She grew more and more unsettled. And then she fell apart. The doctor diag-nosed it as a nervous breakdown. He ordered her to bed. As the trial dragged on, she remained at home for lonely week after week, stranded in her own hopeless world.

Rogers fell apart, too. He disappeared from the case. Sometimes for a day, sometimes longer. Darrow had no choice but to find him, and he went to Rogers's home.

"Where is your father?" Darrow demanded of Adela, Rogers's eighteen-year-old daughter.

"He's taking a rest," she tried. "He hasn't had much sleep lately."

Darrow was not fooled. "Do you know where he is?"

"I always know where he is."

"Is he drunk?"

Adela had answered enough questions, and she was worried, too. "If he is, you're enough to drive anyone to it."

That night she went searching the city for her father. She visited the bars, and when they failed to yield a clue, she tried the houses of pleasure. Her father's favorite was Pearl Morton's; Dolly, the piano player, was his longtime friend and companion. But he was not there. So Adela continued on.

Later that night Adela found him. He had taken refuge in another house of pleasure. The sight was startling. Her father, she would write, was "sitting in a stately teakwood chair, shrunk into the rich embroidered silk. He seemed small, and his face was gray white."

And for a while, he had escaped the case.

It was all becoming too much for Darrow. After a day in court when Rogers once again couldn't keep his footing against the advancing waves of incriminating evidence, Darrow lashed out.

"A fine fool you made me look," Darrow moaned. "I cannot sit there day after day and hear you make a fool of me."

"Nuts," Rogers answered finally. "We must insist that if you, Clarence Darrow, had taken to a life of crime, you would have been as good as Caesar, Borgia, or Moriarty. You couldn't have left such a trail."

But Darrow knew he had. Worse, the jury was now following it.

And so Darrow came to understand that he had to make a choice. Either he must surrender, or he must try to rally his cause by enlisting a powerful yet untapped force.

Darrow had measured out his life in a steady allegiance to losing causes, and now he decided to champion another. He took control of his own defense. He ignored Rogers's wounded protests and diligently went to work.

Darrow wrote to his old law partner, Edgar Lee Masters, and asked him to obtain depositions from all their Chicago friends— judges, lawyers, city officials—that would be testimonials to his character. They arrived within weeks. When they were read into the record, the jury felt as if they could have been listening to a canonization.

Quickly rediscovering his old relish and instincts, Darrow took over the cross-examinations. Bert Franklin was his chief accuser, and Darrow decided there was value in confronting him directly.

The attorney stared into the witness box with a dismissive authority at the dapper little man, a giant taking the measure of a gnat. He let the moment stretch on in a hostile silence so that the entire courtroom could appreciate it. And when Darrow finally spoke, his words were not so much questions for Franklin as they were a public appeal.

"You say that on October fifth I suggested to you that we had better take care of the jury and the next day said it was time to work on Bain and gave you a check for a thousand dollars for this purpose . . .

"If I was sending you out to bribe a prospective juror would I give you a check that could be traced back or would I give you cash?

"If I wanted a prospective juror bribed would I send you out, my chief investigator whose every move was being watched by Burns operatives, or would I have imported a stranger for the dirty work? . . .

"If I knew you were passing a bribe there would I let myself be seen in the vicinity?

"Would I have crossed the street to talk to you, after the bribe had been passed, when I saw Detective Browne walking right behind you? . . .

"Would I have so blithely and callously betrayed the cause for which I have given my heart's blood for twenty-five years, put my hands in the fate of a private detective whom I had known for only three months? . . .

"Or is your entire testimony against me the price the district attorney made you pay to keep yourself out of prison?"

Dozens and dozens of questions. Each was hurled like a sharp spear: an armory of doubts. But Franklin was never the real target. Darrow's only hope was to pierce the jury's certainty.

Still, as Darrow kept doggedly at it, it must have been hard going. For he knew Franklin had been telling the truth. And that he was guilty.

And then it was August 14 and time for the closing arguments. Inside the courtroom every chair was filled, and in the rear people stood shoulder to shoulder. Another thousand spectators jammed the corridor outside, pushing and shoving in the sweaty heat to get in. The bailiffs closed the doors, but that only incited the crowd. They surged forward. A woman fainted. People were having difficulty breathing; there was a solid mass of bodies with little space for any air. But the crowd was determined. They pushed, shoulders banging and banging against the locked but quivering courtroom doors. So the bailiffs raised their truncheons and waded into the turmoil. It was madness and confusion, but still the crowd wouldn't disperse. They wanted to hear Darrow, and only when he rose and walked slowly toward the jury box did they fall into a sudden and absolute silence.

The old warrior began with his hands thrust deep into his pockets and his voice as low and weak as a small child's moan. He seemed uninterested in arguing the facts of the case. Instead, his words were a valedictory. He summed up the life he had lived and the causes he had believed in. He wanted people to know the choices he had made, and the deep pride these decisions still gave him. He was addressing the jury, but he might just as well have been explaining to himself why he had done what he had. His was a confident, defiant tautology.

Darrow started at 2:22 P.M. and continued without stop until the judge recessed for the evening. The next morning he resumed as if he had simply paused in midsentence. And with this heartfelt fluency he continued until the bells at St. Vincent's Cathedral a block away tolled noon and he had had his final say.

It was a masterwork, a song of constant passion. His own intimate tribute to his life.

He argued:

"What am I on trial for, gentlemen of the jury? You have been listening here for three months. If you don't know, then you are not as intelligent as I believe. I am not on trial for having sought to bribe a man named Lockwood. There may be and doubtless are many people who think I did seek to bribe him, but I am not on trial for that. I am on trial because I have been a lover of the poor, a friend of the oppressed, because I have stood by labor all these years, and have brought down on my head the wrath of the criminal interests in the country."

He cajoled:

"Do you suppose they care what laws I might have broken? I have committed one crime, one crime which is like that against the Holy Ghost, which cannot be forgiven. I have stood for the weak and the poor. I have stood for the men who toil. And therefore I have stood against them."

He apologized:

"Now gentlemen, I am going to be honest with you in this matter. The McNamara case was a hard fight. Here was the district attorney with his sleuths. Here was Burns with his hounds. Here was the Erectors' Association with its gold. A man could not stir in his house or go to his office without being attacked by these men ready to commit all sorts of deeds . . . We had to work the best we could."

He offered dignity to the McNamaras:

"I would have walked from Chicago across the Rocky Mountains and over the long dreary desert to lay my hand upon the shoulder of J.B. McNamara and tell him not to place dynamite in the *Times* Building . . .

"Lincoln Steffens was right in saying this was a social crime. That does not mean it should have been committed. But it does mean this: It grew out of a condition of society for which McNamara was in no wise responsible. There was a fierce conflict in this city exciting the minds of thousands of people, some poor, some weak, some irresponsible, some doing wrong on the side of the powerful as well as the side of the poor. It inflamed their minds— and this thing happened.

"Let me tell you, gentlemen, and I will tell you the truth. You may hang these men to the highest tree; you may hang everybody suspected; you may send me to the penitentiary if you will; you may convict the fifty-four men indicted in Indianapolis; but until you go down to fundamental causes, these things will happen over and over again. They will come as the earthquake comes. They will come as the hurricane uproots the trees. They will come as lightning comes to destroy the poisonous miasmas that fill the air. We are a people responsible for these conditions, and we must look results squarely in the face."

He cried, tears racing down his face:

"I know my life. I know what I have done. My life has not been perfect. It has been human, too human. I have felt the heartbeats of every man who lived. I have tried to be the friend of every man who lived. I have tried to help in the world. I have not had malice in my heart. I have had love for my fellow men. I have done the best I could."

———

As he finished, the jury wept unashamedly along with him.

At 9:20 the next morning, the judge offered a final word of advice to the jury. "May God give you the wisdom to see the right and the courage to do the right." Then the twelve men went off to decide Darrow's fate.

Forty minutes later the jury returned.

"What does it mean?" Ruby asked her husband.

"Maybe they want some instructions," he said. The trial had lasted three months. There were five thousand pages of transcripts in eighty-nine volumes. It seemed impossible that a verdict could have been reached so quickly.

Judge Hutton addressed the jurors: "Your pleasure?"

"A verdict," said Foreman Williams.

"You may read it."

The foreman paused and then spoke in a loud, clear voice: "Not guilty!"

At lunchtime the celebration moved from the courtroom to the nearby Café Martan. A photograph was taken of the victory luncheon, and it remains a revealing memento. There is Ruby in a wide-brimmed dark hat, hair pulled up to reveal a long stately neck, and her face is radiant. With the verdict, her worries lifted. Next to her is Darrow. A lock of hair falls carelessly over his forehead as he bends to read the afternoon papers' reporting on the verdict. He has been vindicated, but there is no look of triumph on his face. His pouchy face is set in stern resolve. He was judged not guilty, but he knew he was not innocent. It is the face of a man who understands how narrow was his escape and who realizes the responsibilities he must assume. With today's verdict, the McNamara case was finally over. He must now find the spirit to move forward with the flow of history. And standing behind Darrow, her sharp eyes craning over his shoulder as she attempts to read the newspaper he's holding, is Mary Field. Hers is a secret smile, for she also knows the truth. She, too, knows how close Darrow came to giving in. She knows he has been blessed. Mary and Darrow are no longer lovers. But some ties remain, and at this moment it's as if she's looking at him filled with a wondrous question: What will my Darrow do with this unexpected gift of the rest of his life?

# FORTY-FIVE

MERICA BEGAN TO CHANGE. With the verdict and the end at last of the McNamara case, it was as if the national equilibrium had been restored. Politics became less rancorous. Terror no longer seemed a sustainable ideal. Strikes continued, but the class war had eased; a new civil war pitting labor against capital no longer seemed a possibility. Entrepreneurial opportunities took shape, and they spread through the nation's cities and towns as a more hopeful alternative to the desperation of violence. Another harbinger: Just three months after the acquittal in Los Angeles, the progressive idealist Woodrow Wilson was elected president. The country was on its way to becoming a different place. And swept along by this transforming flow of modern American energy, Darrow became a movie star.

Frank Wolfe, the McNamara defense team's publicist and Socialist city council candidate, had written and directed an epic. Released in 1913, *From Dusk to Dawn* was a five-reel extravaganza with a cast of more than ten thousand, a rambling story about love and politics. And it was a film, as Wolfe was the first to acknowledge proudly, that would not have been possible without the precedent of D.W.'s genius.

The Biograph movies had been Wolfe's entire film education. He had sat in the dark and watched and learned. D.W. had taught him that moving pictures could tell a story, and that the story could have a moral and intellectual force. He had been seduced by D.W.'s new aesthetic. Close-ups, cross-cutting, realism, star performers—

Wolfe had unashamedly purloined an innovative cinematic grammar from the Biograph one-reelers.

Wolfe was D.W.'s child, but—his own great intellectual gift—his political passions and experiences ran deeper than his teacher's. And from this hard-won knowledge, he created a film that was a product of its unique moment in American history. It was a story fundamentally about justice. Its tacit message: After the years of terrorist bombings, twentieth-century America needed to find the moral wisdom to do things in a better, more equitable way.

*Dusk* told a wonderfully hopeful yarn. Iron molder Dan Grayson and laundress Carlena Wayne fall in love and battle for better wages and working conditions. Cavalier managers fire them both. A resolute Dan, however, fights backs—not with bricks or bombs but with nonviolence. He organizes the workers. Marching in orderly formations, hands firmly clasped and mouths shut in a defiant silence, the strikers refuse to be intimidated by management. And they triumph. The laundries and iron foundries become more reasonable places to work. In recognition of this accomplishment, Dan is persuaded to run for governor on the Socialist ticket. The workers flock to the polls, and Dan wins in a landslide. The movie ends with this vision of a peaceful, democratic solution to the inequities in American life; and Dan and Carlena, their hands entwined in a lovers' secure grasp, vow to "become comrades for life."

Visually, the film is a spectacle. Wolfe's ambition was purposefully large. He staged rallies bursting with people, panning his camera over thousands of extras. He interspersed into the narrative actual footage of the masses marching in Labor Day parades, of line after line of stolid picketers staring down real-life management goons, of rows of dismal tenements. The total effect is visceral: The movie is as sprawling, tumultuous, and momentous as the first decade of the twentieth century.

And the film is filled with stars. Wolfe, though, cast from a different yet no less distinguished troupe than his mentor. In *Dusk* labor leaders and Socialist politicians play themselves. But it is Darrow, the instinctive actor, whom the camera adores. He steals the movie.

True, Darrow's part is deliberately tailored to his strengths. But this accommodation makes his performance no less riveting. After Dan's nomination for governor, his wary enemies frame him. He is put on trial for conspiracy charges, and the legendary Darrow arrives to handle the defense. Rumpled yet charged with a remarkable fervor, staring into the camera with a fierce light in his eyes, Darrow delivers a spellbinding speech to the jury. It is, word for passionate word, taken directly from the redeeming summation he made at his own trial. Of course, Dan is acquitted too.

*Dusk* was an unexpected commercial success. In New York it was booked into the entire Loews chain, and a half-million people saw it. In Chicago and nearby towns, it played in forty-five theaters in two weeks and set attendance records. From there it moved on to movie theaters around the country.

And so the ideas flowed, from politics to art and back to politics and on and on across the nation, in a recurring circuit of relevance and inspiration. D.W.'s prophecy that movies would become "a new force in the intellectual world as revolutionary as electricity" was more than a poetic simile. The current of energy now coursing through American life was inescapable and transforming.

And just as the student had learned from the master, D.W. learned from Wolfe, too. He now dreamed of creating a spectacle. He wanted to bring the scale and drama of the nation's defining moments to the screen. But first he would have to break with Biograph.

When he returned from California, D.W. found the new studio in the Bronx a disappointment. The commercial success of his films had paid for the two huge indoor stages—one artificially lit, the other a daylight studio—as well as officelike dressing rooms and oversize prop and wardrobe rooms. But it gave him no pride. He found the structure numbing, as dreary as a factory. He was an artist, and when he walked into the new building, he felt his spirits sink.

The studio heads sensed this resentment; and cautious and ungrateful, they were quick to encourage it. D.W. was making them uncomfortable. The scale of his filmmaker's vision had grown too large. It scared them. It was too ambitious and therefore too expensive.

Jeremiah Kennedy, Biograph's chief money man, made the studio's position clear. "The time has come for the production of big fifty-thousand-dollar pictures," he told D.W. "You are the man to make them. But Biograph is not ready to go into that line of production. If you stay with Biograph it will be to make the same kind of short pictures that you have in the past. You will not do that. You've got the hundred-thousand-dollar idea in the back of your mind."

Kennedy was right; and without bitterness D.W. left. He decided to align himself with Harry Aitken's Mutual Films. "Mutual Movies Make Time Fly" was the independent studio's slogan. But with ruthless determination D.W. was preparing to make a film that did much more than that.

Just days before his deal with Mutual was announced, a full-page ad appeared in the *New York Dramatic Mirror*. The ad was signed by Albert H.T. Banzhaf, who identified himself as "counselor at law and personal representative." But D.W. was the advertisement's guiding force.

The ad was a celebration of all D.W. had accomplished in the five years—an implausibly brief time—since he had so casually been given the opportunity to direct *The Adventures of Dollie*. It

publicly identified D.W. as the "producer of all great Biograph suc-
cesses," the films "revolutionizing motion picture drama and
founding the modern technique of the art." It was D.W., the ad
boldly insisted, who had invented the close-up, the long shot, cross-
cutting, and "restraint in expression." And it listed, incredibly, 151
of the most famous Biograph films he had made.

What self-promotion! D.W. had proclaimed to the nation that
he was a director, an artist, and the inventor of a new industry. He
had declared himself the biggest star in the moving-picture business.

Yet, it was inspired. There was more than a megalomaniac ego
pushing D.W. The director understood fame. The man who had created the Biograph girls, Pickford, and the Gishes grasped the country's easy infatuation with celebrity. And he realized it would now
be essential to establish his image, too, in people's minds. For he
was contemplating a creation on a scale unprecedented in the art of
America. He was ready to throw himself into it without hesitation,
but at the same time he shrewdly began working the levers of
celebrity in the hope of commanding the audience's support even as
he took the first preliminary steps.

He had an idea for a new movie. "A big movie," he told people.
Frank Woods, who wrote scenarios, had suggested to the director
that he take a look at Frank Dixon's best-selling novel *The Clans-
man.* D.W. read the book—an odd, sour, and disturbingly racist
reinterpretation of the Civil War and Reconstruction—and it took
an immediate hold over his filmmaker's mind. Its fraudulent
mythology of gallant white-sheeted Ku Klux Klan riders defending
the downtrodden southern gentry from the nefarious clutches of
libidinous former slaves reinforced the saga he had invented to
explain his own Kentucky family's sad decline. From the start D.W.
saw the opportunity to create an American epic. Large, magnificent
screen images started appearing to him as if summoned from a

trance. "Now I could see a chance to do this ride-to-the-rescue on a
grand scale," he explained. "Instead of saving one poor little Nell of
the Plains, this ride would be to save a nation."

As D.W. worked the movie out in his mind—he never used a
formal script—its message and visual power grew not just out of his
southern childhood but also from his recent years in Los Angeles.
He wanted to make a movie that was a "a true history" of the Civil
War, but many of his ideas were inspired by the near second civil
war he had lived through in that city, the raging battle between capital and labor that had culminated in the crime of the century.

D.W.'s ambition was to show audiences how the war had
brought the South down low, leaving the white plantation gentry
victimized and powerless against the carpetbaggers and unscrupulous former slaves. Crushed to near despair, its women threatened,
the only hope for the southern white man was to fight back. And
therefore, as D.W. creatively (and rather disingenuously) spun the
tale, the Ku Klux Klan came into being. Galloping through the
night, white sheets flying in the wind, the Klan were avengers. Men
on a mission. Violence, D.W. believed, was the only possible
response by proud men to their oppression.

It was a complexity—logic as paradox as well as moral justification—that had first taken shape in the director's mind as he
sorted through the uproar and trial surrounding the bombing of the
Los Angeles Times. Labor, he had come to believe, had no choice
but to fight back against the powerful forces grinding the workingman down. It was war, and dynamite was a cruel but necessary
weapon. Like Steffens, D.W. had come to accept "justifiable dynamiting." He, too, felt that a conspiracy of capital had left labor with
no choice but to turn violent. And like Scripps, he mourned the
twenty-one dead but nevertheless sympathized with the argument
that those killed were "soldiers enlisted under a capitalist employer
whose main purpose in life was warfare against the unions."

D.W.'s South was only a distant childhood memory, but the events in Los Angeles were more recent, more affecting, and more involving. They held center stage in his thoughts. And as D.W.'s vision of the past took shape, as the movie he wanted to make began to play out in his mind, it was all filtered through his understanding of the McNamara case. A combative, retributive urgency, powered by the same exaggerations of sentiment and desperation that had led reasonable men to resort to terror or to bribe jurors, now fused through the director's consciousness and energized his creator's vision. And he saw a story of tremendous power, filled with magnificent images, a movie unlike any that had ever been made.

D.W. had Aitken acquire the rights to Dixon's novel for the colossal price of $25,000. Then he returned to Los Angeles and threw himself into making *The Birth of a Nation*.

D.W.'s intent was to rewrite history. In the process the director, like Darrow, like Billy, would help America—its art, its ideals, its imagination—move into the modern world. It was a confident time. So much had been accomplished, yet there was the untamed promise of still grander gifts. D.W. felt certain that his great success, and the nation's, was still to come.

# THE ALEX

# EPILOGUE

---

THE THREE MEN DID, in fact, meet. The detective, the lawyer, and the director found themselves at the same moment one spring evening in 1912 in the lobby of the Alexandria Hotel.

It was just days after Billy and Rogers had come to blows in the courthouse corridor.

D. W. was sitting on a brown leather couch in the high-ceilinged lobby. It was his habit to smoke an after-dinner cigar before returning to the studio projection room to review the day's rushes.

Darrow, as it happened, was making his slow, ponderous way to the bar. Steffens had returned to town to testify about his earlier role in the McNamara settlement negotiations; that the talks had been so far along that Darrow's bribing a juror would have been unnecessary. The writer had checked into the Alex that afternoon and now was waiting in a booth in the bar.

And Billy was striding across a large reddish Oriental carpet on his way to the dining room. Since finishing up on the witness stand, he had stayed in Los Angeles to meet with Mayor Alexander and several of the M&M officers in the hope of persuading them to release the city's share of the reward money. But the conversations had not been encouraging, and he had made plans to return to Chicago.

As Billy headed to the dining room at the rear of the lobby, D. W. noticed his old acquaintance. The director rose and took a couple of long, looping strides toward him. Billy saw the tall, thin man approaching and veered to greet him. And at the same moment his route intersected with Darrow's.

All at once they were standing together: D.W., Billy, and Darrow.

The lawyer took one look at the man fate had put in his path, and for a moment he seemed too stunned to speak. "Mr. Burns," he managed at last, the words sounding flat and hollow. Then without another comment he continued across the long lobby on his way to meet Steffens in the bar.

D.W. asked Billy if that was who he thought it was.

Indeed it was, said the detective.

The director made a small, amused face. Then he focused all his attention on Billy. He had read about the fight with Rogers, D.W. began. And he had a question.

Billy frowned. He had grown weary of discussing the McNamara case and more recently the bribery trial. Everyone hoped to hear the inside story. There was even a New York theatrical manager who wanted to book a lecture tour. He had promised a thousand dollars a speech. Billy needed the money, but the prospect of night after night re-creating his manhunt, the arrests, and sharing stories about the many intrigues during each of the trials, left him low. He wanted to busy himself with new cases, new challenges. He did not want to live in the past. So it was with little interest and even a bit of impatience that Billy waited to hear the director's question.

"What did you hit him with, Mr. Burns?" the director asked.

Billy laughed out loud. This was not the sort of question he had been expecting, he told D.W.

D.W. explained that on the set he often had to keep people in line with his fists. Extras were one problem, but the actors were another. One time Charlie Inslee refused to get into makeup and came at him with a beer bottle. D.W. had had no choice but to knock him out with a punch. Since then he made sure to get in some shadow-boxing each day even if he had to do it between takes. "A man must perspire once every day to keep in reasonably good health," he was fond of saying. His curiosity, he went on, was strictly professional. He repeated the question: "What did you hit him with?"

Billy didn't answer. He showed him.

The detective hunched his broad shoulders, clenched his fists, brought his arms up high, and let loose with a flurry of punches.

Full of mischief, D.W. joined in. The director shot his long arms into the air in a very precise and elegant left-jab, right-cross combination.

It was all done with smiles, and people in the lobby stopped and watched with amusement. They realized they were fortunate to be witnessing a unique performance, and caught up in the high-spirited moment, they applauded the two celebrities.

Darrow heard the commotion and, curious, turned. He found himself staring at the spectacle of D.W. Griffith and William J. Burns trading mock punches in the lobby of the Alexandria Hotel.

D.W. called to him. "Got to fight for what you believe in. Right, Mr. Darrow?"

"Indeed you do, Mr. Griffith," the attorney called out.

"I'll second the sentiment," said Billy. "Sometimes fighting is the only way."

And then as abruptly as it had begun, the exhibition stopped. Darrow went off to meet Steffens in the bar. Billy went on to the dining room. And D.W. returned to the studio.

The three fighters never met again. After the McNamara case their lives took different paths.

Darrow was forced to remain in Los Angeles despite his acquittal in the bribing of George Lockwood. The district attorney wanted a second chance, and this time he indicted Darrow for bribing Robert Bain. The second bribery trial was fought by both sides without much conviction. By now everyone was drained, even the jury. On March 8, 1913, they voted eight to four for conviction—still not the unanimous verdict needed to find Darrow guilty. The district attorney considered trying the case again, but in the end he didn't have the will. He extracted a promise from Darrow that he would never again practice law in California. Then Darrow and Ruby left for Chicago.

Darrow had made his peace with the settlement of the McNamara case. Jim would spend his life in San Quentin. J.J. would be released in fifteen years. But Darrow felt he had made the right decision. He had saved their lives. If he had taken the case to the jury, he knew, both of the brothers would have hanged.

Darrow would never discuss his bribery trials in any meaningful way. In *The Story of My Life*, his chatty autobiography, he recounted a conversation with Lincoln Steffens. It offered, at best, an opaque denial of the charge: "I told him that if any one thought I had done anything in connection with the jury or any other matter he should be left free to prosecute."

Yet Darrow found the philosophy to live with his guilt. The bribery trial—the entire McNamara case—had transformed him. He had traveled without enthusiasm to Los Angeles, a man reluctantly pressed into service. But in the course of the trial, in the intensity of the fight to save two men's lives and to validate Labor's mission, the crusader's passion had retaken hold of his spirit. He had been reckless; he had privately acknowledged his deep shame to Mary. He had come perilously close to ending his life. But in the final, struggling moments of decision, he had recovered a deeper understanding of his purpose. He now saw the wasteful foolishness in trying to step aside, in immersing himself in the suffocatingly banal intricacies of corporate law. The country was rumbling into a new century, and Darrow knew he had a duty and a responsibility to help lead the way.

His summation to the jury was genuine: a plea for the opportunity to be allowed to live his own important future. When he spoke with earnest poignancy about the need to create "fundamental changes" in the nation, he was sharing his own redemptive plan for the rest of his life. The statement he released after his acquittal in the first trial was no less of a vow: "I shall spend the rest of my life as I have that which has passed, in doing the best I can to serve the cause of the poor."

Darrow returned to Chicago and to a life that used the law as a weapon and as a conscience to transform the world around him. He went on to fight for John Thomas Scopes's right to teach evolution, to crusade against the death penalty in the Leopold and Loeb case, to work for tolerance and justice. By the time he died on March 14, 1938, his excesses in Los Angeles had become a distant episode in another man's life.

Billy moved on to take new cases and make new headlines. He grew rich and opened offices in Montreal, London, Brussels, and Paris. But even after he finally collected $80,000 in reward money (only the city of Los Angeles, at Earl Rogers's urging, still refused to pay the $20,000 it had promised for the arrest of the men responsible for the *Times* bombing), the McNamara case stayed with him. He personally brought McManigal to testify at the federal trial in Indianapolis, and when the jury in 1913 found that thirty-eight union officials shared guilt for the bombings, he celebrated. But Billy could still not close the case. Caplan and Schmitty, the two anarchists who had helped Jim McNamara obtain the dynamite for his bomb, the two men Billy had hunted in the Home Colony, were still at large. He pledged that they would "be made to answer to the charge of murder."

Only they had vanished. Then in 1915 a bomb exploded in an Upper West Side apartment in New York City. When police arrived, they discovered a bomb factory. The man who had been killed died when the device he was making blew up. Several unexploded bombs, however, were recovered, and Billy, working on a hunch, went to New York to inspect them. Their alarm clock and circuit design, he saw, was very similar to that of the suitcase bombs that McNamara and McManigal had planted. The next day he distributed photographs of Caplan and Schmitty to his operatives and sent them out to patrol the streets near the bomb factory. On February 13, 1915, Matthew Schmidt left his furnished room at Broadway and West 66th Street and was surrounded by Burns's men.

Letters found in Schmitty's room provided another clue. Two Burns operatives left that night for Chicago. From there they continued on to Seattle. They rented a boat, crossed Rolling Bay on a dark, starless night, and docked on Bainbridge Island. They found David Caplan asleep in his bed in a cabin deep in the woods. They arrested him before he could extract the revolver hidden under his pillow.

Schmitty and Caplan went on trial in Los Angeles. When they were convicted and sentenced to life imprisonment, Billy felt his work on the McNamara case was finished.

He turned to other cases, murders and even another terrorist bombing. In September 1920 a driverless wagon exploded on Wall Street across from the offices of J. P. Morgan. Billy tracked the bomber to Russia but lost him in the vastness of a strange land. There was never an arrest. Disappointed, feeling he had accomplished all he could as a private detective, Billy turned to politics. President Warren G. Harding appointed the nation's most famous sleuth as the first director of the Bureau of Investigation, the agency that would later become known as the FBI.

His tenure was a disaster. He became embroiled in the charges and countercharges swirling around the Teapot Dome oil scandal and was called before the Senate in April 1924 to testify. The *New*

*York Times* described him as "ashen-faced" as he responded to the senators' pointed and often accusatory questions. Two weeks later he resigned. His young assistant, J. Edgar Hoover, became director.

Billy retired to Sarasota, Florida. He spent his days writing about old cases and trying, with varying success, to sell his stories to the motion pictures. When he died in 1932, he left behind a corporation that bore his name. But it was an enterprise that Billy would have found unfamiliar, a business with little of the spirit and sense of historical duty that its founding father had always brought to an era of significant, challenging cases.

D.W. threw himself into his great gamble. In making *The Birth of a Nation* he risked his entire career. If the picture failed, he would never again have the opportunity to make a "big" movie and would spend his life churning out one-reelers. But only halfway through production, he had already spent the studio's $40,000 and needed, he estimated, at least another $40,000 to finish. He contributed all his salary and all his previous earnings and lived on credit at the Alexandria. Still he needed more. He sought out financiers, and when the banks offered only part of what he needed, he went looking for small investors, anyone who would put in a few hundred dollars. One afternoon he marched through the newsroom at the *Los Angeles Times* with his hat literally in his hand, begging people to buy shares in the production. He thought the newsmen would understand his vision; after all, the story he was filming was in many large ways indebted to what had happened at the paper on the night of October 1, 1910. D.W. was relentless. And he finally succeeded in raising the $100,000 he ultimately needed.

By the time he was finished making his movie, D.W. had harnessed all he had discovered during the experimental Biograph years, all his previously untapped grand cinematic visions, all the ferocity in the war between capital and labor. With exhaustive energy, an intensity of focus, and true art, he created the first American movie masterpiece. It was in many ways a flawed work, a product of the era's narrow southern prejudices. But there was no denying either its power or its inventiveness. It was the first movie to be shown at the White House, and afterward President Woodrow Wilson said, "It is like writing history with lightning."

*Birth* was an unprecedented hit. In New York alone it played to an estimated 825,000 people during its initial eleven-month run. The film was such a success that it is impossible to estimate accurately how many people throughout the country—the world, in fact—ultimately saw it. Or how much money it grossed. It can, however, be documented that during its first run *Birth* did more than $60 million in box office business—at a time when a film that sold $10,000 in tickets was considered a roaring success. D.W. had revealed a dazzling mathematics; and with dreams of such treasure, the Hollywood movie industry was born.

But D.W. could not sustain his own success. In many large and unfortunate ways, the rest of his life was a struggle to recover the vision and relevance of his early accomplishments. By the time D.W. died on July 23, 1948, the originality and miracle in his art seemed to many out of step with the advancing times, and his life was dismissed as simply a small episode in the adventure that became Hollywood.

This judgment was a mistake; just as it would be an error to categorize Darrow and Billy as distant, historical figures. For at the beginning of the twentieth century, the nation had been struggling to find its way. Terror had raged, a second civil war had threatened to split the nation into new feuding armies, and the inequities of industrial life had brutalized too many lives. Three men who were caught up in those traumatic times, shaped by them, found with their talents, energy, and ideals a way out of it, both for themselves and for the nation. Darrow, Billy, D.W. were all flawed—egotists, temperamental, and too often morally complacent. But as their careers and lives intersected in Los Angeles at the tail end of the first decade of the twentieth century, each in his own way helped to move America into the modern world. They were individuals willing to fight for their beliefs; and the legacy of their battles, their cultural and political brawls, remains part of our national consciousness.

# A NOTE ON SOURCES

---

**I**'D BEEN RESEARCHING this book for more than a year when I found myself standing for the first time in the lobby of the Alexandria Hotel. I'd hoped to find the approximate spot where my story's three principal characters—Billy, D.W., and Darrow—stood together for a few brief moments nearly a century ago, but it was impossible. The Alex was a muddle of Dumpsters, scaffolding, and scurrying construction workers in hard hats. The booming echo of demolition pounded through the high-ceilinged space, and a swirling blizzard of noxious gray soot fell from above. A large, brightly lettered sign explained that a $14 million "face-lift" was in progress.

I walked across the lobby toward a makeshift office, my footprints leaving a trail in the thick dust, and was handed a promotional brochure for the "new Alex." It grudgingly acknowledged the hotel's "amazing history," but the decision had been made to bring the Alex into "a new era." The building's 463 rooms will become "micro lofts." The once grand dining room will be partitioned into an "eclectic restaurant" and a "hip bar." The hotel will be transformed to keep up with the times.

Discouraged, I quickly left. More than two years before, I'd set out to tell a story that was in many ways anchored by the formidable edifice of the old Alex. I was writing a true-life tale of intersecting lives caught up in transforming political and cultural events, but I also hoped to capture the energy of the turn of the century—a spirit that, to my mind, was in part personified by the bustle of daily life in the Alex. And now this history, this spirit, was undergoing a "face-lift."

For most of my professional life I'd been a reporter. It's an occupation that lives in the present. Yet I was pursuing a story set in the early 1900s. In my mind, however, there was no large discrepancy between these two ambitions. I'd originally become intrigued by the bombing of the *Los Angeles Times* because the attack so clearly resonated across the intervening decades. I became transfixed by the intersecting lives of my three principals because they helped to shed light on the way we think and act today. I'd set out to write an account that demonstrated the past was never past. I had no ambitions to be a historian. I was still a reporter with notebook in hand chasing down a story, still tracking down "sources." It was only a minor investigative inconvenience that everyone involved in my story was long dead.

Yet, after leaving the Alex I began to have second thoughts. Was the story I was researching, the lives of the men I'd been living with for so long now, merely a curiosity? Something that possessed no immediacy for a "new era" of "hip bars" and "micro lofts"? Was it simply an excursion into the past?

Doubts, of course, are an author's constant companion. The prospect of a new Alex, however, seemed to fuel my uncertainty about the relevance of the trail I'd set out on.

But I plowed on. And as the days passed and I continued my research, as I excavated new material from archives and libraries, I grew reassured. The image of the renovated Alex began to have less prominence in my thoughts. Instead I found myself mulling one of Darrow's sly wisdoms: "History repeats itself. That's one of the things that's wrong with history."

And I realized that my original reporter's inspiration was correct. The McNamara case, with all its complexities and paradoxes, was relevant. The events defied time. They continued to engage and shape the national narrative. For in this century there is a new Age of Terror. And the legacy carried forward from the destruction in

Los Angeles was uncanny. Consider this shared searing image: people jumping in panicked desperation from flaming buildings to their death; a terrorist attack on a building in Los Angeles, and nearly a century later another on towers in New York.

But the connections, I found as I continued my research, were more substantial than pictures. In one era, the precious commodity of water stirred intrigue. In another, oil helped to drive the plot. One century's detectives sought out dynamite caches, another's hunted downs WMDs.

Then there was the debate over the nation's moral and legal responsibilities to those suspected of using terror to further their cause. At the turn of twentieth century, kidnapping, the suspension of habeas corpus, and covert detentions were justifiable. Today some urge torture, rationalize "water boarding," and establish secret prisons while disregarding laws designed to protect the accused.

There were other parallels of dubious, disturbing logic. Scripps and his cohorts, for example, believed that the employees killed in the *Times* bombing "should be considered what they really were— soldiers under a capitalist employer whose main purpose in life was warfare against the unions." Bin Laden and Al-Qaeda preached a similar reckless argument, branding the workers in the Twin Towers "combatants" and justifying the killing of the innocents. And both eras looked to the cinema to help make sense of the confusion; there were films about and inspired by the McNamara case just as there is a growing inventory of 9/11 movies.

Encouraged, convinced I was engaged with contemporary events even though my story was set in the past, I kept at it. In the end, the book I've written is more a narrative, an expansive and hopefully dramatic and resonating story about the past, than a historian's narrow, fact-laden tome. It's a reporter's story. And it is, therefore, a true story.

I was often frustrated by the paucity of historical specifics that could be unearthed (for example, what was said at the initial meeting between Billy and D.W. at the Biograph Studios). I was often troubled by the elusive nature of emotional truths from another era (is it possible for anyone today to know why D.W.'s marriage fell apart, or why Darrow's bond with Ruby prevailed despite all the strains?). And considering the politicized and partisan fervor surrounding the McNamara case, it was no surprise when I found there were very often two—or more—conflicting versions of events (even the number of the dead from the blast differed in book and newspaper accounts; I settled on the total of twenty-one that was cited in the indictments). The more I delved into the past, I came to realize that finding the "true story" was often difficult, if not impossible. Yet, the reader should know that there were no inventions in my account. I have tried to re-create events as accurately and objectively as possible. I have searched for intersecting circumstances and ideas, and then presented them without conjecture, and in a way that made informed sense to me.

To accomplish that, I (with the help of my indefatigable researchers Mark Wind and Andrea Scharf) went through government, union, university, and private archives, as well as newspaper morgues. I read voluminous trial transcripts, memoirs, periodicals, and compiled a stack of 172 books on the era and its principals. These were my sources. And in using this deluge of material—to reach my desk each day, I had to navigate through the tall piles of books, periodicals, and notes that filled my small office—I adhered to a reporter's standards.

If quotation marks bracket any dialogue, then at least one of the principals was the source. Of course, I was not able to conduct any interviews with the participants. I had to settle for other first-person accounts: memoirs, articles written by the principals, or interviews they had given. Burns, for example, wrote a biased, rambling, yet often compelling account of his hunt for the McNamaras, *The Masked War* (George H. Doran, New York, 1913), which I was able to track down on the Internet from an antiquarian bookseller. He also wrote several revelatory articles about the case in publications as diverse as *Popular Mechanics, The Saturday Evening Post,* and *True Detective.* Griffith started an autobiography that was edited by James Hart and published after Griffith's death (*The Man Who Invented Hollywood,* Touchstone, Louisville, Kentucky, 1972). Griffith also gave numerous interviews (two that appeared in *Moving Pictures World* were particularly candid) and wrote several articles for the *Los Angeles Citizen.* His wife, Linda Arvidson, wrote her own memoir (the front cover credited her as "Mrs. D.W. Griffith" despite her ex-husband and her having been separated for decades when the book was published), *When the Movies Were Young* (E.P. Dutton, New York, 1925). So did Mary Pickford: *Sunshine and Shadow* (Doubleday & Co., Garden City, New York, 1954). And Richard Schickel's seminal biography (*D.W. Griffith, An American Life,* Simon & Schuster, New York, 1984) quotes many of the director's conversations with friends and several of his letters. Darrow, too, wrote an autobiography, *The Story of My Life* (Charles Scribner's Sons, New York, 1932) and gave hundreds of interviews, and his wife cooperated with Irving Stone on the very readable *Clarence Darrow for the Defense* (Doubleday & Co., Garden City, New York, 1941). Then there are Darrow's letters to Molly and her letters to him. This treasure trove of information was unearthed and first published by Geoffrey Cowan. Cowan's *The People v. Clarence Darrow* (Times Books, New York, 1993) is a monumental work of writing and research, and I often was inspired and guided by this groundbreaking effort. I owe Cowan's book a large literary debt. Ortie McManigal also published his account of the case. And there are the thousands of pages of depositions and testimony from both the McNamara trial and then Darrow's in government archives in Los Angeles; Washington, D.C.; and Stanford, California. The directly quoted conversations that led to Darrow's indictment, for example, were taken from testimony in these transcripts. As I've said, when dialogue is directly quoted, at least one of the participants is the source.

Also, when I share what an individual is thinking or feeling, it is no casual narrative device but a reporter's using the facts as he discovered them to describe a scene as accurately and completely as possible. For example, Burns's thoughts when he first went to the scene of the *Los Angeles Times* bombing were found in his memoir about the case. Darrow's feelings about Molly were revealed in the letters Cowan discovered and first published. And Griffith's initial reluctance to give up playwriting for the more dubious business of making movies was recalled by his wife in her memoir.

Yet while there were, as I've stated, many books and articles that were used as sources for this book, readers interested in learning more about the era might want to consult the books I found myself relying on most frequently. Morrow Mayo's *Los Angeles* (Alfred A. Knopf, New York, 1933) is a witty and insightful history of the city. Steven J. Ross's *Working-Class Hollywood* (Princeton University Press, Princeton, New Jersey, 1998) is a particularly insightful documentation of the political roots in American film. Professor Ross's thesis that much of Griffith's early work was shaped by political sentiments is at odds with Schickel's analysis. Yet I found myself persuaded by Ross, and his view fueled and inspired this book. Those wanting more of a feel for Burns's career should consult Gene Caesar's *Incredible Detective* (Prentice Hall, Englewood Cliffs, New Jersey, 1968) and Alan Hynds's *In Pursuit* (Thomas Nelson & Sons, Camden, New Jersey, 1968). An elucidating view of the period and its various labor disputes can be found in the archives of the Cleveland Public Library, the Chicago Historical Society, and the Los Angeles Times History Center at the Huntington Library. The website of the Iron Workers Union as well as the official *History of the Iron Workers Union* (Mosaic, Cleraly, Maryland, 2006) gives a subjective but still informative account of the events surrounding the McNamara case and trial. And I originally found great inspiration for the writing of this tale of intersecting lives and ideas in Louis Menand's wonderfully erudite *The Metaphysical Club* (Farrar, Straus and Giroux, New York, 2001).

Finally, while I don't feel it's necessary in this sort of nonacademic history to give a full account of all the sources I consulted (for example, the many books on anarchism I delved into to write with some authority about Burns's time in the Home Colony), let me share the major sources of information for each chapter of this book:

## Prologue

William J. Burns, *The Masked War* (MW); Alan Hynd, *In Pursuit* (IP); Gene Caesar, *Incredible Detective* (ID); *New York Times; Asbury Press;* Richard Schickel, *D.W. Griffith: An American Life* (RS); Museum of Modern Art Archives, D.W. Griffith Collection (MOMA); Linda Arvidson, *When Movies Were Young* (WMWY); Tom Grunning, *D.W. Griffith and the Origins of American Narrative Film,* University of Illinois Press, Urbana, 1991 (ANF); Geoffrey Cowan, *The People v. Clarence Darrow* (PvCD); *Clarence Darrow, The Story of My Life* (SML); Irving Stone, *Clarence Darrow for the Defense* (CDFD).

## Chapter One

MW; Iron Workers' *Official History* (IW); ID; Philip S. Foner, *History of the Labor Movement in the United States,* International Publishers, NY, 1964 (HLM).

## Chapter Two

Morrow Mayo, *Los Angeles* (LA); Huntington Library archives; PvCD; Robert Gottlieb and Irene Wolf, *Thinking Big: The Story of the Los Angeles Times,* GP Putnam, NY, 1977 (TB); IW.

## Chapter Three

Steven J. Ross, *Working-Class Hollywood* (WCH); MOMA; RS; WHWY; ANF; Academy of Motion Picture Arts and Sciences, Margaret Herrick Library (AMPAS).

## Chapter Four

LA; Huntington Library archives (HL); HLM; TB; LA Times archives.

## Chapter Five

Indianapolis Public Library; PvCD; MW; IW; ID; IP.

## Chapter Six

SML; CDFD; TB; MW; HL.

## Chapter Seven

HL; PvCD; IW; *New York Times; LA Fire Dept Official History.*

## Chapter Eight

MW; TB; William J. Burns, "My Greatest Cases," *True Detective,* October 1951; October 1952 (TD).

## Chapter Nine

TB; MW; PvCD; ID; LA; HL.

## Chapter Ten

*New York Times;* RS; Mary Pickford, *Sunshine and Shadows*

(S&S); WHWY; Kenneth S. Lynn, "The Torment of D.W. Griffith," *American Scholar,* Spring 1990.

# Chapter Eleven
CDFD; Chicago Historical Society; PvCD; HL; MW.

# Chapter Twelve
MW; TD; ID; IP; *Los Angeles Times;* LA; PvCD.

# Chapter Thirteen
RS; WHWY; LA; PvCD; Daniel J. Johnson, "The Socialist Municipal Campaign in Los Angeles," *Labor History,* vol. 41, 2000 (LH); HL; MW.

# Chapter Fourteen
WHWY; MW; ID; TD; IP.

# Chapter Fifteen
SML; CDFD; PvCD; HL.

# Chapter Sixteen
MW; TD; ID; IP; trial transcripts; Ortie McManigal, *The National Dynamite Plot,* The Neal Company, LA, 1913 (NDP).

# Chapter Seventeen
RS; WHWY; MOMA; PvCD.

# Chapter Eighteen
ID; MW; trial transcripts; TD.

### Chapter Nineteen

"Home Colony, Its Philosophy and Beginnings," www
.Redlandsfortnightly.org; "A Nest of Vipers in This Country,"
Tacoma Press; MW; trial testimony.

### Chapter Twenty

MW; trial testimony; ID; NDP.

### Chapter Twenty-one

ID; *New York Times;* MW; IP; NDP; trial testimony.

### Chapter Twenty-two

MW; trial testimony; TD; RS; WHWY; Karl Brown, *Adventures
with D.W. Griffith,* Da Capo Press, NY, 1974 (KB).

### Chapter Twenty-three

MW; ID; IP; NDP; trial testimony; TD.

### Chapter Twenty-four

MW; RS; ANF; MOMA; IP; NDP.

### Chapter Twenty-five

MW; TD; ID; RS; WHWY.

### Chapter Twenty-six

NDP; MW; CDFD; IW; TD; PvCD.

### Chapter Twenty-seven

MW; NDP; trial testimony; IP; ID; IW.

### Chapter Twenty-eight

MW; PvCD; Chicago Historical Society; IW; *Los Angeles Examiner*; LA.

### Chapter Twenty-nine

*Los Angeles Times*; IW; HLM; MW; *Los Angeles Examiner*; trial transcript.

### Chapter Thirty

MW; LA; IW; Chicago Historical Society; PvCD; Eugene Debs, "The McNamara Case and the Labor Movement," *International Socialist Review,* February 1912; HLM.

### Chapter Thirty-one

CDFD; PvCD; SML; IW; HLM; Huntington Library.

### Chapter Thirty-two

IW; WCH; MW; Sam Gompers, *Seventy Years of Life and Labor,* E.P. Dutton, NY, 1935; ANF; RS; MOMA; MW.

### Chapter Thirty-three

*New York Call; Los Angeles Citizen;* RS; WCH; S&S; WHWY; ANF; MOMA.

### Chapter Thirty-four

CDED; PvCD; WCH; Huntington Library; *Los Angeles Times; Los Angeles Examiner.*

### Chapter Thirty-five

LA; Johnson, in *Labor History;* WCH; SML; PvCD; IW; MW; Justin Kaplan, *Lincoln Steffens,* Touchstone Books, NY, 1974 (LS).

### Chapter Thirty-six

MW; ID; IP; TD; trial testimony; Dictaphone Company website; PvCD; RS; WHWY; KB.

### Chapter Thirty-seven

Trial transcripts; CDFD; SML; PvCD; *Los Angeles Examiner;* LS.

### Chapter Thirty-eight

ANF; WCH; RS; MOMA.

### Chapter Thirty-nine

LS; LA; PvCD; Lincoln Steffens, various articles collected as "Explosion of the McNamara Case," Stanford University; E.W. Scripps Papers; E.W. Scripps, *Damned Old Crank: A Self-Portrait,* Charles McCabe, ed., Harper & Brothers, NY, 1951; CDFD; MW; IW.

### Chapter Forty

LA; *Los Angeles Examiner;* PvCD; MW; trial testimony; *Los Angeles Times;* Johnson in *Labor History;* TB; CDFC; SML.

### Chapter Forty-one

*Los Angeles Times;* trial transcript; LS; Steffens articles; PvCD; CDFD; HLM; RS; WHWY.

### Chapter Forty-two

PvCD; Huntington Library; MW; TD; S&S; RS.

### Chapter Forty-three

SML; CDFD; PvCD; Adela Rogers St. Johns, *Final Verdict,* Doubleday, Garden City, NY, 1962 (FV); trial transcripts; *Los Angeles Examiner;* MW; TD; ID; IP.

## Chapter Forty-four

PvCD; CDFD; FV; trial transcript; *Los Angeles Times;* Hunting-ton Library.

## Chapter Forty-five

WCH; RS; MOMA; KB; WHWY; S&S; *NY Dramatic Mirror.*

## Epilogue

MW; TD; LA; PvCD; CDFD; SML; ID; IP; trial transcripts.

# ACKNOWLEDGMENTS

---

From my desk, I can look out through a wall of windows toward a helix-shaped pond. I was writing this book one winter's day when I lifted my head up from my computer, gazed absently toward the frozen pond, and noticed something in the distance making its unhurried way across the ice. Anchored to my desk for months, I'd become accustomed to animal sightings; beyond two grassy rectangular fields fronting the wooden house, deep, dark woods stretched on and ominously on. A variety of creatures—foxes, turkeys, deer, even coyotes—would emerge, and I'd admire them with the fascinated scrutiny of someone who'd been raised in the Bronx. But this animal was something I hadn't seen before. It was bigger, mangy, and walked leisurely but with a confident air of menace. Curious, I got up from my chair and headed out to the weathered deck that faced the pond. I looked, and in an instant I was certain: My visitor was a gray wolf. I watched him anxiously for a while. When at last he'd slunk back into the woods, I sighed with relief and returned to my desk.

I never saw the wolf again. Months passed, and soon the frogs were once again croaking and lily pads blanketed the pond. The seasons had changed, but I was still sitting at my desk struggling to write this book. As I worked, the image of the wolf making his slow way across the ice would often pop into my mind. In fact, I'd begun to feel there was a bond of sorts between the two of us. In my self-imposed isolation, in the midst of grappling with the challenges I faced daily while trying to tell the meandering story that would become *American Lightning*, I'd decided he wasn't so much a frightening apparition as an appropriate visitor: one lone wolf calling on another.

But now that the book is done I realize I was being more than a bit indulgent. I was never really alone while writing this book. In fact, I was constantly buoyed by the wisdom and friendship of others; and without their help, I, like my solitary wolf, most probably would've slunk without a trace back into some deep and foreboding woods. So with gratitude, I want to acknowledge their aid.

From the first days when I began seriously thinking of writing about the bombing of the *Los Angeles Times,* my agent, Lynn Nesbit was a voice of encouragement. I've worked with Lynn on eight books, and over the years she's become a friend, an advisor, and a model of how one should conduct one's self in the often rough-and-tumble world of publishing. I count on her wisdom enormously. Also at Janklow-Nesbit, I was helped by the ever gracious Tina Simms, the tenacious Richard Morris, and my friend Cullen Stanley.

This is my first book with Crown and with Rick Horgan as my editor, and it's been a pleasure. Not only is Rick insightful, but he's also a gentleman: someone who actually does what he says he'll do—and throws himself into the task with intelligence and energy. Julian Pavia, Rick's assistant, was always helpful, smart, and, perhaps most astonishing, never once told me he was too busy to answer one of my anxious questions. And Tina Constable's enthusiasm for the book, as well as the support of the entire Crown team, has been the sort of response of which an author dreams. They have made the process fun, and I am very grateful.

Bob Bookman, of CAA, has been a friend for many years, and his help in shepherding the manuscript through Hollywood has been invaluable. Alan Hergott, too, has been a wise Hollywood advisor, and, no less important, a valued friend. And at *Vanity Fair,* Graydon Carter's early interest in the story and Dana Brown's skilled editorial touch were much appreciated.

I was also helped by my researchers. Mark Wind was able to ferret out the most fascinating bits of information. And Andrea Scharf was indefatigable; I gave her the slimmest of leads and yet she would manage to track everything down.

And I owe a lot of people for their friendship and support as I toiled (with often grim self-absorption) on this book. My sister Marcy was, as ever, the best: funny, smart, and always there when I needed her. As also were Beth DeWoody, whose generosity of spirit, kindheartedness, and unique, vivacious involvement in the bustling world around her were invaluable gifts; Jane and Bob Katz, who rushed to the rescue when it was needed; Sarah and Bill Rauch, whose hospitality allowed me to escape and whose friendship was a rock I clinged to; Susan and David Rich, with whom I shared many meals, many laughs, and too many drinks; Lacey Bernier, who has a knack for putting things into perspective; Pat and Bob Lusthaus, who were always there to help; and Gary Cohen, a very smart man and a generous friend. My children, Tony, Anna, and Dani, are a blessing; their accomplishments fill me with pride and our time together is a heartfelt joy. And, not least, Ivana, who helped to keep things interesting, and wonderful.

# The LOS ANG

PER ANNUM, $9.00; Per Month, 75 Cents. Or 2½ Cents a Copy.

SATURDAY MO

# UNIONIST BOMBS V TIMES; MANY S

## Terrific Explosion at 1 o'Clock This Morning Starts Fire Which Engulfs Score of Employes in Great Newspaper Plant---Many Victims ---Great Property Loss.

Many lives were jeopardized and half a million dollars' worth of property was sacrificed on the altar of hatred of the labor unions at 1 o'clock this morning, when the plant of the Los Angeles Times was blown up and burned, following numerous threats by the laborites.

Not quite as many of the employes were on duty as would have been the case earlier in the night, when all departments were working in full blast, but even so, the murderous cowards knew that fully 100 people were in the building at the time.

With the suddenness of an earthquake, an explosion, of which the dry, snappy sound left no room to doubt of its origin in dynamite, tore down the whole first floor wall of the building on Broadway, just back of the entrance to the business offices. In as many seconds, four or five other explosions of lesser volume were heard.

In the time it took to run at full speed from the police station to the corner of First and Broadway, a distance of less than half a block, the entire building was in flames on three floors. Almost in the same instant flames and smoke filled the east stairway on First street, driving down in a frenzied panic those employes of the composing room who had been so fortunate as to reach the landing in time.

Elbowing past the last of these fugitives, men fought their way up to the first floor with flash lights and handkerchiefs over their faces. There efforts were unavailing, the blistering hot smoke and the lurid light of the flames almost upon them and licking down at

## INJURED

E. B. ASPINALL, linotype operator. C nose cut; right wrist strained.

S. W. CRABILL, foreman composing room with flying glass.

WILL LATTA, sterotyper. Burned arms

U. S. G. PENTZ, linotype operator. Jump wrist broken.

G. RICHARD, cut.

M. WESTON, cut on shoulders.

RANDOLPH ROSS, lynotype operator. J story window; abrasion left knee; ankle sprain

CHARLES VON VELSEN, fireman. Cut

MRS. J. B. ULRICH, fell down elevator.

CHARLES E. LOVELACE, editorial sta third floor window; injuries perhaps fatal.

AUGUST KOTSCH, compositor. Slightly

J. F. LINK, glass cuts on head.

CHURCHILL HARVEY-ELDER, burne head; broken right leg; will probably die.

RICHARD GOFF, slight burns and cuts.

## MISSING

J. C. GALLIHER, 40, linotype operator, ma dren.

W. G. TUNSTALL, 45, linotype operator,

FRED LLEWELLYN, 36, operator, marri

JOHN HOWARD, 45, printer, married and

GRANT MOORE, 42, machinist, married

ED. WASSON, 35, printer, married.

ELMER FRINK, 25, operator, married.

EUGENE CARESS, 35, operator, married

DON E. JOHNSON, 36, operator, married

ERNEST JORDAN, 32, operator, married

FRANK UNDERWOOD, 48, printer, mar

J. WESLEY REAVER, stenographer.